Psycho-spiritual ascent, witness detachment.

Willard L. Bright

ABSTRACT

This dissertation proposes a pathway for White people in the United States to become liberated from a culture of whiteness that cut its teeth on anti-Black racism.[1] I focus primarily on the Black–White paradigm to represent two ends of a spectrum in hopes of providing insights into dismantling other forms of racial oppression. Martin Luther King, Jr., defined racism as "a philosophy based on a contempt for life. . . . [It] is total estrangement. It separates not only bodies but minds and spirits."[2] The struggle against racism is a matrix for psychological, social, and spiritual transformation that resists dualism. Though important, I assert that it is not enough to perform anti-racist acts. Rather, we must undergo a transformative process of *becoming* antiracist. Applying an integral, liberatory lens, I articulate a psycho-spiritual process of *unbelonging* from a culture of whiteness. The process is akin to Jungian individuation and moves through stages: apocalypse, education, elucidation, catharsis, and transformative action grounded in transpersonal love that challenges misguided ideals of hyper-individualism and racial superiority. Building on James Baldwin's insight that fear of dying fosters irresponsibility for the complex and beautiful conundrum of life,[3] the process I develop calls upon White people in the United States to overcome their fears by symbolically dying, or unbelonging, to a culture of whiteness. My methodology is autoethnographic as I examine my ancestry to place the self in a larger social and political context.

I aim to disrupt "ontological expansiveness" and epistemologies of ignorance by speaking truths about our racialized history. Embracing a radical, transpersonal love teaches us to see and be with the wounds of whiteness and White racism to facilitate meaningful, lasting repair and explore the tension between what is and what can be.[4]

---

[3] Baldwin, *Fire Next Time*, 65.

[4] *Ontological expansiveness* is the presumption that "geographical, physical, linguistic, economic, spiritual, bodily [spaces] are or should be available for [White people] to move in and out of as they wish." Sullivan, *Revealing Whiteness*, loc. 166.

DEDICATION

To all the mother-scholar-activists types who want to be good ancestors. You belong here. You are enough.

To all the kids who need this world to be FOR them; we are working on it. And you are loved. You are so loved.

TABLE OF CONTENTS

Abstract..

Dedication..

List of Figure ....

Introduction | Apocalypse 1

    In the Grip of the Shadow of Racism 1

    Thesis 8

    Theoretical Frameworks 9

    Methodology 26

    Overview 37

    Limitations 40

    Language Choices and Terms 45

Part I: Education 56

Chapter 1 | Autoethnographic Grounding 57

    Seeds of This Study 57

    Perspective 62

    Standpoint 64

Chapter 2 | Past Is Present 72

    From CRT to CART 74

    Explicating Whiteness 85

        The Shadows of Whiteness 95

        White Innocence 103

    Emergence of Anti-blackness 112

Chapter 3 | Impacts of White Racism Today 127

Economic Impact 127

    Zero-Sum Paradigm 135

    Universal Programming 141

Psychological Impact 149

    Myopia 150

    Primitive Narcissism 156

    Shame and Denial 161

Spiritual and Religious Impact 172

    Individualism 177

    Spiritual Shame and Misguided Transcendence 184

    "Thinking Black" 192

Part II: Elucidation 201

Chapter 4 | Liberation 203

Defining Liberation 203

Types of Freedom 208

Problems with Liberation Movements 217

Love as the Practice of Freedom 225

Chapter 5 | Practicing Liberation 231

A Philosophy of Liberation 231

A Psychology of Liberation 245

    Principles of Liberation Psychology 248

        1. The role of psychology is to assist people in understanding their realities by reflecting on their social and historical experiences, both the positive and negative, the light and shadow aspects. 248

        2. Psychology needs to develop a critical consciousness that moves toward an ethical praxis to which the issues of human liberation are central. 252

       3. Liberation psychology bleeds into depth psychology and spirituality with the goal of individuation, or the ability to embrace the tension of opposites. 255

    From Me to (Mature) We 259

A Spirituality of Liberation 263

    Decolonizing Transcendence 274

    Self-awareness 276

    Curiosity 278

    Uncertainty 279

    Personal Responsibility 281

    Change 284

    Institutional Responsibility and Change 288

Part III: Transformation 295

Chapter 6 | Human Becoming and Human Being 297

Love in Action 298

    Sacrifice and Struggle 302

    Death 308

    Lament 310

    Care 315

    Honesty 323

    Patience and Persistence 329

    Justice 331

    Mutuality 339

    Repair 345

Unbelonging to Belong 354

LIST OF FIGURE

Figure 1: Ladders in the Sky 1

INTRODUCTION | APOCALYPSE

Figure 1. Ladders in the Sky. Author's image.

The Greek meaning of apocalypse, from *apokalyptein*, means to uncover, disclose, or reveal in a prophetic sense.[5] Rather than being an imminent end, it is an indication that something needs to or is about to change. As a country, the United States has been on such a precipice before, when it became clear that present conditions were unsustainable. Periods of darkness reveal what needs to change, but the darkness persists when we do not allow it to transform and recreate us.

In the Grip of the Shadow of Racism

Behold! Human beings living in an underground den, which has a mouth open towards the light and reaching all along the den; here they have been from their childhood, and have their legs and necks chained so that they

---

[5] *Online Etymology Dictionary*.

cannot move, and can only see before them, being prevented by the chains from turning round their heads . . . and you will see, if you look, a low wall built along the way, like the screen which marionette players have in front of them, over which they show the puppets. . . . They see only their own shadows, or the shadows of one another.[6]

Aphrodite is a goddess born of the sea: she is primeval, oceanic in her feminine power. . . . She reigns in the unconscious . . . in service of personal development and wields terrible power to make those around her grow. When it is time for growth, the old ways and the old habits must welcome the new.[7]

Our nation is in the grip of shadows stemming from an unhealed and unfaced past. We are foreclosing quickly on a brighter future because greed, violence, and racism seem to outweigh generosity, love, and justice. In 2019 Congress issued a bill to authorize dedicated domestic terrorism offices within the Department of Homeland Security, the Department of Justice, and the Federal Bureau of Investigation.

IN THE SENATE OF THE UNITED STATES: March 27, 2019

SECTION 1. SHORT TITLE.

This Act may be cited as the "Domestic Terrorism Prevention Act of 2019."

SEC. 2. FINDINGS.

---

[6] Plato, *Allegory of the Cave*, 10.

[7] Johnson, *She*, 13–15.

Congress finds the following:

> (1) White supremacists and other far-right-wing extremists are the most significant domestic terrorism threat facing the United States.
>
> (2) "... Federal and State levels, [have] been slow to respond.... Killings committed by individuals and groups associated with far-right extremist groups have risen significantly."
>
> (3) "... [s]ince September 12, 2001, the number of fatalities caused by domestic violent extremists has ranged from 1 to 49 in a given year ... exceeded those caused by radical Islamist violent extremists."

The continued growth of "white supremacists and other far-right-wing extremists" represent the worst of a culture of whiteness that manifests as Christian Nationalism and nativism that infiltrates a range of income and education levels.[8] White supremacy persists when non-extremists remain ignorant, unconscious, or in denial that racism is still an issue. A holistic, integrated commitment to transforming a culture of whiteness toward greater belonging is needed at the personal, communal, and institutional levels. Ibram Kendi argues that "efforts to roll back racist policy, to create equity, are not an attack on White people but an attack on racism,"[9] specifically anti-Black racism. Often equity is confused with equality, when in fact they are not synonymous. I align with Critical Race Theorists by affirming equity in place of equality.

---

[8] Hawley, "Demography of the Alt-Right."

[9] Kendi, "Double Terror of Being Black in America," par. 16.

From a legal, constitutional standpoint, the words adopted support impartial treatment under the law regardless of race, class, gender, or ethnicity. In principle, the Constitution is supposed to be colorblind. However, the application is far from it. While constitutional colorblindness is an admirable goal, it becomes perverse when it interferes with taking historical inequities into account to address specific needs.[10] The primary concern when creating and debating laws ought to be how they might add to or ameliorate the distress of poor or marginalized groups. Equal opportunity does not always result in equal outcomes, such as the case in affirmative action in college admissions criteria.[11]

Lately we have seen an increase in affirmative action reversal to benefit White applicants because of the rising tide of complaints that Whites are victims of "race hatred" and reverse discrimination.[12] When admissions committees or interpreters of cases brought to state and federal courts are mostly White or ignore historical exclusion and inequity, the law is much less likely to be equitably applied. Critical Race Theory helps illustrate that deeply held biases inform the application of the law; thus those biases ought to be openly considered and mitigated as much as possible. I discuss this further in Chapters 2 and 3.

Even if we have the framework for equal rights under the law, social equity is grossly skewed by class, race, gender, and the like. In 1989, Peggy McIntosh compiled a now widely disseminated list of forty-six privileges White people enjoy in

---

[10] Delgado and Stefanic, *Critical Race Theory*, 49.

[11] Delgado and Stefanic, 52.

[12] Delgado and Stefanic, 117.

the social world, from the assurance that store clerks will not follow us to being able to find a Band-Aid that matches our skin tone.[13] While greater awareness of "white privilege" exists today, and Band-Aids come in multiple shades, associated privileges have not vanished. Social and economic equity remains elusive even though the mechanism for legal equality exists. Legal equality is intended to be a universal principle, but it has been inadequately applied because of social inequity. Some critics say that the only solution is to change everything at once. As long as white privilege and normativity remains intact, changes that address outright racism are overshadowed.[14] While laws and processes can mitigate white privilege as a factor, truly relinquishing it requires a psycho-spiritual conversion. The many intersections in one's experience of privilege, equality, and equity are entangled with our society's race- and class-based hierarchy.

Our systems have long rewarded certain demographics more than others, such that we confuse who is deserving with who has access. Equity is more complicated than equality because defining justice and freedom is often subjective. For my purposes, I define justice as more than the lack of injustice. It is the intentional pursuit of equity in a society. How the legal justice is interpreted and applied correlates with social equity. A culture that privileges whiteness conditions us to believe we live in an unbiased meritocracy when in fact many people—poor Whites included—experience unequal access. While both the application of legal

---

[13] McIntosh, "White Privilege."

[14] Delgado and Stefanic, *Critical Race Theory*, 93.

equality and the achievement of social equity require political and legal transformation, I am making the case for psycho-spiritual transformation as well.

White supremacy and resulting racialized inequity are our nation's long shadow, and confronting it is necessary for this country's survival. The body politic is wounded, and the wounds of racism are as complex and deep in our flesh as blood and nerves with varying degrees of consciousness.[15] The wounds demand a meaningful response from White dominant culture.

Viktor Frankl named numbness to horrific circumstances "a kind of emotional death" in which we become apathetic to what should otherwise horrify.[16] I add that it is also a kind of moral death as our feelings of disgust, horror, and outrage diminish as racism is normalized, ignored, or minimalized. Unmetabolized trauma, even when inherited from a lineage of oppressors, is a kind of soul wound. Left unaddressed or unacknowledged, it is re-enacted from generation to generation.[17] Alternatively, when horrific events in the present produce reactions of shock and disbelief, we display naïveté and denial. Such tendencies are evidence of intergenerational unconsciousness around our traumatic, racialized history. I wager that no Black person in this country thinks the murder of an unarmed Black person unbelievable. Rather it is continued evidence of brutality long endured.

Many White people espouse disbelief when racism or implicit bias is a factor in state-sanctioned violence, expressing an unwillingness to look at this shadow that

---

[15] Berry, *Hidden Wound*, 6.

[16] Frankl, *Man's Search for Meaning*, 28.

[17] Menakem, *My Grandmother's Hands*, 28.

leaves what Wendell Berry calls "a silence, an emptiness, of exactly the shape of the Black [person]."[18] The more we avert our eyes from the persistence of anti-Black racism, the more we become "the brutal thing itself."[19] Plato's *Allegory of the Cave* is relevant to our current situation. The prisoners represent those who abide in a culture of whiteness without question or critique or remain in denial of its existence altogether, while the puppeteers represent the systems and structures upholding it. The prisoners have no concept of light. Our present challenge is to inhabit the role of the prisoner who exits the cave and later re-enters as a witness and teacher.

I am hopeful that a shift, a rising discomfort is emerging from within the cave. We are increasingly aware of the darkness. The metaphor of the cave invites us to contemplate, build awareness of what is, and perhaps truly see it for the first time. In referencing "the shadows of late night," bell hooks writes about "the need to see darkness differently"[20] without succumbing to overwhelm or complacency. The shadows on the cave wall obscure a history of white supremacy's impact on our social, political, and spiritual systems. Adapting to illusory shadow projections is protective, a well-established defense mechanism that promotes a shallow sense of belonging. Seeing the shadows for what they are allows us to overcome them by embracing darkness as the womb of creative transformation.

The cave is explicitly feminine. Not only is it womb-like, but representative of depth and wisdom, a tehomic container with endless creativity and possibilities for

---

[18] Berry, *Hidden Wound*, 19.

[19] Berry, *Hidden Wound*, 5; W. Williams, *American Grain*, 107.

[20] hooks, "Aesthetic of Blackness," 113.

growth.[21] Process theologian Catherine Keller offers that the face of the deep is a woman's, that to wrestle with the dark is an act of love, and "to love is to bear with the chaos."[22] Transformative change seeks balance between masculine and feminine, light and dark, thought and action while always recognizing the eternal process of becoming. I argue that anti-racism requires an embrace of the feminine in a culture long dominated by patriarchal values.

"To go into the dark with a light is to know the light.

To know the dark, go dark. Go without sight.

and find that the dark too, blooms and sings,

and is traveled by dark feet and dark wings."[23]

Once we embrace the dark, "there is no place for you to go but onward / into greater freedom."[24] The freedom I propose is from a culture of whiteness that perpetuates anti-blackness that extends from a fear of the dark, which is to say a fear of consciousness.

Thesis

My research integrates insights from the fields of philosophy, psychology, spirituality, and critical theory to address how White people can meaningfully

---

[21] C. Keller, *Face of the Deep*. In Hebrew, *tehom* means "ocean," "deep," and "abyss," related to the Babylonian goddess Tiamat. Keller "depersonifies" it to mean "the depths of great life." See p. xvi and fn. 4.

[22] C. Keller, *Face of the Deep*, 29.

[23] Berry, *Selected Poems*, 53.

[24] Hafiz, "Selling Your Art," 60.

contribute to an already complex conversation about racism. Many recognize the need for change but often feel paralyzed by the task.

Notions of white superiority continue to fracture our social, psychological, and spiritual well-being; thus, our systems, policies, and institutions remain inequitable. A more healed, whole society is possible if enough White people submit to critically examining our history and the impact of race and racism on our current beliefs and behaviors. This dissertation aims to deconstruct the effects of racism on economic, philosophical, psychological, and spiritual development and apply radically reimagined approaches to these disciplines to reconstruct a nation freed from it. If our philosophies, psychologies, and spiritualities are framed by liberation and transpersonal love, we can transform white supremacy. I propose an integral, psycho-spiritual process for White people to *unbelong* from a culture of whiteness and anti-Black racism.[25]

Theoretical Frameworks

When my oldest son asked one night before bed, "Mommy? What is the human element?" I wanted to tell him it was love. However feeble in the moment, I wanted to give him hope. I wanted to say that *being* human is the most beautiful thing and to expect a world where love is not a lie but the most transformative human truth. At the same moment I had to recognize that he is a brown-skinned boy whose experience of being loved by the world could be very different from mine, that some

---

[25] An integral approach honors multiple truths and ways of knowing; critical thinking; experience, reflective practice; an integration of the academic and spiritual; bodily and spiritual experience; examining one's unconscious and disowned aspects; and healing and wholeness. See Arora, "Women's Spirituality at CIIS."

of his Black ancestors were the recipients of some of his White ancestors' abuse. Is it fair to tell him that love wins? Or must I simply teach him that becoming more human requires holding the tension of our capacities for love and hate? Throughout this work, I insist that we infuse our communities, spiritualities, philosophies, cosmologies, histories, and social systems with love as if it is the quintessential "human element." We can demonstrate love as remembering, naming truths, celebrating courage where it existed, and summoning needs for change. As I wrestle with the question of the "human element," I am struck by how often issues of oppression are framed by what the oppressed must do to heal their own plight. I take the position alongside activists like Martin Luther King, Jr., and Fannie Lou Hamer that no one is free until all are free,[26] but it remains an abstraction until those historically aligned with power are willing to engage in the psycho-spiritual work of liberation.

Several years ago, I took a course on liberation theology. Reading scholars like Vine Deloria, James Cone, Delores Williams, and Mary Daly, I wondered what it could look like to develop a *White* theology of liberation. It seemed paradoxical to even consider. I was reminded, however, that the theology I am most familiar with (Christianity) was inspired by a radical, anti-imperial Jewish mystic who was *not* White. I am already embedded in a liberatory tradition that was co-opted by a culture of whiteness. I need only return to its roots. I argue in this dissertation that genuine liberation requires a psycho-spiritual dimension to have the deepest impact. As two

---

[26] Hamer, *Speeches of Fannie Lou Hamer: To Tell it Like It Is*, 126.

sides of the same coin, liberation seeks freedom from oppression whereas transformation requires future vision, what I am naming "ladders in the sky."[27]

In applying theories of liberation to deconstructing whiteness, I am aware of the looming dangers of appropriation. However, if we are truly able to know genuine freedom and justice, White people must take seriously the role in freeing ourselves from the mental slavery that perpetuates systems of oppression. Yes, we are all *just human*, and there may not be meaningful racial differences between us, but there are meaningful racial experiences that make us different. As such, White people need to understand the role our racial experience plays in maintaining hierarchies prohibitive of a *just* human experience.

Ultimately, I could not find literature on a specifically White theology of liberation without venturing toward Christian Nationalism, which is precisely the opposite of my striving. There is also no White philosophy or psychology of liberation, but liberatory theories profoundly shape my ideas about what it means to unbelong from a culture of whiteness. If I am to become free from it, I must first see how I am captured by it. Aware again of the dangers of appropriation, I borrow from WEB Du Bois's concept of "twoness" and the necessity to reconcile my whiteness and my humanness, my inner/contemplative and outer/action-oriented worlds.[28] In adopting twoness, one comes to recognize that what one hopes for the world is very often at odds with what is; thus we must adeptly embrace paradox. Shelly Tochluk wrestles with this premise in her work, *Living in the Tension*. Our

---

[27] Tochluk, *Living in the Tension*, 15.

[28] Du Bois, *Souls of Black Folk*, 10–11.

psycho-spiritual unfolding is entangled with our social-political awareness and emancipation. As such, liberatory theories grounded in transformative praxis are relevant to my work.

A second theoretical framework informing this dissertation is depth psychology's understanding of archetypal feminine values that diverge from what Catherine Keller calls "divine dominance" so often carried out by humans and in patriarchal religious spaces.[29] In a psycho-spiritual sense, Carl Jung asserted that each person possesses both feminine and masculine aspects. He also suggests that culture has tipped in favor of masculinity, thus subjecting the feminine to the unconscious realm.[30] In offering passages from Plato's *Allegory of the Cave* and Robert Johnson's *She* to introduce each part of this dissertation, I seek to illustrate how descending into the oceanic cave of the unconscious will reconnect us to feminine qualities of interconnectedness, wisdom, transformation, and creativity necessary to birth more holistic approaches to social change.

In Chapter 2 I discuss the connection between White racism and a culture of domination, and to deconstruct both we need to approach it with radically different energy. Complementary to Riane Eisler's partnership model that brings the life-giving feminine into balance with the masculine and links rather than ranks, Keller uplifts divine relationality that is feminine, creative, and connective in nature.[31] She writes that our greatest potential can only be realized in relation, justice is love

---

[29] C. Keller, *Face of the Deep*, 97–98.

[30] Jung, *Archetypes and the Collective Unconscious*, 48, par. 58.

[31] Eisler, *Chalice and the Blade*, 189; and C. Keller, *Face of the Deep*, 13.

realized through engaging deeply with conflict, and love is the practice of difference in relationship.[32] The archetypal feminine resonates with aspects of spiritual feminism as defined by Shelly Tochluk and Alka Arora. I combine some of their principles with Keller's and distill bringing the feminine into balance with the following values.

1. Honoring the interconnection between the spiritual and material, therefore contemplation and action.[33]

2. Committing to the transformation of hierarchy, patriarchy, and exclusion based on understanding ourselves as an autonomous and embedded part of a larger whole. Arora references "the Divine Oneness underlying all apparent difference."[34] Throughout this dissertation, I reference it as unified diversity.

3. Understanding that the personal is both spiritual and political by engaging with the "politics of the intimate" that upholds intentional relatedness and truth-telling to unlearn patriarchal dominance and internalized white supremacy in public and private settings.[35] In the intimacy of my home where I am one White woman among four Black

---

[32] Eisler, *Chalice and the Blade*, 233.

[33] Tochluk, *Living in the Tension*, chap. 1.

[34] Arora, "Feminism and Spiritual Citizenship," 4.

[35] Arora, "Feminism and Spiritual Citizenship," 1–2. Arora makes the point that we need to unlearn and speak to the abuses of patriarchy in our private and public lives so that we may better participate in undoing dominator cultures.

males, we work to create a culture of transparency, equity, consent, and accountability. My hope is that my sons experience a partnership model in the microcosm of the home and work toward it in the outer world.

4. Get beyond the hero complex. We do not need a single, dynamic, male leader to show us the way. Similarly, we need not depend on non-whites to lead us out of white supremacy. An integral, feminine approach to spirituality and "transformative leadership" calls us to dig deeply into our own capacities for courage, wisdom, creativity, and change to co-create a more inclusive world.[36] Post-heroic leadership is a shared practice that incorporates participants at all levels rather than sustains a hierarchical model.[37]

5. Adopt a sense of embeddedness. As I write about what it means to unbelong, it is helpful to trust that there is a deeper web of belonging that not only honors difference but depends on it. Keller indicates that the deeper web is the feminine energy of the tehomic abyss that is the birthplace of all. To be out of alignment with it is to disconnect from "infinite intimacy; the desire for a mothering matrix" that contains and creates.[38]

Feminine and feminism are not mutually exclusive, but distinct differences exist. Feminism is activist-oriented, and activism is often associated with masculine

---

[36] Arora, "Feminism and Spiritual Citizenship," 3.

[37] Arora, "Feminism and Spiritual Citizenship," 3.

[38] C. Keller, *Face of the Deep*, 121.

energy, in part defined by going, doing, providing, and protecting. On the other hand, feminine energy aligns with pausing, being, creating, and nurturing, which can also sustain and enrich activism.[39] Feminine is usually associated with beauty ideals or a hyper-focus on body image, whereas feminism historically seeks freedom from such restraints.[40] In addition, feminine ideals related to the body tend to have homophobic undertones.[41] I do not refer to qualities of the body; rather to feminine qualities of the soul relevant to the entire gender spectrum. Despite differences between feminine and feminism, I draw upon spaces of overlap while ultimately emphasizing the need to make archetypal feminine values more visible in social change. As an example, Riley and Scharff noted the seemingly deep connection between Black feminism and femininity where embracing Black womanhood as beautiful is a message of political and social empowerment that challenges traditional, White concepts of beauty.[42]

I take a minority position within feminist discourse by highlighting depth psychology's approach to the archetypal feminine. While I center Jung's contribution, I do not minimize the numerous feminist Jungians who continue to

---

[39] These are my descriptions, but I interpret that such qualities are relevant to concepts of spiritual feminism as defined by Shelly Tochluk and Alka Arora. They also describe C. Keller's explication of "tehom" in *The Face of the Deep* and bell hooks's actions of love in *All About Love*.

[40] Riley and Scharff, "Feminism versus Femininity?"

[41] Riley and Scharff.

[42] Riley and Scharff note that this balance of feminine/feminism among Black women is a short-coming in their research.

expand and challenge his work.[43] Adding my mothering and feminine voice to the lineage personalizes, pushes, and pays homage to his contribution. We are in constantly shifting waters; as gender categories evolve, so do our understandings of the feminine and feminism. My goal is to champion our relatedness.

All movements benefit from a balance of masculine and feminine aspects, and I prioritize the feminine because our culture is woefully imbalanced, again expanded upon in Chapter 2. Eisler asserts that the problem with domination is not with men as such but with our conditioning within a dominator system that also happens to be patriarchal.[44] Feminine qualities are not essential to those who identify as female, as they can be embodied by all people to shift culture and approach wholeness. We have the choice to recondition our minds and co-create new realities. Thanks to feminist scholarship and a resurgent interest in concepts of love, even in the halls of science, the themes of interconnectedness and relationship are becoming more integral to theories of change than pyramids and hierarchies.[45]

Included in the archetypal feminine is the mother archetype, a role I cannot separate from my work. Mothering as social and political empowerment is an often overlooked, missing piece in the broader landscape of feminist theory. Yet the path to wholeness requires reclaiming our mothered or mothering selves so that we have a

---

[43] Examples include Marion Woodman, Clarissa Pinkola Estés, Maureen Murdock, Jennifer Embry, Mary Watkins, and Helene Shulman, all of whom have influenced my journey; some of whom I reference in this work.

[44] Eisler, *Chalice and the Blade*, 188.

[45] Eisler, *Chalice and the Blade*, 193.

fuller picture of our origins.[46] Like any archetype, the mother has an almost infinite variety of aspects with both positive and negative meanings.[47] She is complicated and complex. Left in the cave of the unconscious, the mother archetype emerges as vengeful, jealous, frightening, and terrible. Brought to consciousness, her fierceness transforms into passion, nourishment, and depth.[48] She can transform chaos into creativity, reveal our missing aspects, and create the conditions for something new. I aim to embrace the mother image who represents "the mysterious root of all growth and change" that transforms consciousness.[49]

In some sense, writing through the acquisition and deconstruction of whiteness explores the motherline. Countries are often referred to as "mothers," thus on a very personal and collective level, mother is the first world we know, the source of our lives and our stories, the connection to our roots both old and new.[50] "Motherland" suggests a nurturing place of birth whereas "fatherland" implies heritage, tradition, government, and order.[51] Qualifying these is subjective and will change from group to group, but I make the point that the United States is conditional and exclusive about who it nurtures.

---

[46] Lowinsky, *Motherline*, xi.

[47] Jung, *Archetypes and the Collective Unconscious*, 109, par. 156.

[48] Jung, *Archetypes and the Collective Unconscious*, 110, par. 158.

[49] Jung, *Archetypes and the Collective Unconscious*, 93, par. 172.

[50] Lowinsky, *Motherline*, xi.

[51] Lu, "Fatherland vs. Motherland."

Culturally speaking, our country has nursed and distributed the primacy of whiteness. Individual mothers were raised on this same milk and passed variations of it or resistance to it to their offspring, consciously and unconsciously. If we accept liberation as an ongoing process and democracy as continual revolution, then we must also accept responsibility for questioning the traditions of the "mother country" prohibitive to both.[52] The mother complex emerges in the form of cultural pathology when she is subjugated and untransformed.[53] As an archetype she represents the tension between tradition and transformation.

One myth that illustrates the ever-evolving feminine and mother archetype is Psyche and Aphrodite, where Psyche represents the breath of life and Aphrodite the tehomic depths. Psyche is forward movement and Aphrodite regression. Within the context of the mothering relationship, they also signify attachment and individuation where Psyche must complete psychological tasks to healthfully separate from the mother-in-law and gain a new sense of self.[54] As an aspect of the firm, traditional mother, Aphrodite holds a mirror that reflects experiences back to our own consciousness. She is in service of personal development. Whereas Psyche, as an aspect of transformation, represents and softens the great, oceanic archetypal

---

[52] hooks, *Teaching Critical Thinking*, 17, 26.

[53] Jung, *Archetypes and the Collective Unconscious*, chap. 3.

[54] Jung's work on archetypes mentions this myth and he refers to the feminine aspect as the Anima, the Roman translation of Psyche. For a succinct Jungian explanation of the story of Psyche and Aphrodite, see also Johnson, *She*, 1989.

feminine.[55] Both soft and strong characteristics are necessary. To reconcile and bring forth feminine energy is to contend with the continuum, the comfort of tradition in tension with the instinct for change and revolution.

The individual and collective task with the feminine and maternal archetypes is not to deny them, but to dissolve projections to avoid developing complexes and neuroses that keep them in the shadows.[56] Their purpose is to exemplify our capacities for birth, growth, and transformation—all necessary to unbelonging from a culture of whiteness. Racial hierarchy and division deny the feminine whose highest expression seeks balance with masculine principles. Inasmuch as something new must be midwifed into existence to change a culture of whiteness, feminine and mothering archetypes inform my work.

To illustrate qualities and behaviors of the archetypal feminine, I rely on bell hooks in addition to Catherine Keller. Keller because her lens is specifically spiritual, especially in *Face of the Deep* where the origin and evolution of wisdom is aligned with feminine energy. In her approach to theology, the direction of spiritual becoming is relational and feminine. From her work, I conclude that our wrestling with the most profound questions as well as our human becoming includes embracing the sacred feminine. Neither racial justice nor any move toward wholeness can occur without engaging with feminine energies of chaos and creativity, death and rebirth, introspection and change.

---

[55] Johnson, *She*, 13–14. Aphrodite was said to have had an attendant readily available with a mirror so the goddess could constantly look at herself.

[56] Jung, *Archetypes and the Collective Unconscious*, 114, par. 161.

I consider Catherine Keller's work the esoteric feminine whereas bell hooks is a practical feminist who defines feminism as a movement for everyone interested in ending sexism, sexist exploitation, racism, and oppression of any kind.[57] Beyond emphasizing gender equity within existing structures, hooks's approach to feminism brings concepts traditionally aligned with the feminine, like love, belonging, compassion, and interdependence, into political and academic arenas. I relate to hooks as a feminist scholar, but for the purposes of this dissertation, I expand upon her insistence that we reify feminine qualities in public spaces so that our political discourse is more intimate and relational. Reorienting our public lives to incorporate feminine values is a means of raising consciousness. Foundational to hooks's body of scholarship is a conviction that love should be the driving force of any social and political movement.[58] Taken together, Keller and hooks represent a body-soul, action-contemplation continuum.

While there are many definitions of spiritual and spirituality, I imply it as interfaith experience of striving to transcend the separate self in favor of interdependence and relationality. I cannot fully escape the Christian lens of my upbringing even though my current definition of spirituality is not tied to a particular religious doctrine but to a belief that spiritual experiences extend beyond the self and are fulfilled between selves regardless of faith tradition. I uphold the rich differences between religious traditions while also calling forth a shared devotion to love that

---

[57] hooks, *Feminism Is for Everybody*, xii.

[58] hooks, *All About Love*, Introduction.

aligns with the meaning and purpose of existence.[59] As such, a feminine lens on spiritual transformation ought to emphasize our connectedness and combine contemplation, personal responsibility, and group accountability.[60]

A third theoretical framework is transpersonal love, foundational to many theologies. While he is not a theologian, I borrow from James Baldwin and define love not "in the infantile American sense of being made happy, but in the tough and universal sense of quest and daring and growth."[61] Love does not just happen to us but requires something from us and is fulfilled between us. As I challenge White racism, I determine that "quest and daring and growth" necessitate practicing transpersonal love that include sacrifice, death, lament, care, honesty, patience, justice, mutuality, repair, and ultimately unbelonging to dominance. Over time, these behaviors facilitate a psycho-spiritual, interfaith process that honors each person's irreducible "transcendent otherness" and furthers deeper belonging.

Though I have come to understand the theological underpinnings of love mostly in a Christian context, a common thread that connects wise religion is the mandate to love one another. In the Christian scriptures, we are called to "Love others as well as you love yourself."[62] This is both specific to Christianity and universal to human becoming. To love well requires an inward and outward gaze.

---

[59] Thurman, *Mysticism and Social Action*, 9.

[60] Arora, "Feminism and Spiritual Citizenship," 2.

[61] Baldwin, *Fire Next Time*, 44.

[62] Peterson, *The Message*, Mark 12:31, Matthew 22:40.

Therefore, to love the other well in the context of dismantling White racism requires examining our personal and ancestral relationship to it to approach the self and other with greater depth and humanity. For me, this requires examining how White Protestantism has upheld racism while also asking whether Christianity can be a means of liberation. I disaggregate the liberatory roots of Christianity from mainline White expressions of it. Even though there are interfaith applications in my work as I assert that love is both transpersonal and trans-religious, I cannot fully separate from a Christian matrix. I also do not intend to settle on false universalism that erases difference, but to elevate love as the complex web that heals division and continually creates. Love is not an abstraction for me, but the quality of the highest self that stretches across difference beyond the isolated self, beyond what is known and familiar, toward an unknown, liminal space.

Dietrich Bonhoeffer, whose wisdom I draw upon, writes that "Love, therefore, is the name for what God does to [humans] in overcoming the disunion in which [humans] live. This deed of God is Jesus Christ, is reconciliation."[63] As a Christian, I concur that Jesus was an incarnated example of radical, transpersonal love, but I also believe that we must push past notions of love limited to a single religion. Love is the way of reconciliation; Jesus was one messenger. The radical nature of his teaching was that we too are couriers of love. We do not need a mediator. The ability to love beyond and across the limits of the self is a tenant of all wise religions. A saying attributed to Jesus in the Christian scriptures is, "I'm only

---

[63] Bonhoeffer, *Ethics*, 51.

quoting your inspired Scriptures, where God said, 'I tell you—you are gods.'"[64] *We are the ones we've been waiting for*; we are love incarnate. In Jungian psychology, the purpose of human becoming is to allow abstract concepts of God to manifest through right relationship with the self and others.[65]

Transpersonal love, then, is a movement toward who we are meant to be in a cosmos stretching toward communion. A deep, abiding love is inseparable from justice and therefore liberation from a culture of whiteness. James Baldwin's succinct definition of love as "quest and daring and growth"[66] is a call to participate in the action of love. Baldwin cautions,

> White people in this country have quite enough to do in learning how to accept and love themselves and each other, and when they have achieved this—which will not be tomorrow and may very well be never—the Negro problem will no longer exist, for it will no longer be needed.[67]

This is not easy, for we must be simultaneously self-critical and self-accepting. Consider this, in some sense, a love letter challenging White people to embrace that tension to love the self and the other.

Transpersonal love does not require transcending human reality but encourages us to further the "human element" in our own lives and relationships.

---

[64] Peterson, *The Message*, John 10:34.

[65] Edinger, *Transformation of the God-Image*, 25.

[66] Baldwin, *Fire Next Time*, 44.

[67] Baldwin, *Fire Next Time*, 29.

Thus, through our lived realities and relationships with one another, we may access transcendence. Martin Buber's mystical, Jewish philosophy speaks of love as expansive, integrative, and transformative in that it creates peace and empathy in the world.[68] It is also the premise of the Beloved Community that calls us to expand our limiting ideas about who we perceive as our neighbor.[69] My understanding of Beloved Community is based on the lineage of several scholar-activists. It is a loyalty to visions of a diversified unity made manifest through relationships and participation in ethical communities. I am especially inspired by Howard Thurman's dedication to practicing the Beloved Community in his interfaith, interracial Church for the Fellowship of All Peoples in San Francisco.

Thurman once wrote that the sanctions dividing us "are so much a part of society that to tamper with them is to throw the society itself into confusion."[70] In Chapter 5 I discuss uncertainty as a necessary aspect of psycho-spiritual liberation. As such, aligning ourselves with the lineage of the Beloved Community is uncertain and subversive to the status quo. In a sense it is loyalty to uncertainty and openness to change that I am asking of us. I am asking that we disrupt the foundations of separation and domination that define this country. It means that in both like-minded and discordant communities we will be loyal to racial equity and full

---

[68] Buber, *I and Thou*.

[69] The Beloved Community lineage extends from Josiah Royce to Howard Thurman to Martin Luther King, Jr. and has been adopted by contemporary scholars like Barbara Holmes and bell hooks. It has to do with the ethical, spiritual, and social quality of human relations that values communalism over individualism.

[70] Thurman, "Desegregation, Integration, and the Beloved Community," 2.

inclusion, a concept larger than any one person's devotion to it. Though an incomplete blueprint framing the edges of human existence like some fleeting ghost, the Beloved Community is made concrete by our commitment to fulfilling our "high destiny" to become like gods through loyalty to a higher love.[71]

The Beloved Community is neither naïve nor sentimental. It can hold disturbance and discomfort as it seeks to eradicate artificial barriers and honor what Thurman calls the transcendent and "precious ingredient in each personality, unique unto itself . . . that it will enrich the common life even as it creates its own light in which to stand."[72] It is both deeply personal and transpersonal. From the myriad pools of light, new forms and patterns emerge in communities committed to the general health and well-being of everyone in them. Achieving this is not conflict free, but a commitment to honesty and dialogue so that we may be released from a history that traps us.[73] To achieve such a community, we need an apocalypse, or uncovering, of what stands in the way. A basic tenant of liberation philosophy, psychology, and spirituality is a commitment to the fundamental dignity, worth, and interrelatedness of all beings—all values of transpersonal love.

Love is a lens through which to view theory. I still wrestle with whether love is the universal, cosmic force that keeps us from flying apart, as there is so much evidence that humans behave to the contrary. Regardless, the fundamental principle that draws matter together is attraction. Ultimately, I decided I needed to write this

---

[71] Thurman, "Desegregation, Integration, and the Beloved Community," 16–17.

[72] Thurman, "Desegregation, Integration, and the Beloved Community," 19.

[73] Baldwin, *Fire Next Time*, 11.

work as if love could be at the heart of a "theory of everything" and hold fast to the hope that humans can evolve toward it. We are—love is—a work in progress. Love is the connective tissue between philosophical, theological, psychological, and social liberation.

A spiritualized social transformation requires that we be and become love. If we awaken to the fact that we already are nested in an interconnected reality, we can more consciously attend to it. My approach to transforming White racism is integrative, informed by liberatory theories, a feminine ethic, and a diverse body of historical, philosophical, psychological, and spiritual texts. I weave theory, practice, and personal narrative to center love as a transformative force that shepherds us in the psycho-spiritual process of unbelonging from a culture of whiteness toward deeper belonging.

Methodology

While I analyze relevant literature and apply liberatory frameworks to it, my primary methodology is autoethnography. Throughout my dissertation, I include vignettes narrating my ancestral and personal story (forthwith identified by ellipses and italicized text) because they provide a relevant, sometimes-uncomfortable illustration of the formation and proliferation of a culture of whiteness. In the process of uncovering my history, I became more aware of the indirect and direct messages I inherited about what it means to be White, American, and female, how subtle but persistent the teaching is from generation to generation. Autoethnography allows me to be transparent with my own psycho-spiritual process of unbelonging from a culture of whiteness, a process I believe to be lifelong, multilayered, and demanding of consistent awareness. It is my own way of "re-mothering" myself and the world more whole.

I employ autoethnography for the following reasons:

- It is consistent with bringing forth the archetypal feminine as it challenges patriarchal, dualistic paradigms, therefore shifting relations between power and inequality.[74]
- It is vulnerable, creative, and wrapped in and ethic of care.
- It is liberatory because it does not let the past remain content in the past but brings it forth to envision an altogether different future. It is a method of casting ladders in the sky because it combines lived experience with theory and imagination.

Several practices inform my application of autoethnography. My daily practice combines mindfulness, contemplative writing, reading, and Jungian dream work. For six months leading up to my dissertation, I wrote one page a day on my topic, unfiltered and unedited. All these practices deepened my relationship to my body, my conscious awareness, and the collective unconscious. Over the last few years, even prior to embarking on this academic journey, I journaled about my personal learning about race in my familial and social context. I pored over the largest family database I have access to, the Chandler Family Association, and created an interior, often imagined dialogue with my ancestors' stories recorded there. I can't pretend to know the totality of their minds, but I am interested in what got passed along to generations versus what got left out. How did we believe so

---

[74] Elizabeth Ettore, *Autoethnography as Feminist Method*, 1.

firmly in the "self-made man" and meritocracy while maintaining indifference about the human suffering and exploitation that enabled success? I attempt to fill in the gaps with other historical accountings, so it felt like assembling a patchwork quilt. I also continue to participate in interracial dialogues, workshops, and seminars to continue unpacking my relationship with white racism and systems of power. Of course, I read many books on anti-racism, social justice, spirituality, and whiteness which facilitated deeper introspection and learning.

  I mined my own life for pivotal moments in developing racial consciousness. I thought about Joel Kelley, the Black boy I had a crush on in fourth grade. I didn't simply jump from Joel to my husband Josh twenty years later. There were moments in between in which I realized, "Oh, I am White. And my experiences are not the totality of human experiences." There were some times I wished I weren't White because I didn't want to be "normal." There were other times I didn't want to be White because my mostly non-white students felt guarded with me. Of course, it is useless to wish to be anyone other than who I am, so I dove deeper into introspection. I repeatedly asked, "How did I learn about whiteness? How has it shaped me?" The trajectory of my life where I intentionally pursued diverse experiences and access to liberal arts, including an incredible arts high school in which intersectionality was happening without us consciously knowing, has led to greater awareness and deeper inquiry around race, gender, and class awareness.

  Most significantly, perhaps, is my participation in my daily life with my sons and husband. In our ordinary lives we deal with both mundane and complex questions, from "Can I have this granola for breakfast?" to "What does it mean that this boy called me an 'Oreo?'" On my best days, I can be both observer and participant. It is the messiest, most beautiful, and challenging love project I have ever encountered. The many difficult and creative conversations around our table about what we are trying to co-create as a family are the breath that hold this work together. I journaled about the raw anger and hot shame I felt the first time one of my children experienced racism. I remember the fear I felt the first time I confronted it as their advocate. Each successive time, and sadly there are multiple, was an invitation to examine yet another layer of my inherited beliefs and how they are upheld in our social milieu. I notice the powerlessness I feel in my inability to shield them from the sometimes-cruel world, less and less as they get older, so I spend time imagining the world I want to create, the one I'm asking readers to help me build. I keep lists and make artwork about it in hopes that I, too, am casting ladders in the sky. I don't have a special badge that certifies me an anti-racist; I am still becoming. This tender awareness is one I try to hold with grace, humility, and accountability.

In addition to the contemplative and participatory practices above, I started with a research question informed by my son's asking about the "human element." Because I wanted it to be love, and couldn't quite get there with integrity, I circulated around the question of what stands in the way of love. In my context, and in the context of this country, I concluded that racism is a major barrier to love. The next question became, "How might we deconstruct White racism to access deeper belonging and greater love, and what authority do I have on this topic?" First, I am human. Second, I am a mother and have been mothered. Third, I am embedded in an intimate, interracial context committed to loving one another despite a social context that feels increasingly divisive. Fourth, I know that what is possible on the small scale is repeatable at the large, so I examined the behaviors of love in my everyday life and looked for resonance in the research.

As I wrote, I realized that the process I describe closely follows Jung's process of individuation that includes elucidation, education, catharsis, and transformation but with some nuances and differences described in Chapter 6.[75] I began to see that unbelonging from a culture of whiteness is a process of moving from unconsciousness to consciousness and organized my research under the headings of that process in this dissertation. I am writing through something that has not happened on a broad scale, which requires submitting to and trusting the imagination.

To address my questions, I dove into the acquisition of whiteness acquired over generations and in my lifetime. Because I draw upon memory and collected stories as data, it is difficult to know what is objectively "true." I approach memory and constructed narratives as indicators of what holds meaning for me around White racism rather than as objective facts.[76] Many of these memories and revelations reflect cultural values relevant to current events and scholarship around race and racism. When combing the research, I looked for consistency of thought (i.e., whiteness as "normative," anti-blackness as persistent, and radical love as transformative) to support the narrative data. The stories I convey play a crucial role in meaning-making, honoring my situated knowledge, and interpreting my

---

[75] Jung, "Problems of Modern Psychotherapy."

[76] Cooper and Lilyea, "I'm Interested in Autoethnography," 199.

experiences in relation to a culture of whiteness.[77] Combing the narrative data led to my finding that transpersonal love is a powerful path toward the psycho-spiritual process of unbelonging from a culture of whiteness.

My personal history is, in many ways, parallel to the formation of modernity since this country's colonial origins. As such, the forms of ethnography I employ include narrative and layered accounts, presenting the personal and historical arc alongside analysis of relevant literature.[78] The process of doing and writing research, of moving between inner and outer experience, deepened my understanding of the self in a cultural and ancestral context. Knowledge is emergent, and autoethnography offers a more fully human method of inquiry that highlights both process and product. It also engenders creative analysis of a problem and in some sense, allows me to be in dialogue with the characters in my own life, an experience echoed by researchers Katherine Allen and Fred Piercy.[79] It also allows me to narrow the gap between the creative and academic.

Autoethnography sits firmly within the tradition of feminist narrative writing and the literary turn within ethnographic research.[80] It challenges paradigms of rationality and dualism, as it does not presume objectivity possible in the

---

[77] Cooper and Lilyea, 202. A further note on situated knowledge: Donna Haraway asserts that all knowledge is situated and subjective and that elevating what we know is a feminist move. See Haraway, "Situated Knowledges."

[78] Ellis, Adams, and Buchner, "Autoethnography," pars. 17, 20.

[79] Allen and Piercy, "Feminist Autoethnography," 156.

[80] Allen and Piercy, 156.

accumulation of knowledge. It trusts personal experience and seeks to make the most intimate experiences relevant to universal human becoming. It gives voice to the moments unseen and unspoken that might otherwise be discounted. In my case, it gives voice to the unspoken inherited patterns of my family of origin and reveals the tenderness inside the family I am creating.

Autoethnography embraces a both/and approach that helps researchers navigate paradoxical tensions, or interdependent opposites to balance inner experience and outer social, historical, and cultural aspects of life.[81] As an example, it helps me make sense of how whiteness and blackness emerged in concert and continue to reflect one another today. Similarly, I can simultaneously see myself as an individual worthy of grace, love, and joy as well as embedded in a system of whiteness that perpetuates harm. If tended to, my individual self is better poised to address larger societal inequities with grace and compassion. Likewise, if I honor my embeddedness, I experience greater empathy and more clearly see the self. From this place, social liberation and personal transformation are not separate but complementary.[82] Self-reflection and social change are ongoing as both occur in relation to present circumstances. I am convinced that our dreams about positive social change ought to occupy our spiritual practices so that our spiritual standpoint holds both me and we.

Autoethnography includes the experience of the researcher as part of the process, making way for the use of I as a crucial voice. It is a method of being and

---

[81] Tochluk, *Living in the Tension*, 14.

[82] Tochluk, 15.

knowing that makes good use of personal experience to evaluate larger trends and recognizes that all knowledge is situated within a specific context. The goal of ethnography is to deconstruct "what is" and demystify a strictly scientific formation of ideas.[83] In many ways it is a subversive approach as it pushes against the boundaries of traditional academia and spans the distance between analysis and revelation. In my case, personal narrative, my role as a mother, and elevating archetypal feminine values are evidence of the analysis. The cultural and personal dynamic I confront is the legacy of White racism, specifically anti-blackness.

I aim to write from my social position. Thus, I examine my relationship to acquiring "whiteness" as an upper-middle-class White woman in a patriarchal society to highlight the personal as political. "Personal as political" emerged from second-wave feminists for whom telling one's stories to create societal changes and spaces for healing personal and collective traumas.[84] Untold stories live in our bodies. Telling them not only raises consciousness but restores the teller to their body. Telling is a way of mapping the body in time and space and addresses disassociation. In my experience, White Christians, and perhaps it is broader than a particular religious trend, are encouraged to distrust the body as a site of knowing and transformation.

I hold the tension between envisioning a future where our common humanity is celebrated and our ancestral wounds healed without losing sight of how a racialized history shapes each of us differently. As James Baldwin reminds us,

---

[83] Allen and Piercy, "Feminist Autoethnography," 156.

[84] Etorre, *Autoethnography as Feminist Method*, 10–12.

"History is not the past, it is the present. We carry our history with us. We are our history. If we pretend otherwise, we are literally criminals."[85] Left unexamined, history repeats and perpetuates ignorance, making perennial criminals out of all of us. Left unexamined, our history becomes cultural pathology, and racism is central to a culture of whiteness. My analysis of our national history, braided with my personal history, treats research as a necessarily political, social justice–oriented, self-conscious, and reparative act in hopes that I produce an artful and analytical work that changes the world, if only slightly, for the better.[86]

My epistemological and ethnographic perspective on matters of whiteness and theories of healing racism are informed by subjective knowledge, that which I have experienced; procedural knowledge, that which I have studied; and constructed knowledge, that which I have created based on experience and learning.[87] My hope is that research can liberate both the reader and the researcher and construct new possibilities from existing paradigms and experiences. Autoethnography is heart centered, emotionally vulnerable, and at times, painful as new truths emerge in the process of research and writing.[88] What this looks like for me is a willingness to bring my full maternal, spiritual, and justice-centered self into an academic setting while bearing the tension that I am here because of colonialism and despite

---

[85] Peck, *I Am Not Your Negro*, 01:36:32.

[86] Ellis, Adams, and Buchner, "Autoethnography," pars. 1, 3, 40.

[87] Belenky et al., *Women's Ways of Knowing*, 15.

[88] Etorre, *Autoethnography as Feminist Method*, 1.

patriarchy. It means investigating the personal and ancestral aspects of my history that need unraveling so that my descendants have different stories to tell. It means being willing to take a long, hard look at what is and daring to imagine that something else is possible.

I aim to take the role of "inner observer" to my experience in the context of a broader community and history. A hermeneutic-discernment approach to my research is useful, as it allows the researcher to place herself in the phenomenon being examined. The four key steps are as follows:

1. *Describe the phenomenon in context:* White racism/Anti-blackness in the United States.
2. *Describe my standpoint:* White-identified people can help to heal anti-Black racism if we confront and integrate our personal histories, perspectives often left out of learned history, connect with our bodies, and seek repair personally and communally.
3. *Understand the phenomenon without necessarily arriving at a singular, definitive answer:* The origins of racism and impact on economic, psychological, and spiritual development.
4. *Take a position:* We need a psycho-spiritual process of unbelonging from a culture of whiteness that is individual, communal, and political. We need to imagine that we can be liberated from a culture of whiteness and in so doing imagine a different society.[89]

---

[89] Franzmann, "Hearing Voices." 21.

A personal hermeneutic is a spiral continuum, constantly moving forward and backward, upward and down, especially between steps 2 and 4. Historical and personal contexts allow movement and dialogue between the macro and micro, the past and present. As I participate in remembering, reckoning, and healing, I become alert to my blind spots and areas for growth.[90] As a branch of religious and spiritual analysis, the hermeneutic process implies continuous transformation from an initial understanding to a new one through iterative recontextualization. It is a process of unlearning, relearning, and openness to change.

The work of racial justice and unbelonging to whiteness is deeply spiritual precisely because it unsettles and transforms us in the process. It is also deeply feminine because it requires a basic commitment to interconnectedness, care, and introspection. Here I borrow and add to Shelly Tochluk's perspective and argue that feminine values, spirituality, and racial justice may require one another. Awareness of one unfolds and deepens awareness of the other two. As she notes, both racism and patriarchy have been justified and perpetuated by religion.[91] Particular to my experience, both are perpetuated by Western, White, patriarchal Christianity. In undoing one, we teeter toward undoing the other. Undertaking a personal hermeneutic requires that I remain open to deconstructing my spiritual formation and internalized messages about power, a process that remains incomplete.

These pages are an exercise in imagining the possibilities for love to radically transform the habits of whiteness and White racism and perhaps, even, the world.

---

[90] Franzmann, 18–19.

[91] Tochluk, *Living in the Tension*, 11.

"Whiteness needs to be made strange,"[92] as do the systems of oppression and violence it continues to construct. I hope this work serves as a tool to critique a cultural norm (White racism) as well as moves readers to greater awareness and action. My commitment to a psycho-spiritual process of unbelonging from whiteness that incorporates my role as a mother, autoethnography, and transformative love, constitutes my unique contribution to the evolving conversation around anti-racism.

Overview

Analysis of relevant literature is woven throughout this dissertation. Thus, my intention here is to present the guiding questions and primary influences for each chapter. By integrating the various scholars and subject areas, I aim to make a call for unbelonging from a culture of whiteness as an act of transformative love more powerful and holistic. Some of my guiding questions include the following: How can dominant culture apply tenets of liberation philosophy to increase reflexive awareness? What might it look like to apply a framework of love to political rhetoric and action? How does one's psycho-spiritual unfolding relate to addressing racial justice? To this end, my dissertation seeks to address White racism though the integration of mind, body, and soul akin to the process of Jungian individuation. Within each section I move between the personal and theoretical.

Chapter 1: Autoethnographic Grounding provides the personal background for this study. My role as a mother and partner in an interracial family is entangled with the intensity of recent events that have forced a "racial reckoning" for many White folks in the United States. My voice is one among many, one that I hope

---

[92] Dyer, *White*, 78.

offers a unique perspective that is both scholarly and personal. I also provide rationale for focusing on the spiritual, moral, and psychological aspects of transforming White racism.

Chapter 2: Past is Present uses Richard Delgado and Jean Stefanic's *Critical Race Theory: An Introduction* as a primary text. It explicates how and why Critical Race Theory provides a framework for understanding the impact of race and racism on systems, institutions, and the law. George Sefa Dei's work on Critical Anti-Racist Theory provides action and thought based tools that offer individuals and communities ways to unwind the impact of race and racism in our day-to-day realities. Also important to this chapter are explications of whiteness and anti-blackness that emerges from it. Here I draw primarily upon the work of Shannon Sullivan, Reverend Thandeka, and Richard Dyer to explicate whiteness and Gerald Horne on the history of anti-blackness.

Chapter 3: Impacts of White Racism explores the impact of racism on our economic, psychological, and spiritual realities. Using Heather McGhee's *The Sum of Us* and john a. powell's *Racing to Justice* as guiding texts, I offer a broad view of how a history of racism continues to affect economic inequity. Further, in thinking about the psychological impact of racism on White people, I explore how a tendency toward myopia leads to primitive narcissism, creates a lack of awareness around the existence and impacts of race and racism, and furthers shame and denial around our ability to reshape a more loving, equitable society. James Baldwin's short story "Going to Meet the Man," Adam Breakey Hinshaw's work "Pale Narcissus," and Reverend Thandeka's *Learning to Be White* are primary texts.

Finally, I discuss the spiritual impact of racism on White people, beginning with the assertion that Western spiritualities tend to be overly focused on individualism, shame, and misguided ideas about transcendence. To expand on the spiritual impact of White racism I draw primarily from Shelly Tochluk, Catherine Keller, and Willie James Jennings, all of whom critique Western spirituality and religion (predominately Christianity) for distorting our theological and relational imaginations. I make the case for relational, embodied transcendence as a way forward if we are to include racial justice as part of a spiritual practice.

Chapter 4: Liberation introduces a philosophy of liberation as conceived by Enrique Dussel and Eduardo Mendieta. Based on definitions of freedom by Erich Fromm, I propose that liberation is not solely the work of those who are historically marginalized, but necessitates participation from those Dussel identifies as "the center" to decenter their own philosophies by recognizing that their position is a result of reinforced ideological dominance. I also discuss the limitations of liberation movements. Inspired by cultural critic bell hooks and psychologist Viktor Frankl, who even in the darkest circumstances found himself able to love beyond pain, I propose that transpersonal love is the practice of freedom. Here I braid philosophy and spirituality with praxis or seeking *metanoia*, allowing that we may be converted by a call to love because of our differences, not despite them. In this chapter I explore how White people can conceive of liberation independent of another's oppression.

Chapter 5: Practicing Liberation is an antidote to Chapter 3 in that it explores how a liberatory philosophy, psychology, and spirituality could radically transform a culture of whiteness. I seek to concretize liberation as a philosophy and action of unbelonging from dominance rather than an abstract idea. On a psychological and spiritual level, integrating the individual self into a broader context is the soul's work.

Drawing again upon the work of Eduardo Mendieta and Enrique Dussel, I also look to psychologists Martín Baró, Fritz Künkel, and Viktor Frankl; theologians Dietrich Bonhoeffer, James Cone, and Catherine Keller; and philosopher-theologian Martin Buber to apply liberation to psycho-spiritual growth. These and other thinkers support the chapter's inquiry as to how White people may consider practicing liberation to further a more just world.

When it comes down to it, we must seek and allow change at the level of soul to radically transform the self and the world. Using bell hooks's *All About Love* and King's *Where Do We Go from Here?* as guiding texts, Chapter 6: Human Becoming and Being explores what it means to *become* and *be* love. This chapter engages the creative imagination and aims to generate hope about our ability to transform the soul of our nation. My hope is grounded in pragmatism, and I cannot resist offering tools to motivate a culture of whiteness to individuate from anti-Black racism. As I draw deeply from my own life, I begin this work with a child's inquiry and end it with a mother's plea to love one another better by choosing the psycho-spiritual path of unbelonging from whiteness to remake our social, political, economic, and spiritual systems.

Limitations

I write for a White audience who may feel nudged awake by recent events and desire a deeper change in consciousness. I write for those interested in anti-racism who have at least danced close to its edges. My audience may be rather small, but I write in response to an often-irrational hope that a better world is possible and that a relatively small group can bring it into being. While there are many forms of racial oppression, I focus primarily on anti-Black racism in a culture defined by whiteness. It is This is both a limitation and a strength as we must get beyond the Black–White binary to situate the experiences of other groups and develop a more robust conversation about race.

To extrapolate differences between a *binary* and a *paradigm*, john powell states that seeing race as a paradigm suggests a gradient with White at the top and Black at the bottom whereas a binary is just that: strictly Black and White.[93] Delgado and Stefanic highlight that the United States cut its teeth on discrimination against Blacks and to understand this is to learn to analyze and address racism against other groups as well. They also acknowledge that each marginalized group in this country has been uniquely racialized according to the whims of the dominant group.[94] To situate racism solely between Blacks and Whites is an oversimplification that dangerously limits analysis and reduces opportunities for coalition building as whiteness often casts marginalized groups against one another.[95]

In no way do I intend to minimize the impact of race-based discrimination on other groups, nor do I want to cause further injury to Black people by placing them at the center of a discussion on White racism. It is a strange kind of exceptionalism to spotlight one group's discrimination as one pitfall is for other historically marginalized groups to compare grievances and determine theirs less

---

[93] powell, *Racing to Justice*, 196.

[94] Delgado and Stefanic, *Critical Race Theory*, 90.

[95] Delgado and Stefanic, 91.

worthy of redress because of the intensity of Black suffering. Another pitfall is that binary thinking can cause other non-white groups to over identify with whiteness so as not to experience being "raced."[96] However imperfect, it is helpful to examine the opposite edges of a paradigm to understand why they exist and use it as guidance in other circumstances. In many ways, we cannot understand whiteness in this country without also understanding anti-blackness as its literal and metaphorical darkest shadow. With a measure of humility, I ask that we employ a paradigm mindset that can hold the many complex shades of racism between Black and White. My primary purpose is to challenge a culture of whiteness rather than limit White racism solely to anti-blackness.

I acknowledge the existence of anti-Black racism among other non-white groups. While it is a phenomenon that needs to be named and examined, it is beyond the scope of this study. Relatedly, there are White identified people—many Jewish people for example—who benefit from white privilege but inherit historical traumas and face present-day prejudice and persecution. Each one of us has unique and intersectional identities and traumas, and I intend to stand among the intersections and work on behalf of a more just world.[97]

---

[96] Delgado and Stefanic, 88, 92.

[97] "Intersectionality" was coined by Kimberlé Crenshaw in 1989. "Rooted in Black feminism and Critical Race Theory, intersectionality is a method and a disposition, a heuristic and analytic tool . . . to address the marginalization of Black women within not only antidiscrimination law but also in feminist and antiracist theory and politics." The term also highlights the ways in which social movement organization and advocacy around violence against women elided the vulnerabilities of women of color, immigrants, and socially disadvantaged communities including those who identify as LGBTQIA. See Carbado et al., "Intersectionality," 303.

While I cannot imagine writing about this topic without employing an autoethnographic and personal hermeneutic lens, there are limitations. Autoethnography is a bridge between the literary and scholarly and receives criticism for being too artful and not scientific, or too scientific and not sufficiently artful.[98] Because I draw from my personal history, I run the risk of having a too narrow study group, interpreting the data with a biased lens, and too much ancestral "navel gazing." My hope is to generate a conversation so that White readers may be compelled to understand themselves in the broader context of a racialized society that impacts inherited ideas about the self that did not originate with us. In choosing autoethnography as a method, I seek to disrupt the binary between social science and art, the personal and the universal. Naturally there are limitations in *not* choosing to be fully embedded in one or the other. However, I am convicted that conversations about race belong in the space of both/and made possible by autoethnography.[99]

Throughout my research, the complex relationships between gender and race, sexism and racism, race and feminism, became more apparent. My own relationship with the patriarchy, how I benefit from proximity to it even as I challenge it, was thrown into sharp relief throughout this work. I am aware of the irony that I am using logos, the paternal principle of logic and knowing, that extricates itself form the primal warmth of the maternal womb, to bring forth eros, the maternal principle of love.[100] It is my own attempt to balance the two, which I

---

[98] Ellis, Adams, and Buchner, "Autoethnography," par. 36.

[99] Tochluk, *Living in the Tension*, introduction.

[100] Jung, *Archetypes and the Collective Unconscious*, 94–96.

hope is evident to the reader. That said, I acknowledge that analysis of gender and feminist theories in my work remains incomplete. They are not influences I quieted entirely and represent opportunities for future inquiry.

Along these lines, I felt conflicted about featuring Carl Jung's work prominently in this dissertation because of his understandings of the primitive and civilized mind that he associated with non-white (including Black, Asian, and Native American) and White people, respectively.[101] He fell prey to scientific racism, or the assumption that certain races are inherently less intelligent than others, a theory that has been thoroughly disproven. Furthermore, his mythological associations with the unconscious are often Eurocentric. He allows that Europeans project their shadow onto the more "primitive" person while also supporting that the primitive (i.e., non-white) person is unable to see their shadow because the unconscious is so dominant in them.[102] Nevertheless, Jung's contributions to the fields of psychology and spirituality remain significant and continue to be expanded by women, non-white, and non-European practitioners who shed light on similarities and differences between cultural symbols and archetypes. It is a testament to the power of the unexamined unconscious to consider that even our great teachers have significant blind spots. I decided not to throw the proverbial baby out with the bath water and offer some of the tools to deconstruct the thinking that created them. However, the entangled topic of racism and depth psychology warrants further attention.

---

[101] Many articles reference Jung's misconceptions of the races. For an overview see Dalal, "Jung: A Racist."

[102] Dalal, 271–72.

I have taken a relatively small bite out of a complex issue. Because I approach it through an integral lens that combines spiritual, ethical, psychological, and political ideas, it is hard to "place" this work into any one category. I acknowledge that each section could be a springboard for an entire dissertation. To that end I hope it is a sketch for future work or presents a tapestry of threads with which another person might interact. I view writing and research as truth and social justice seeking activities, and my goal is to be changed, to change the reader, and to do my small part to change the world.[103]

Language Choices and Terms

Unbelonging is a deconstructive process that involves peeling back the layers of our assumed and inherited identities. As I demonstrate in this dissertation, it involves educating ourselves about how collective and personal histories define current racial awareness. It also entails understanding that in the context of this country, we are embedded in a culture of whiteness that resists being challenged. As I unpack the impact of a culture of whiteness on our psycho-spiritual formation, other ways of being based on inclusion and liberation are elucidated. As a deconstructive process, unbelonging will likely bring up fears of racial exile.[104] Thus, there is a reconstructive aspect aimed at creating pathways for deeper belonging rooted in transformative love. For my purposes, I define *unbelonging* as a process of deconstructing and reconstructing through education, elucidation, catharsis, and transformation. While it is the underlying framework for this dissertation, I go into greater detail in Chapter 6.

---

[103] Ellis, Adams, and Bochner, "Autoethnography," par. 40.

[104] Thandeka, *Learning to Be White*, 9.

I intentionally address those who identify as White as "we." A prohibitive factor in healing White racism is the insistence that White people are unique and wholly separate individuals, distinct from a collective racial category with some common experiences. I consistently hear, "But I am not racist. I did not own slaves. I have [insert ethnicity or race] friends." Our belief that we exist apart from the problem also separates us from the solution. We have so long benefitted from individualism, recused ourselves from complicity with any sort of oppression by demanding that "I am one of the good ones." We have, in effect, othered one another by creating distance from "the bad White folks." While I do not imply that White people are a monolith with uniform experiences and beliefs, no one who identifies as White in this country knows systemic discrimination based on skin color. To better understand ourselves as individuals, I believe we must learn to see ourselves in the context of a larger cultural story, in the context of we and how we are shaped by a culture of whiteness.

White people have the luxury of individuality not granted to non-white people. However, we lack a sense of community, a sense of we that could equate with a healthy racial identity that is not created from superiority. Our sense of I is strong, but the issue of racism is more significant than our personal responses to it. Showing kindness or doing acts of charity are inadequate responses to a pervasive societal sickness. Yes, transformed personal behavior and beliefs matter. More importantly, though, White people need to willingly embrace our discomfort around race and challenge a culture of whiteness so that it can sustain equity and anti-racism at the level of systems and structures as well as psychology and spirituality.

I insist on using we even though the process of individuation is ultimately personal. It will take the sustained attention of multiple generations to imagine and teach new ways of being. White is an inherited, physiological characteristic. On the other hand, whiteness is a learned habit that can be broken. The process of dismantling White racism and a culture of whiteness is emergent, layered, and complex. It will require a groundswell of multiple generations of White people committed to cultivating and embodying repair over time. It is necessary to address the "sins" of disunion we inherit from our ancestors, so we don't pass them on to future generations. It is individual, communal, and transgenerational we work.

White is defined by anyone with light skin who might check the "White" or "Caucasian" box on a demographic survey. White is a physical characteristic that varies from creamy to olive, just as Black ranges from deep coal to light caramel. There are hardly distinctions between the two at the darkest and lightest ends of each respective spectrum. The primary difference is that White relates to European ancestry whereas Black relates to African. There are dozens of cultural and ethnic expressions within both races. Alas, the skin-deepness of skin color has come to signify so much more. While it is important to understand White as a racial experience, I also want to name the often-absurd and -vague territory that racial classification can slip into. I struggle with it even here. In the United States, White is an aggregate term resulting from a pan-European identity that set competing European colonizers apart from enslaved Africans and Native Americans.[105]

---

[105] Horne, *Dawning of the Apocalypse*, 6–28.

Many people of different ethnicities have been socialized to "become White" or "act White," so while the term is broad, it is also an invitation to reflect on an experience of socialization in the context of this country.[106] White is not a singular culture or ethnicity, just as Black does not encompass a singular culture or ethnicity. They are both racial identities that pertain to skin color. However, in contrast to African, Asian, Arab, and so on, White is rarely hyphenated with -American. We must unpack why it is okay for other people to be raced while we hold on to the cloak of "just human" or in the context of the United States, as "just American" when our cultural identities are extremely varied. While I recognize that "The Americas" collectively refers to all of North, Central, and South America, for my purposes and except where noted, I define Americans as persons living, naturalized, or born in the United States where the term *United States* does not fit.

Definitions of "whiteness" continuously evolve, and for my purposes, I define a culture of whiteness as the system of privileges and advantages afforded to those who appear White by government agencies, corporations, schools, judicial systems, economic entities, and the like. Non-white people participate in a culture of whiteness because it pervades systems, institutions, and laws and requires assimilation. However, those who identify with the White race inherit a culture of whiteness predicated on superiority and expectations of assimilation without offering full inclusion to non-whites. Even if we actively work against racism, we still benefit

---

[106] Take, for example, the varied and rich European subcultures that migrated to America. While each group has unique cultural and ethnic traditions, all eventually became racially categorized as "White" because of light skin and benefited in varying degrees from white privilege.

from belonging to a culture of whiteness. Whiteness often operates in individuals unconsciously and undetected, resulting in three levels of advantages: personal, societal, and systemic.[107] Personal advantages are often unconscious, an acquired habit, status, or ability to think of oneself as "just human." Socially, the advantages of whiteness may result in receiving the benefit of the doubt for belonging in an academic institution, for example. White people are not often suspected or reacted to with fear by those in positions of power or leadership. I refer to "ontological expansiveness" as the assumed right to belong, situate their bodies anywhere without recourse, or refusal to adapt to cultural or local customs. It is not a privilege felt by many non-white people. Laws, policies, state-approved curriculums, home-buying, and many other systems we navigate regularly privilege whiteness. It is imperative to expanding our racial consciousness that White-identified people learn to recognize the many ways we are privileged.

A culture of whiteness informs our attitudes and beliefs about the self and our position in society. It is characterized by an overvaluation of individualism, paternalism, either/or thinking, competition, transactional relationships, defensiveness, power hoarding, aversion to discomfort, and reluctance to develop inclusive leadership.[108] Individuating from a culture of whiteness entails embracing and creating opportunities for community, partnership, complexity and paradox, collaboration, transformational relationships, curiosity and vulnerability, power

---

[107] Tochluk, *Living in the Tension*, 31.

[108] Adapted from Okun, "White Supremacy Culture."

sharing, growth, and representative leadership. There are spaces where such values exist; it is just not the norm. I address this further in Part II.

That a culture of whiteness is so difficult to pin down is one of its most insidious characteristics. It is a shape-shifter, a bit of a trickster, both a marker of its power and fragility. At any point when whiteness fears its own demise, it changes the rules of belonging. Unbelonging from it feels risky, but I offer that it is also freeing.

If there is a "religion of whiteness," it worships economic power, violence, and hyper-individualism.[109] At times a religion of whiteness is openly supported in religious denominations. The persistence of "Christian Nationalism" among White mainline Protestants and Evangelicals is alarming to say the least. Many White Christian churches' past endorsements of slavery and present indifference to ongoing racial injustice are cause for sustained question and criticism. Robert P. Jones examined the relationship between racism and White Christian churches, concluding that "recruiting for a white supremacist cause on a Sunday morning, you'd likely have more success hanging out in the parking lot of an average White Christian church—be it evangelical Protestant, mainline Protestant, or Catholic—than approaching Whites sitting out services at the local coffee shop."[110] Even more incriminatory is Gerald Horne's assertion that a culture of whiteness has a general religious pallor, "indicative of its tangled roots, with lynchings of Negroes emerging as a kind of sacrament."[111] I assert that a culture of whiteness is un-Christian.

---

[109] Emerson, "Divided by Race."

[110] Jones, *White Too Long*, 191.

[111] Horne, *Dawning of the Apocalypse*, 6.

Not all White people or White Christians abide by a culture or religion of whiteness. Still, unbelonging from it requires consciously challenging inherited beliefs that whiteness is the accepted norm in the United States. It requires a conversion or change in perspective that seeks to deconstruct whiteness and dismantle structures and systems that reward it. Participating in a culture of whiteness without examination damages all people and allows racism to persist.

An overt white supremacist chooses deliberate forms of white domination demonstrated by groups like the KKK, Proud Boys, and recently factions of the Republican Party. White supremacist thinking, however, infiltrates every part of our culture to varying degrees. It refers to how we have been taught to think about differences in dualistic terms based on who is inferior or superior. White supremacist thinking is a political-economic-social system of domination that continues to elevate White people as a group and provides large-scale institutional and systemic benefits to Whites.[112]

When referring to an individual or group's race or ethnicity, I capitalize the first letter (White, Black, Native American, Hispanic/Latinx, European).[113] However, when referring to an idea (whiteness, white supremacy, anti-blackness, or

---

[112] Menakem, *My Grandmother's Hands*, introduction.

[113] While Latinx is popular in social justice circles, and even more so among younger females, only about 3% of Hispanic/Latino people refer to themselves as such. (See Noe-Bustamante, Mora, and Lopez, "About One-in-Four U.S. Hispanics Have Heard of Latinx, but just 3% Use It," 2020). It is a label often adopted and forwarded by Latin Americans who desire to "futurize" the Spanish Language, which is very gendered. The caution is not to colonize the term, make it our own, but allow people of Latin descent to determine their own labels. Many younger people of Latin descent I know are quite politically involved and refer to themselves as Latinx. I use it here to honor the way they reference themselves. However, many of the older Latinos I know reference themselves as Latino,-a.

white body supremacy), I do not capitalize. When drawing distinctions between White and other races collectively, I use non-white, though it must be said that I am not satisfied with this term. "Non" implies negativity, "as if people who are not White only have identity by virtue of what they are not."[114] Furthermore, it delegitimizes White as a race or color, reserving it for anyone other than White people, a paradigm I want to challenge. I don't currently have a better alternative succinct enough though "people of the global majority" is commonly used to reference people who are not of White, European ancestry.

I am aware that my work centers whiteness, which I acknowledge happens often enough in our culture. I hope, however, that I present in such a way that makes whiteness visible and challenges the insistence that White is simply "normal." Normal is not critiqued, and whiteness needs to be critiqued. The point of racializing Whites is to dislodge a culture of whiteness from a position of power. Although White studies as an academic category deserving of critical analysis has grown, the presumed ubiquity and assigned dominance of a culture of whiteness renders White as a racial position invisible and furthers denial that White racism and White patriarchal rule are at the core of our social issues.

The use of the word *other* merits attention, as there are several ways I refer to it and hope they are clear in context. First, I use it as a casual adjective to indicate a person or group of persons distinct from one previously mentioned. "The self and others" is an example. I don't intend this usage as a value statement, just as a distinction between two people, groups, or things.

---

[114] Dyer, *White*, 73.

Second, there is the verb form of "being othered." In this context it is a negative implication in that the one othered is made to feel separate and intrinsically different from another group or individual, especially one that wields power. In the context of my work, usage indicates how a culture of whiteness has othered Blacks, Native Americans, and other non-whites. The invention of the strange and lesser other gives White people the illusion of normalcy, power, and superiority.[115] It is the habit of othering and persisting in the delusion that we are separate that I aim to challenge.

Third, I refer to the *sacred* or *transcendent other*, which is the opposite of demeaning. Every person is distinct from another, but that distinction does not qualify one as lesser or more. Everyone has an aspect of transcendence and an aspect of otherness. It is what makes us alike and different. It could also be called our "transcendent relatedness" and the necessary way of seeing if we are to experience a shift in consciousness. Each person is a unique other which is precisely what makes us sacred.

I define spirituality in a broad sense and do not refer to a specific belief, practice, or path. The context in which I grew up is mostly informed by White Protestant Christianity, but my evolving beliefs derive from interfaith mysticism and perennial wisdom teachings. Loosely, I believe spirituality is the pursuit of belonging and meaning in a broader context that extends beyond one religion toward greater connection with others and Ultimate Reality. As interpreted in Paul's letters to the Galatians, "In Christ's family there can be no division between Jew and non-Jew,

---

[115] Morrison, *Origin of Others*, 24.

slaves and free, male and female. Among us you are all equal."[116] If interpreted both beyond and within the Christian context, Jesus and his early followers seemed to advocate for an interfaith, inclusive, relational community that extended beyond institutionalized religion It is not a verse supporting color-blindness but a diversified unity in which all people are deserving of love, dignity, and freedom. Jesus was just one mystic, and coincidentally the one I am most familiar with, who offered a path of greater belonging. While much more needs exploring on the topic of mysticism, liberation, and transpersonal love, it is beyond the scope of this dissertation. However, I point to the mystics as a source of inspiration in my work to offer a relational, embodied, interfaith commitment to transformative love as outlined in Chapter 6.

By psycho-spiritual I mean the integration of theoretical traditions like depth and liberation psychology with spiritual practice and awareness. I borrow from Shelly Tochluk in trying to outline a process of personal and social transformation that is as much mystical as it is intellectual and psychological, thus the use of psycho-spiritual to describe the process of unbelonging from a culture of whiteness.[117] Anti-racism is soul work, and soul is an abstract concept. The definition that resonates most with what I am trying to achieve references Michael Meade and Shelly Tochluk's combined explanation:

> [Soul] descends into the depths, the darkness, the earth, the shadow, the mud, and the messiness of life. . . . Soul is grounding. [It] is another kind of

---

[116] Peterson, *The Message*, Galatians 3:28.

[117] Tochluk, *Living in the Tension*, 17.

body, a subtle body that partakes of both spirituality and physicality . . . [filling] the space between spirit and matter. . . . Soul is the connecting principle of life, the "both-and" factor, the unifying third between any opposing forces . . . and needed to heal the divisions and make things whole again. . . . Soul would have us incarnate fully and would help us grow deep roots that allow the spirit of our life to branch out.[118]

Naomi Lowinsky goes on to emphasize that soul is not separate from body, that we become ensouled through honoring bodily experiences, one of which is an embodied experience of race.[119] As we transform, through confusion, suffering, and subsequent enlightenment, we acquire more feminine depth, more soul.

Finally, I want to acknowledge the use of demand language with words like *must*, *should*, *require*, or *ought*. When these words are spoken to me, I have an impulse to cringe and a desire to do the exact opposite of what is being asked. Where they occur, they illustrate the urgency of attending to the problem of White racism and my intention to persuade others of its importance. It is not shame I wish to impart, but a collective call to action.

---

[118] Tochluk, 43.

[119] Lowinsky, *Motherline*, xiii.

PART I: EDUCATION

Part I is educational and follows the apocalypse or "uncovering" of racism as a founding principle of our society. It seeks to increase knowledge of the impact of racism on individuals, communities, and systems. I provide rationale for this study, then move to Critical Race Theory as a lens through which to understand the impact of chronic, systemic racism, and defining whiteness and anti-blackness. I close with an analysis of the impacts of White racism on economics, psychology, and spirituality. This section is about learning to see racism operating and understanding its impact in context.

> The power and capacity of learning exists in the soul already; and that just as the eye was unable to turn from darkness to light without the whole body, so too the instrument of knowledge can only by the movement of the whole soul be turned from the world of becoming into that of being, and learn by degrees to endure the sight of being, and of the brightest and best of being, or in other words, of the good.[120]

> "Psyche, which means soul . . . will take us on a journey to the inner world."[121]

---

[120] Plato, *Allegory of the Cave*, 16.

[121] Johnson, *She*, 12.

CHAPTER 1 | AUTOETHNOGRAPHIC GROUNDING

The purpose of this chapter is to provide a sense of my own awareness of where I stand in the complex, ongoing conversation of racial justice. I hope to convey the deeply personal reasons for embarking on this study and offer my perspective as a White mother to Black-biracial boys and partner to a Black man. Further, my perspective informs my standpoint from the margins in that I am neither fully invested in whiteness nor can I ethically appropriate blackness. I hope to illustrate how I exist in tension with a culture of whiteness and "thinking Black."[122]

Seeds of This Study

In the wake of the tumult of 2020 and what colloquially came to be called "America's racial reckoning," I began to think more earnestly about what it meant to untangle the roots of racism in this country and whether it was even possible. I am married to a Black man for whose public safety I fear routinely and yet feel powerless to protect. I have three sons who are privately loved so hard, but whose public right to make mistakes and learn from them is limited. Our ancestries in this country have been entangled for generations, as I hail from early colonizers, enslavers, and capitalists and my husband from enslaved Africans who remained in the South post-Emancipation and -Reconstruction. The seeds have long been planted and cross-pollinated.

The life we are co-creating is not a social or political project. However, it does provide opportunity to better understand current and historical circumstances

---

[122] Cone, *Black Theology of Liberation*. I explore this concept further in Chapter 2.

through the lens of autoethnography. My personal story is a microcosm of a larger cultural drama. Though one's experience is ultimately unique, the personal has a collective dimension. Much of my acquired knowledge converges in this study as I integrate psychology, spirituality, philosophy, creativity, and ethics in my work through the lens of a mother and partner.

Current political and racial division brought my entrenchment in a culture of whiteness into sharp relief. I've held an internalized, inherited culture of whiteness in tension with learning to "think Black." I've come to understand this process as adopting a kind of "double consciousness" and specifically "second sight," by which I've learned to become simultaneously more self-aware and self-critical.[123] It is a willingness to reconcile how I see myself and how I am seen through the eyes of non-white others. "Thinking Black" is learning the history of this country and understanding how the past has shaped current inequities and distribution of power—who has it and who does not. To that end, we must also create a new way of looking at history independent of the perspective of the oppressor.[124]

I've learned that I, too, have a racial identity shaped by my embeddedness in a culture that privileges whiteness yet renders it invisible. It's confusing because would *not* having a race render us *less* human in a world socially constructed by our various identities? Because whiteness is 58invisible by its "normalcy," it is a difficult aspect to recognize as part of me, let alone implicate as a shadow aspect. In recognizing that I am White, I must also accept my participation in whiteness and its

---

[123] Du Bois, *Souls of Black Folk*, 18.

[124] Cone, *Black Theology of Liberation*, 14.

collusion with racism. As George Sefa Dei et al. note, it is easier to relegate racism and oppression to historical circumstance rather than analyze my own complicity with ongoing cycles of injustice.[125] Divesting from whiteness is a deeper shift than simply showing kindness, charity, signing a petition, or reading all the right books. Rather, it involves internalizing our diverse but interconnected humanity that embeddedness in a culture of whiteness does not amplify. It is an understanding that all people are injured by forms of oppression and need liberation from it.[126]

"Thinking Black," I understand the exhaustion Black mothers with Black children feel even though it is not imprinted in my body in the same way. I understand Claudia Rankine's assertion that "the condition of Black life is one of mourning"[127] because I do not know if someone will deem my child unworthy of life or love because he walks down the street in the wrong way. I understand why my husband and I must teach our sons all the ways they can't be children, that they can be killed at worst or suspicious at best simply for being Black. I understand that they are forced to carry a constant vigilance, a psychological harm that many of their White counterparts do not bear. The not-entirely-irrational thought of losing them to someone else's unaddressed bigotry triggers pre-emptive grief.

I feel a visceral fear when my husband walks alone at night (he once had beer bottles thrown at him in our "progressive" neighborhood) or when I see "White

---

[125] Dei, Karumanchery, and Karumanchery-Luik, "White Power, White Privilege," 82.

[126] Tochluk, *Living in the Tension*, 46.

[127] Rankine, "Condition of Black Life," par. 2.

Jeep" as the vehicle listed for Amber Alert highway signs.[128] I understand both my White friends' impulse to apologize to me for anti-Black racism and the fury my Black friends feel at how flimsy apologies seem. Signs with rainbow proclamations of "IN THIS HOUSE, WE BELIEVE . . ." scattered our neighborhood in the wake of George Floyd's murder. Today those signs are limp, crooked, faded, or completely gone. What would happen if my child climbed one of those fences to retrieve an errant ball or my husband knocked on a door at dusk for help or sugar?

The crucible of this moment, rife with division and extremism, calls for a deeper inquiry and radical imagination about what it means to be(come) more human. This time begs for a deepening of consciousness, a vision of belonging resulting from the transformation that arises from a kind of death. I argue that White people need to die to a culture of whiteness. We must understand and dismantle white supremacy in all areas of life, which requires us to "see [our own] darkness differently" and at least become aware *that* it operates, even if we cannot fully grasp *how*.

A second seed for this study was planted a few years before entering the process. One of my son's teachers asked students to imagine how their ancestors *chose* to come to United States and what transportation they used. She could not see the problem with this question. His Black ancestors were once enslaved, forced here

---

[128] This needs explaining. My husband drives a white Jeep. One day, a kidnapping in our area listed a Black male driving his same make and model car as the kidnapper's vehicle. My mind immediately went to what could happen if he were pulled over by a cop as a suspect, even if he could prove otherwise. He might not get the benefit of the doubt, given the privilege of an individual identity. In my world and in my very active imagination, this is not an impossibility. This felt too much to leave to chance, so I immediately went to his office and traded cars with him for the remainder of the day. The reality of racism is a disruption.

in the hold of a cargo boat. His White ancestors were among the early Jamestown colonists, unshackled atop a ship sent by the queen. Many would become farmers, some became enslavers, and a handful of others were supposedly abolitionists. Many were indifferent. His teacher asked that we leave it as "they came by boat" because, admittedly, talking about slavery made her uncomfortable. We did not abide. Such discomfort needs to be challenged and, at the very least, push educators to ask inclusive questions that allow for complete and honest answers.

When he answered his assignment, he wrote a story about his Black ancestors arriving in a slave ship, then drew a picture of them building a house, brick by brick, for a White enslaver. In his drawing, one of the enslaved conjured a ladder in the sky that my son called an "escape hatch" through which they could climb to freedom. It dangled precariously above a half built, multistoried building from which one must jump to grasp the bottom rung. His ladder points to a future yet to be realized. He intuited that his ancestors had to trust the possibility of him, a future where he existed, freer than they, however hazy and far off. His ladder in the sky offers us a clue about the "human element:" imagination. Radical imagination, however aspirational, is a form of resistance that calls upon future possibilities and ancestral wisdom to transform the present. It evokes a capacity to think critically, reflexively, and creatively about the social world.[129]

I borrowed the ladder image from my son as it is an archetypal symbol of ascension, evolution, and higher levels of thinking. Somehow, he clued into this. In Plato's *Symposium*, Diotima's Ladder of Love culminates as love for love's sake, in the

---

[129] Haiven and Khasnabish, *Radical Imagination*, 2.

ability to love all bodies and souls as sacred others. Her ladder eschews dualism and suggests that the highest form of love is utterly nondual and transpersonal. I aim to reconfigure the ladder as indicative of process rather than a symbol of hierarchy and competition. If we hold fast to the ladder of love and liberation, we can dismantle white supremacy and racism.

Policies and practices impact systemic and structural racism, but these alone will not address the generational impact of racism on human becoming. Anyone who has lived in the United States for any length of time is impacted by racism, either implicitly or explicitly. For White Americans, it is a moral wound, often hidden, whose redress is psycho-spiritual so that we relinquish control of structures and systems and participate in changing them. Maintaining innocence that we are not responsible for what we've inherited allows racism to persist.

Racism is the air we breathe, a quiet handshake some of us did not know we made. It is not the responsibility of the historically marginalized to perpetually demonstrate resilience and creativity nor to illuminate the detriments of racism to us. In this undertaking, I hope to elucidate the importance of White participation in transforming the ills of racism so that we may evolve the "human element." More than anything, I want to show my sons that I tried.

Perspective

First and foremost, I maintain the perspective that creating a world that works for everybody is possible. As stated, I want to contribute to creating that world for my sons. Their very existence feels both hopeful and precarious. Any academic question worthy of sleepless nights should envision a world where they can soar. Further, the most urgent and vital inquiries require answers from the whole self. This work is not just intellectual, for without relating to it emotionally, personally, and spiritually, it remains untransformed and uninspired. Therefore, much of my personal history is woven throughout. I also write from the perspective of a social philosopher-activist, psychologist, and spiritual teacher. I want to imagine a place of belonging and freedom for my children, whose children will inherit this seemingly "loveless world"[130] but expect it, as any child would, to love them back. We are called, in every generation, to respond to "the fierce urgency of now."[131] In so doing, we advance the cause for freedom and love.

When I was young, I did not know I had a race. We whispered "*Black*" as if it were a bad word, and we never spoke overtly about what it meant to be White. Everyone got simplified into broad categories of Asian, Mexican, or Black—all descriptions that flatten unique ethnicities just as White does.[132] Yet, somehow, we must come to understand ourselves both within and beyond these categories. I was implicitly taught that my race/looks/beliefs were "normal," which I interpreted as dull and admittedly exoticized the different other. I was never explicitly told I am White . . . just *human*. I was never expressly told others were *not* human, just *different*, and *different* was *not White*. The meta-communication is that *different* is also *less*. The normalcy of White ran parallel to the patriarchal assertion that White meant I was "a

---

[130] Baldwin, *Fire Next Time*, 10.

[131] King, *Where Do We Go from Here?*, 185.

[132] In Texas, because of the large population of recent Mexican immigrants and generations of Mexican Americans (often identified as Tejanos), many of Hispanic or Latinx origin, are conflated with Mexican regardless of their country of origin. Similarly, I was not taught to distinguish between various Asian or Black ethnicities.

member of the lucky sperm club." If I came to see myself as lucky, that meant others were unlucky, an implication that automatically engenders superiority and a sense of deservedness. Yet these are some of the sentiments that raised me.

I endeavor to understand how a culture of whiteness shapes our habits and systems. I now realize that my race is defined in some ways by negation and denial of the body, my own and others. I learned not to talk about any aspect of the body. Notice color. Revel in it. Paint your walls anything but white. Come to deeply love how blue "draws us after it,"[133] but *do not* notice *skin* color. Like so many in the halcyon days of the post-integration 1980s, I learned racial colorblindness; thus, I could remain innocent of the social issues aligned with it. I could remain ignorant that White is also a race. I aim to challenge the seduction of "White as normal" and participate in dislodging whiteness from a position of dominance and violence.[134] I argue that every person living in the United States is impacted by a culture of whiteness and the expectation to assimilate to it. White racism is a cornerstone of the American social system and continues to perpetuate division and harm. I illustrate how a culture of whiteness continues to impact our economic, psychological, and spiritual well-being.

Standpoint

In proposing an integral, psycho-spiritual process for White people to unbelong from a culture of whiteness, I write from the standpoint of a mother–activist–spiritual–philosopher. Through an inevitably creative and disruptive process

---

[133] Goethe, *Theory of Colours*, 311.

[134] Dei, "Reframing Critical Race Theory," 2.

of learning about the self in context, one discovers empowerment, liberation, transcendence, and reclaims the vitality of life.[135] I am informed by a lineage of philosophers, activists, and theologians in pursuit of Beloved Community. My son intuited a more just world with his ladder in the sky; his ancestors felt it as they dreamt him into being. Some of my own European ancestors danced close to its edges, too. Beloved Community has always existed in pockets and been longed for in the hearts of individuals, for the radical pursuit of love persists and sustains us throughout time.

Examining my social location—a White mother raising Black-biracial sons with a Black husband, both of whose ancestral roots are in the complicated South—substantiates my inquiry with subjective, personal evidence of acquiring and unbelonging from a culture of whiteness. Writing with standpoint theory in mind challenges assumptions that neutrality and objectivity are possible or necessary when examining White racism.[136] Using my lived reality as evidence removes the veil that I am neither impacted by nor relevant to what is being studied. Especially when challenging whiteness, White researchers need to see themselves operating in context. To practice social change, I must see myself as part of what needs changing and an agent of transformation. Etorre asserts that if we can experience ourselves as both insider and outsider, we are better able to bear what is "unstable, always shifting, and yet full of discovery and hope."[137] Writing from the standpoint of a

---

[135] Palmer, "Grace of Great Things," 3.

[136] Wylie, "Why Standpoint Matters," 343.

[137] Etorre, *Autoethnography as Feminist Method*, 8.

White, upper-middle-class woman engaged in interracial social activism is not a powerless, outsider position, but one that needs to be deconstructed and disempowered. It is a kind of inverted standpoint. I must be aware of how whiteness can be silencing. Along the continuum of silences, I am also aware of being silenced because of my gender and because I publicly advocate for racial justice in White spaces. As a mother to my children and as a White woman, I am witness to both ends of the oppressor–oppressed paradigm.

This is not a scientific study, but a philosophical, psycho-spiritual inquiry about how we come to know what we know and how subjective, situated knowledge can inform social change. Subject (my ancestral and personal knowing) and object (deconstructing and disempowering White racism) are deeply interconnected.[138] I make meaning of my experience, lean into what I know, and hope to contribute to human cosmologies that move us toward greater belonging. I know that we are not separate but deeply entangled with one another, emphasizing the case that complete objectivity about the human experience is impossible. Thus, what we come to know about our own lives has philosophical and spiritual value. My unique experience lends credibility to the evolving conversation around race and racism.

Just as my theology is most influenced by Christianity, my racialized experience is most understood in the context of whiteness, one that is too often permitted to remain unselfconscious and non-self-critical. My acquired knowledge around race is simultaneously made by observing my participation in a culture of whiteness and constructed by my academic and personal relationships with voices

---

[138] Haraway, "Situated Knowledges."

outside of it. My chosen standpoint is from the margin, what bell hooks names a liminal space that holds both likeness and difference. It is a site of radical openness and resistance.[139]

Examining whiteness from the margin, I attempt to make visible what is often kept invisible and therefore rendered unknowable and unchangeable. I am Plato's prisoner who exits and later returns to the cave. I am Psyche who questions accepted traditions and seeks to evolve them. I cannot deny the cave of whiteness as formative to my identity, and I attempt to shine a light on it so others may be encouraged to examine their relationship to it. I was formed in the darkness of the cave, but I am learning to see *in* it differently; to see, as Plato suggests, with my whole self.[140] The cave aims to keep things hidden but sit with it long enough and all things become knowable. The demonization of and looking away from darkness is at the root of anti-Blackness and other forms of racism that continue to harm.

I write from the standpoint of a mother, a role too often minimized in academia. I was told, once, that I am perhaps a better mother than a scholar. This felt like a disempowering statement, one intended to poke holes in my belonging. On the contrary, I elevate my role as mother to ensure it is given a voice in this work. Motherhood may be perceived as a limitation, but I assert that maternal qualities of care and interdependence are needed in academic and social justice spaces. As a mother I know something of the gritty, fierce, and tender qualities of love. As a White mother to Black-biracial boys, I know the dangers of whiteness that can only

---

[139] hooks, "Choosing the Margin."

[140] See opening quotes of Part I, by Johnson and Plato.

be transformed by redemptive love. I know that White mothers have sabotaged coalition-building because of our seductive proximity to White men from which we can borrow power. If critically examined, I know that we are also well poised to understand both ends of the oppressed–oppressor paradigm. I know the ways I was mothered and the ways I am trying to mother that are both echoes of the old and seeking new sounds. I cannot fulfill the mother archetype on my own, but I am part of a great and flowing energy mothering the world a little more whole. I cannot set this part of me aside. It is my second skin; a statement made more complex given who I mother.

Although I am not in a position of subservience as implied by Wylie's understanding of the insider–outsider standpoint, I am able to observe patterns and connections in a culture of whiteness as an insider.[141] I am also able to observe and viscerally feel the effects of dominant culture on my most intimate relationships. Perhaps this might more aptly be referred to as an outsider–insider standpoint in that my close relationship to those deemed outsiders are juxtaposed with my insider status to whiteness. I can critique whiteness from the standpoint of insider and elevate outsider voices. There is not a space I enter where I do not consider the safety and belonging of my children and husband. They are my conscience, my mirror, my light. To every room I ask, "Do you see them? Are they welcome, or

---

[141] Wylie, "Why Standpoint Matters," 346–48. Wylie points to the long history of Black women working in White homes and how this role affords them an intimate, insider view of whiteness. Even though Black women are considered subservient in such a role, their acquired knowledge ought to be elevated and empowered when it comes to understanding a culture of whiteness.

more importantly, celebrated? Can you love them?" They are here, in every page of this dissertation.

Some of my mother's words are here because she awakens aspects of myself that need undoing. She represents a group of White mothers who came of age but did not participate in the Civil Rights Movement and may not resonate with the need for ongoing racial awareness. To these mothers, undoing racism did not require undoing whiteness. Racism is a "them" problem, an inability to move on from the past. Like Aphrodite does for Psyche, she brings me toward deeper awareness and reveals parts of me that dwell in the unexamined unconscious or traditions no longer useful. Each generation has the task of questioning tradition and ushering ourselves beyond, of shedding old skin for new even as we retain the memory of the old. In a memoir about mothering, I read that women carry fetal cells from all the babies we've carried and vice versa. The cells mix and circulate in our bloodstreams for decades after birth or loss. They are not invaders, but friends, recognizing each other in the terrain of the body. This integration of cells is called "microchimerism."[142] Mother and child are forever joined; we are not lost to one another at the moment of physical separation. Positive or negative associations with our personal mothers aside, we belong to a collective maternal energy.

Every single one of us was mothered into being. Creation is *ex profundis*, born of a germinating, creative abyss.[143] It is from the depths of that primordial womb that everything arose. The fear of our genesis from the dark denies our deeply

---

[142] Hall, *Without a Map*, 216.

[143] C. Keller, *Face of the Deep*, chap. 9.

feminine origins. Embracing the dark, or the shadow aspect, increases the potentiality for wisdom and transformation. My standpoint is that we need this energy to birth new ways of thinking about ourselves in relation to one another to mother the world more whole.

Not all who mother embrace the archetypal feminine, and not all mothers are caring. For me, however, mothering is explicitly feminine in that I see it as one of the most potent expressions of our interconnectedness. I align with Keller in describing our feminine, and I add maternal, origins as "radical relationalism . . . in which difference is not swallowed up by the self but enhanced."[144] Speaking from a deep place of feminine knowing is an act of resistance. bell hooks points out that women are rarely at the center of public discourses on race, that perhaps we fear it makes us less feminine.[145] This leads to my standpoint that the field of anti-racism requires both feminine and maternal energies that attend to the fact of our relatedness. Embodying both means working in the transformative space between I and you as well as the sacred and profane. Here, love, justice, and experiences of God are undifferentiated.[146]

My dissertation reckons with family history as my story is not separate from our nation's. It is also an expression of my radical commitment to reimagining who we can become if we take seriously a public discourse on the power of love to repair

---

[144] C. Keller, *Face of the Deep*, 87.

[145] hooks, *Killing Rage*, 3.

[146] C. Keller, *The Face of the Deep*, 233.

and begin the world over again.[147] More importantly, it is an offering of defiant hope to my sons. Hope is a controversial standpoint, one that could be considered a privilege. It is different from naïve optimism, however, and can emerge from hopelessness. As an action, it requires that we become active participants in bringing about the kind of world we desire.[148] Adrienne Rich's words served as a mantra.

"My heart is moved by all I cannot save:
so much has been destroyed

I have to cast my lot with those
who age after age, perversely,

with no extraordinary power,
reconstitute the world."[149]

---

[147] King, *Where Do We Go from Here?*, 88.

[148] Macy, *Active Hope*.

[149] Rich, "Natural Resources," 67.

CHAPTER 2 | PAST IS PRESENT

In the Spring of 2021, still locked into the forced monasticism of the Covid-19 pandemic, my family became absorbed by The Falcon and the Winter Soldier *series on Disney+. Every Friday night for six weeks, the five of us crowded onto the couch. We watched, cried, cheered, and gasped. In it, Sam Wilson, a Black man who is the son of a shrimper from Louisiana, is tapped as the next Captain America, a title previously owned by an archetypal, Blond White male. Sam wrestles with his readiness to accept the shield, in part, because of the country's treatment of his ancestors and, in part, because he does not trust its readiness to embrace him. Sam has a lot of White friends, even fellow superhero friends who would give their lives for him. But friendship is different than equity—a truth he knows too well.*

In one especially touching scene, his young nephews play-fight with the iconic shield emblazoned with a star, imagining themselves as future heroes. Possibility abounds. They dare to imagine. Sam feels the weight, responsibility, and love for the community he carries with him, how little his idea of "hero" has to do with an idealized individual and more to do with fostering the dreams of a people.[150]

My boys and my husband loved this scene and cheered with delight, ready for the world to witness what they have long known.

"I, too, sing America . . .

"I, too, am America."

The poem drums in my head.

"I, too . . .

---

[150] Skogland, *Falcon and the Winter Soldier*, "Truth."

"I, too . . ."[151]

Finally, they will see just how beautiful you truly are.[152]

...

I share this vignette because a pop-culture show held the weight of a powerful subtext. I share it to illustrate that none of us enters a room or arrives at a position alone. We carry our histories, our communities, our ancestries, and our future hopes with us at all times. Very often these are at war within us. They knowingly and unknowingly impact how we live and move through the world, both blinding and exposing biases. I share this to emphasize the enormous conflict felt by many Black Americans who love this country, who stand for its unrealized values of "liberty and justice for all" yet do not feel fully loved by it. Finally, I share this to highlight the point that White America often resists being challenged except on its own terms. Without overtly naming Critical Race Theory as a backdrop, *The Falcon and the Winter Soldier* confronted its viewers with a conversation about the history of race and power.[153] It is imperative that we address these issues to imagine a process of *unbelonging* and ultimately transforming a culture of whiteness.

As much as Critical Race Theory (CRT) has become a red herring and "wokism" is parried as a dirty word, it provides helpful data analysis for understanding the intersection of race and systems in this country. It serves the

---

[151] Hughes, "I, Too," 35.

[152] From this point on, personal anecdotes are identified by italicized font, with an ellipsis centered at the top and bottom.

[153] Skogland, *Falcon and the Winter Soldier*, "Truth."

purpose of helping to unlearn generational patterns of thought and long-held assumptions. While this work is not solely under the umbrella of CRT, Chapter 2 offers a brief overview of it to help understand the shifting nature of whiteness and why it is so difficult to divest from it. Further, I seek to contextualize the entangled nature of whiteness and anti-blackness.

From CRT to CART

The election of our first Black-biracial president in 2008 did not render us a post-racial country. Instead, we were confronted by a culture of whiteness that loudly resisted Barack Obama's leadership or hid behind a vote for him as evidence of non-racism. Since then, however, White backlash and fear of irrelevancy grew and festered, deepening fissures between groups of White people and between Whites and non-whites.[154] Conversations about what it means to be White and who was "Black enough" gained national traction. The historical moment rode in on the still-glowing embers of the past. It felt impossible to experience the present without seeing ghosts of the sobering, infinitely more terrible history that created it hovering in the background.

Any remotely conscious marginalized person or group will tell you the fissures are not new, but that White Americans may finally be growing the capacity to see them. We no longer have excuses *not* to see them. We have more tools at our disposal, from workbooks to programs to articles to incredible and challenging works of art, but these are means toward a shift in consciousness, not ends. An aspect of the "human element" lies in our ability to make meaning and change

---

[154] powell, *Racing to Justice*, 32.

behavior based on what is learned. Learning to *see what is* lies at the heart of our social, political, and spiritual evolution. The human project is compromised when we cannot hold the tension of its beauty and terror, its light and dark. As a nation, it feels like we are currently seeing through eyes of nostalgia or progress, torn between nativism and pluralism and unsure of how to wrestle with the process of unlearning and relearning.

Part of seeing is holding tensions between the limitations and possibilities of our inherited thought patterns and histories. If the "human element" is to evolve, it cannot be through colonial domination or complicity with pan-European imperialism but through honoring a multitude of cultural wisdoms. The question is whether enough White people will commit to the grueling and ongoing task of critical examination to make the necessary psycho-spiritual shift toward a more just and equitable society. The task is made more difficult by the wealth and education disparities among Whites, proliferating replacement theories among alt-right and white supremacist groups who demonize and mislabel CRT.[155]

One expert in the field of psychology suggests that shifting race consciousness takes three to ten years at the personal level, and seven to ten generations at the collective if we commit to the work of dismantling White racism.[156] CRT is a tool that provides data and analysis to help shift consciousness.

---

[155] "White Replacement Theory" proliferates violent speech, behavior, and propaganda by falsely asserting an ongoing, covert effort to replace the White population in the United States and beyond. See Wilson and Flanagan, "Racist 'Great Replacement' Theory Explained."

[156] Menakem, "Somatic Abolitionism."

More than dates and analysis, however, changing a culture of whiteness requires moving away from competitive individualism and toward a liberated collective consciousness that values interdependent connectedness. The racial hierarchy in the United States is economically, politically, and spiritually unsustainable if we want to usher in a more humanitarian, integrated society. Dismantling it requires a close examination of whiteness and opening to the extent to which our behaviors around it are unconscious.[157]

The nature of racism in this country makes it unsolvable if addressed only at the individual level. Instead, it must be simultaneously addressed individually, communally, and systemically and taken on as academic, political, psychological, and spiritual work. Too often, racism is seen as a personal failing or belief rather than a systemic problem. The emergence of CRT in the 1970s initiated a legal framework for understanding the impact of race on one's access to systems, institutions, and resources. It builds on the insights of critical legal studies and radical feminism to question the foundations of a liberal society, especially theories of equality and legal reasoning.[158] As individuals, we can understand our connection to systems by inquiring about the historical processes that created our relationships to them.

Inspired by Black thinkers like W. E. B. Du Bois, James Baldwin, and their predecessors Frederick Douglass and Sojourner Truth, whiteness studies is a growing aspect of CRT among White academics. While I look to Black perspectives on

---

[157] powell, *Racing to Justice*, 27.

[158] Delgado and Stefanic, *Critical Race Theory*, 24.

whiteness, I also look to contemporary White scholars and critics like Tim Wise,[159] Shannon Sullivan,[160] and Richard Dyer[161] who successfully challenge White readers to examine their own racialized experiences and the unconsciously absorbed assumption that White is simply the default category for human. Today, as an aspect of CRT, whiteness studies explicate more than White attitudes about non-white groups and instead increases our racial awareness around the acquisition of whiteness, both consciously and unconsciously. It is important to rethinking race and ethnic relations.[162] Studying whiteness with a personal hermeneutic lens underscores that we cannot afford to allow whiteness to remain invisible to itself.[163] A tension to hold is the connection between anti-racist politics and whiteness studies used as a means for progressive Whites to virtue signal by challenging white racism.[164] I am advocating for anti-racism, and I am politically progressive. I also aim to challenge white racism and white hegemony without distancing myself from it.

What I hope to contribute is a way of understanding how to critically examine and pursue unbelonging from a culture of whiteness in such a way that leads to deeper interracial belonging and coalition building to dismantle racial hierarchies.

---

[159] Wise, *Dear White America*.

[160] Sullivan, *Revealing Whiteness*.

[161] Dyer, *White*.

[162] Doane, "Rethinking Whiteness Studies," 4.

[163] Doane, 5.

[164] Doane, 6.

Choosing the path of unbelonging is neither intended to further confuse definitions of whiteness nor demonstrate racial privilege by creating yet another category of exclusive belonging that is both mercurial and fragile. Rather it is a challenge to honestly own how a culture of whiteness shapes us and consciously refuse to remain complicit with upholding hierarchy and oppression without disowning White as a racialized experience.[165] The behaviors performed that constitute belonging to a culture of whiteness are the ones I suggest deconstructing. Over time, whiteness can be recast as a visible part of the racial fabric of this country rather than remain invisible and "unraced." To do this, *unbelonging* asks that we examine the effects of whiteness on interracial relationships in the United States in such a way that transcends and includes it as an aspect of identity. Current iterations of whiteness studies explore the implications of whiteness with an external and internal gaze to expand the evolution of White racial identity, challenge White racial invisibility, and avoid reproducing White hegemony. To achieve social change, it is imperative to critically examine whiteness and its impact on our racial consciousness.[166] I intend to expand on each of these throughout this dissertation.

A culture of whiteness is the very heartbeat of this country, and opening our eyes to it is an act of love that can help us change systems, structures, and ourselves. Whiteness left unnamed clots the flow of love that facilitates repair. As Baldwin wrote,

---

[165] Doane, 8.

[166] Doane, 7.

> Love does not begin and end the way we seem to think it does. Love is a battle, love is a war; love is a growing up. No one in the world—in the entire world—knows more—knows Americans better, or odd as this may sound, loves them more than the American Negro. This is because he has had to watch you, outwit you, deal with you, and bear you, and sometimes even bleed and die with you, ever since we got here—and this is a wedding. Whether I like it or not, or whether you like it or not, we are bound together forever. We are part of each other. What is happening to every Negro in the country at any time is also happening to you.[167]

Deconstructing whiteness is to know ourselves better and come face-to-face with the codependent, interrelated nature of the oppressor–oppressed paradigm.

We can deepen our relationship to CRT if we can see it as a language of love, one that allows us to see ourselves, as Baldwin suggests, through another's eyes.[168] A lens of love understands that all people are injured by racism, require some type of liberation, and deserve compassion while unraveling their relationship to privilege and oppression.[169] We have a chance to grow up, grapple with, and struggle with thinking more creatively and humanely about ourselves and one another. We have an opportunity to understand whiteness as a site of struggle as well as a site of resistance and liberation.

---

[167] Baldwin, *Nobody Knows My Name*, 72.

[168] Baldwin, *Nobody Knows My Name*, 72.

[169] Tochluk, *Living in the Tension*, 14.

Though it continues to be misinterpreted and demonized in conservative media,[170] CRT provides analysis of the impact of race on law, politics, and economic systems in the United States, as well as on the unseen collection of patterns and habits that inform our racialized psychology and spirituality.[171] Racism is not past but continues to have very real consequences today for White and non-white people. The fundamental tenets of CRT are as follows:

- Racism is ordinary, and its ordinariness makes it challenging to address because it is not acknowledged even when it operates.
- Racism advances the interests of both White elites and the White working class. Even if there is widening class division among Whites, there is a growing sense that the lower class is overlooked in favor of "minority interests." Thus, they can blame non-whites for taking their opportunities instead of critique the system that keeps poverty in place. Paradoxically, it also prevents poor and working-class Whites from forming alliances with their non-white counterparts that could aid in overcoming economic oppression. Strides toward equal rights often result from self-interest rather than a desire to help non-white populations. The question, then, is how can anti-racism appeal to the self-interest of Whites? Is moral and spiritual growth enough of an

---

[170] Many articles and news pieces support this claim, from CNN to PBS to *The New York Times*. For clarity on the origin of this demonization, see Wallace-Wells, "How a Conservative Activist Invented the Conflict over Critical Race Theory," 2021.

[171] Delgado and Stefanic, *Critical Race Theory*, 26.

incentive? How can we disaggregate anti-racism from being synonymous with "anti-White?"

- Races are categories that societies invent, manipulate, or retire when convenient. White *skin* cannot be retired, but I argue that whiteness as a culture can be.
- No person or group has a singularly stated, unitary identity. We live in a world of intersections that shift all the time. Naming and understanding our intersectional identities can build a culture of empathy and deeper belonging.
- White people need to increase their stamina for analyzing race and racism so as not to burden or idealize the "voice of color" as teacher and counselor on matters of race.[172]

As an outgrowth of CRT Critical *Anti-Racist* Theory (CART) moves beyond thought and toward action to challenge the limitations of our current systems and essential identities. It is the activity of CRT. One of the habits of a culture of whiteness is to minimize and silence opposition to it and resist constructive criticism that facilitates change. It tends to intellectualize and theorize lived experience, so our solutions are often intellectual and theory-based. However, speaking or writing effectively about race and racism cannot be addressed without emotion and attending to embodied experiences. CART proposes that lived experiences inform

---

[172] Delgado and Stefanic, 51.

theory.[173] Internalized racism lives in the body; anti-racism is exhibited through the body. It is not enough to *think* anti-racist. We must *be* it.

In George Sefa Dei's words, CART simply states that "we cannot read and understand race without being anti-racist."[174] It requires an awareness of our social location. It is embodied and holistic, not merely intellectual. White people cannot participate in anti-racism without also examining our embodied experience. Ibram Kendi posits that anti-racism begins at the policy level, leads to racial equity, and is substantiated by antiracist ideas and actions.[175] He is not wrong that policy significantly impacts changes in systems, however equity must be internalized so that policies are not undermined. There is also the practicality of how to propose, build coalitions for, and enact policy changes. Dei advocates for an integral antiracist approach that addresses inequities in race, class, gender, and sexuality primarily through education. He further argues that racist practices do not require intentionality but are deemed racist by their effects on communities or individuals.[176] Both acknowledge that racist ideas are unconsciously supported in institutional structures and carried out by individuals. Anti-racism, therefore, requires that we engage with the unconscious. Shelly Tochluk proposes that developing racial

---

[173] Dei, "Reframing Critical Anti-Racist Theory," 2.

[174] Dei, 1.

[175] Kendi, *How to Be an Antiracist*, 13.

[176] Dei, "Integrative Anti-Racism," 13.

awareness and antiracist action emerge from one's contemplative practice.[177] Alongside her, I argue that anti-racism is more powerful when addressed through political, psychological, and spiritual engagement. Ultimately, anti-racism seeks to undo the hierarchical ranking of racial difference.

It is not a betrayal of one's race to think critically about it. Later sections explain race as largely a social and historical construct, and CART tasks us with examining and rejecting how race has come to represent good/bad, superior/inferior binaries. Ignoring what race has come to signify and its impact on lived experience is a betrayal of our humanity. Whites have been "raced," and the overvaluation of whiteness deepens our social and political fault lines by insisting we are "innocent, normal, natural, and objective."[178]

If White Americans want to counteract racism and seek to repair the legacy of colonial slavery, then we must engage in a self-conscious, hermeneutic process that seeks to bring about social transformation. We may meet the future by learning from the past and by creating long-term, multigenerational efforts toward dismantling racism. CART asserts that we cannot afford to be objective, rational, unemotional, or indifferent in discussions about race if we want to identify as anti-racist.[179] To see clearly is to internalize that an unexamined, unhealed past continues to be a liability for future generations. If it is true in families, it is also true in communities and societies. While CRT informs my understanding of the entwined

---

[177] Tochluk, *Living in the Tension*, chap. 1.

[178] Dei, "Reframing Critical Anti-Racist Theory," 2.

[179] Dei, "Reframing Critical Anti-Racist Theory," 1.

nature of whiteness and anti-blackness, it extends beyond a legal framework. I employ CRT primarily to elucidate how the past is present, not as a strategy for imposing guilt or suggesting specific judicial, systemic changes. Anti-racism, which includes CRT and CART, receives criticism for implying that all Whites are racist.[180] It is a simplistic argument that closes doors if cultivated. No White person alive invented racist thought, but it is part of the inherited cultural ethos we inhabit. Taking responsibility for changing it is not the same as *being* responsible for it.[181]

Suppose we can use CRT and CART to increase our vocabulary and stamina around understanding hierarchical systems and how they uphold dominator patterns. In that case, we can change systems based on shared values, empathy, and collaboration. I recognize the idealism inherent in this vision. Still, I maintain that part of radical imagination is naming what is (racism) alongside what is desired (a compassionate, anti-racist society) and finding ways to get there. The work of transformation requires braiding intellect, creativity, and action. It is not enough to use anti-racism as a vehicle to change others; we must allow ourselves to be changed, too.

Resistance to CRT and CART further amplifies the need for them as frameworks to analyze systems and policies. They are not ends in themselves but means through which to understand just how pervasive and rigid White racism is. In short, CRT provides language and analysis about how racism persists in systems and institutions whereas CART moves individuals and communities toward changing

---

[180] Thandeka, "Why Anti-Racism Will Fail," par. 5.

[181] Dyer, *White*, 73.

behavior and inherited beliefs. Integrated with a feminine, spiritual lens that allows us to hold polarities and somehow find a middle way that focuses on political emancipation and personal transformation, these are powerful tools for change.

Explicating Whiteness

To engage in the process of unbelonging from whiteness, it is imperative to cultivate some understanding of what whiteness is. The expression of racism is a function of dominator systems that are as old as recorded history. Riane Eisler's Cultural Transformation theory indicates that societies exist on a partnership–dominator continuum, but that during the historical period human societies tilted toward domination.[182] Prehistoric cultures may have balanced masculine and feminine principles and roles until a fundamental social shift occurred after a prolonged period of chaos and disruption. Eisler asserts that humans have lived in dominator societies for 5,000 years with some tilts toward partnership.[183] At the onset of the Common Era, for example, the early Christians threatened the growing power of the "church fathers" as their empowered community preached compassion, nonviolence, and love, undermining patriarchal family structures. Under the rule of Constantine, the Roman Empire eventually extinguished threats of equity by making Christianity the official religion, placing control of it within the domain of the state. Christianity became androcratic, the Roman Empire the "Holy Roman Empire," and God explicitly male.[184] Reasserting a foundational ranking of males

---

[182] Eisler, *Chalice and the Blade*, 13.

[183] Eisler, 188.

[184] Eisler, 138–39.

over females and using Christianity as a tool of power affected patterns of conquer and control in the expanding Western world that eventually shaped racial, ethnic, and religious hierarchies in this country.[185]

Dominator societies are violent and rank one segment of humanity over another. Even though domination can be in the form of a matriarchy or patriarchy, over time it skewed toward upholding a toxic expression of patriarchy. Such societies value force, individualism, competition, and commodity over intuition, collectivism, cooperation, and reciprocity.[186] None of these are inherently "bad" or "good" qualities, but they become abusive or enabling when used to subjugate. Further, they systematically oppress racial and ethnic groups, LGBTQIA communities, disabled people, and women, denying possibilities for a more equitable society.[187] Racism is the abuse of acquired or claimed power based on ethnocentric beliefs that one group is biologically superior to another because of skin color or ethnicity. Ibram Kendi extends the definition of racism beyond personal or group belief to include the collection of policies that sustain racial inequities and injustices that are substantiated by ideas about racial hierarchies.[188] The European colonial powers initiated a racial hierarchy in the Americas; thus, a culture of whiteness functions as a culture of domination.

---

[185] Eisler, 141.

[186] Eisler, 18.

[187] Eisler, 13.

[188] Kendi, *How to Be an Antiracist*, chap. 1.

Dominator culture socializes people to believe that power in the form of force is the inevitable foundation of human relations rather than rational persuasion. It seizes upon a single narrative that maintains rather than dismantles systems of injustice and exclusion and preys upon primitive emotions of fear, anger, and rage. Such societies are pyramids, with the interests of a few upheld at the top.[189] Dominator systems determine policy, incentive structures, legal rights, and access to social power within a given society without public buy-in. Compliance with them provides relative access to power and safety. Disrupting them puts one at risk. Those who maintain security in dominant societies are complicit with the power structure and leave it unchallenged, and the system is reinforced and strengthened. This "old order" needs to be contested and dismantled; the present system is breaking down. I do not address the entire history of domination, but apply it as a baseline concept for understanding the roots of a culture of whiteness and White racism in this country. I seek to counter dominator frameworks with integral approaches that value partnership, intersectionality, transpersonal love, and a balance of healthy masculine and feminine qualities.

The arrival of Europeans in the "New World," who decimated Native Americans with disease and violence and bought and sold enslaved Africans, set in motion a dominator paradigm based on race intertwined with religious superiority. Race is a category that has little to do with genetic or biological differences, but it has come to signify so much about one's social and political experience in the United States. That a White mother can give birth to Brown sons challenges neatly defined

---

[189] Eisler, 66.

racial categories and proves that race is a skin-deep characteristic that has come to symbolize static qualities of one's character and potential. We must endeavor to understand the impact of racism on the body, mind, and soul and how it limits the ability to access the true self and transcendent other. Racial differences are real without being essential, and the realities of those differences need recognition if racism is to be challenged.[190] In the United States, racial categorization signifies who belongs and who does not. Challenging the idea that race is essential and static allows for more spaciousness and fluidity of the self to develop freely in the world. Racism cannot be erased with platitudes like "We are all human." That we are all human is a premise, not prescriptive.

Humans are 99.9% similar in their genetic makeup. No accepted scientific data supports biological racial categorization. Genomic difference would imply divergent evolutionary tracts, whereas the primary difference in humans is because of migratory pathways and resulting linguistic patterns that inform social habits. Racial categories such as White, Black, or Asian do not accurately encapsulate unique ancestral lineages, nor are they confined to specific geographical locations.[191] A White, Black, or Asian person can also be American, Canadian, or Brazilian and have very different experiences in each place. Even if not a verifiable biological difference, race is at least historically, socially, culturally, and politically real.[192] Race, like culture, exists as a social construct with continually changing definitions, and racialized

---

[190] Sullivan, *Revealing Whiteness*, loc. 403.

[191] Baker, Rotimi, and Shriner, "Human Ancestry Correlates."

[192] MacMullan, "Facing Up to Ignorance and Privilege."

experiences are specifically located. In truth, no matter what we "know" or "understand" about race, the White race assigned itself superiority, is motivated by retaining power, and artificially created a standard of "normalcy" by which all other people should be measured. The question of race in the United States was made into a species question: Who is more human?[193]

The social and lived reality of *being raced* has enormous consequences. Until White is understood as a racialized experience rather than an unmarked or neutral category, we recuse ourselves from understanding its impact on current and historical divisions. We remain unable to leave the shadowy cave of a culture of whiteness that is just a euphemism for domination. Richard Dyer argues:

> As long as race is something only applied to non-white peoples, as long as [White] people are not racially seen and named, they/we function as a human norm. Other people are raced; we are just people. There is no more powerful position than that of being "just" human. The claim to power is the claim to speak for the commonality of humanity.[194]

If Whites are "just human," then it follows that non-whites are something else entirely. Imagine if I had told my son that the "human element" was White. Said that way, I hope the faulty logic is obvious. As we move toward racial awareness, we come to realize the prevalence of white supremacist culture and its insistence that

---

[193] Menakem, "Somatic Abolitionism."

[194] Dyer, *White*, 38.

White people deny our understanding of race. In fact, embedded in a sense of White superiority is that we are somehow beyond thinking about race.[195]

White is rarely named in reference to race, and we often blanch at being called White. Reverend Thandeka initiated a simple social experiment to prove this point. When White colleagues expressed curiosity or a desire to support the work of racial awareness, she challenged them to spend a handful of days referencing White people as such in casual conversation with others, the same way one might with a person of Asian or African descent. Most could not sustain it and reported discomfort and awkwardness. Some said naming people White made them feel aligned with white nationalists or neo-Nazis.[196] I do not quarrel with race as a descriptive category with specific shared experiences. However, those of us who want to move beyond racism are so desperate to distance ourselves from "the real racists" that we lack the tools to develop racial awareness that could situate us in time and space and help us to understand our histories. Racism does not have to be the inevitable outcome of acknowledging race. There are white supremacists just as there are black separatists; neither of these is ubiquitous. Ironically, by negating White as a race, we are inadvertently raced and thrown into an entire drama governed by unwritten rules of social control, denial, and negation. These create shame and confusion, especially for children.

In Chapter 3, I offer an analysis of the social construction of a culture of whiteness and the consequences on economic, psychological, and spiritual well-

---

[195] hooks, *Teaching Community*, 26.

[196] Thandeka, *Learning to Be White*, 3–4.

being. If we can come to know ourselves as White, then we can begin to understand how a history and culture of whiteness moves through us. If we can understand how race moves through us, it can be dislodged from a position of power and privilege. We can begin to address the harm done by oppression and retire a culture of whiteness that obscures our respective ancestries and dominates American systems. Addressing how difference is exploited is not an argument for colorblindness but for a genuinely pluralistic society that responds to the fact of diversity by engaging it with curiosity and authenticity.[197] Those involved in the work of "[making] the world a more human dwelling place"[198] are called to push against oppressive boundaries and systems of domination that thrive on maintaining abusive and exclusive power. Such systems have a deep investment in the myth of sameness, even as their actions and outcomes reflect the primacy of whiteness.[199] Part of the human project is deciding whether we will be creatures of domination or communion, whether we can learn to see difference as a function of equity.

The connection between White and whiteness is like the relationship between race and racism. Both whiteness and racism are socially conditioned ways of being and thinking. As a function of domination, a culture of whiteness upholds binary relationships between self–other, subject–object, dominator–dominated,

---

[197] hooks, *Teaching Community*, 47.

[198] Baldwin, "Creative Process," 315.

[199] hooks, "Representations of Whiteness," 209.

center–margin, universal–particular, and so on, and arranges them hierarchically.[200] In looking at the shifting impact of race on social programs, Heather McGhee asserts that "race isn't a static state; it's better understood as an action, and one of its chief functions is to distance White people from people who are 'raced' differently."[201] If we identify as White, understanding the social ontology of a culture of whiteness from an objective and subjective perspective deepens awareness of a personal and cultural experience. Whiteness is more than a sum of privilege, power, and identity, but intimately connected with the reality of racism.[202]

Race is a story that was embedded into the founding of our nation. Increasing diversity and corresponding trainings is not enough; we must also transform the narrative of racial division.[203] The story reads that White skin color, regardless of ethnic origins, symbolized power, privilege, and preference. The primacy of White skin triumphed over culture and ethnicity and created a wall of whiteness that ultimately negated unique ethnic origins in favor of social belonging. In the formation of colonial America, even poor Whites, who often labored alongside enslaved Blacks, aligned themselves with the ruling aristocracy just by virtue of skin color. Encouraged by the planter elite, they deceived themselves about the realities of their own class degradation. Even they had to pay for the delusions of

---

[200] Birt, "Bad Faith of Whiteness," 87.

[201] McGhee, *The Sum of Us*, 58.

[202] Dei, Karumanchery, and Karumanchery-Luik, "White Power, White Privilege," 81.

[203] Wallis, *America's Original Sin*, xxi.

whiteness, which arise from the fact that they were not visually Black and therefore not treated as Black.[204] We see this today as working-class Whites align themselves with powerful Whites, demanding that immigrants and non-white citizens stop taking their jobs.[205]

It could be said that Englishman John Smith—confident, rugged, adventurous, and motivated by self-interest—served as the founder and preserver of the Western White male archetype as early as 1607.[206] The French and Spanish also rivaled for what eventually became the United States. Competing colonization resulted in violent encounters with coastal Indigenous peoples and other invaders for much of the early seventeenth century. At various times, the colonial empires attempted to enlist both Indigenous and African populations to their aid, often with conditions attached. Ultimately, a race-based, pan-European mobilization equally crushed African and Native American rebellions.[207] Violence and colonization would become hallmarks of a culture of whiteness.

John Smith was shrewd in his dealings with the Powhatan and worked to maintain a tenuous, if not self-serving, peace based on his swagger and ability to convince the Chief that he was a man of great importance. When ill health led to his eventual return to England, the collaboration between the Native American and the

---

[204] Birt, "Bad Faith of Whiteness," 90.

[205] powell, *Racing to Justice,* 112–13.

[206] Horne, *Dawning of the Apocalypse,* 167.

[207] Horne, *Dawning of the Apocalypse,* 17.

colonial settler deteriorated. Interactions were increasingly hostile, revealing a fundamental lack of interest in developing a covenant of respect and cooperation. As the English inched ahead in establishing the original thirteen colonies, White was indistinct from *free*, *Christian*, and *English*, and I would add *self-interest*. Gradually the French, Spanish, and Portuguese with interests in the New World were subsumed into a White racial category, too. Many who arrived and established legacies in the United States traded their ethnicities and religions for nationalism and whiteness.[208]

If we want to challenge beliefs that White racism is indelible, we must endeavor to understand how whiteness shapes us. A culture of whiteness revealed its violent nature during the conquest of Indigenous peoples, the enslavement of Africans, the Civil War, and Jim Crow. It proved its power when it undermined Reconstruction and the New Deal. It shows its persistence in the era of mass incarceration and continued targeting of Black and Brown bodies by law enforcement.[209] In short, it has created standards of belonging, freedom, and citizenship in this country, and it will not change without increased awareness. Still, genuine transformation will occur only when we commit to the psycho-spiritual work of unbelonging from a culture of whiteness and practicing public behaviors of love, both of which I discuss in more depth in later chapters.

---

[208] Horne, *Dawning of the Apocalypse*, introduction.

[209] Coates, foreword to *Origin of Others*.

The Shadows of Whiteness

As a dominator construct, a culture of whiteness is in the grips of the following stories and shadow archetypes:[210]

- *Flawed notions of creation and clinging to the myth of Adam:* Colonialist reinterpretations of the Genesis narrative of a seven-day creation story in which humans assumed dominion over the natural world and fell from grace because of Eve's temptation in the Garden led to the alignment of toxic patriarchal values with White Christianity.[211] Only in the last century and a half have we begun to understand humans in the context of a multi-billion-year evolutionary history. While interpretations of the creation narrative span a wide range, in the United States, colonial domination of the land and people fed the metanarrative of Euro-American progress and superiority.in which the rugged White male adventurer was the rightful conqueror of the land. He was considered the New Adam, the one created in God's image to recover man's original divine likeness.[212] Credible religious scholars now reject the literal seven-day creation story and the ensuing appointment of humans, especially

---

[210] These archetypes are an amalgamation of many conversations with my mentor, Dr. Bill Kerley. In our teaching together, we attempt to deconstruct these archetypes even as they continue to function. The rise of the patriarchy, ranking males over females, and their influence on the "New World" are also supported in Eisler's *The Chalice and the Blade.*

[211] Peterson, *The Message*, Genesis 2:5–3:24.

[212] Delio, "Racism and the American Dream."

males, as superior, but upholding the myth enabled a rapacious attitude toward the land and the domination of the masculine over the feminine.

- *Patriarchy:* Because the patriarchy in the United States was established and upheld by White, predominantly Protestant men who created our governing bodies and documents, it directly influenced the persistence of white supremacy.
- *Dependence:* A culture of whiteness has made its constituents dependent in that belonging, representation, and "success" are directly related to standards of behavior created by White men. Ironically, one of the most prevalent myths a culture of whiteness depends on is a "pull yourself up by your bootstraps" independence that interferes with cultivating the types of interdependence necessary to dismantling white racism. We come to depend on the myth of individual success more than the strength of supportive communities of belonging and inclusion.
- *Meritocracy:* The seductive belief that we deserve what we get because of hard work and relentless participation in a capitalist system that has long benefitted those at the top of the social pyramid. It is a myth that if one just works hard enough, they will achieve financial success. I know many laborers who work infinitely harder than executives, but have no pension, investments, or paid vacation.
- *Colorblindness:* This archetype is a call for an end to racial categories that does not seriously challenge race or racism as a factor in one's sociopolitical experience. It precludes intervention and supports the racial status quo. Colorblind conservatives guard against noticing race and

racism as a factor in the minds of those in power while blaming historically marginalized groups for their status and conditions. Colorblind liberals lean toward "post-racialism" to believe themselves beyond race. Such a stance is supported by saying, "Race doesn't matter to me," therefore allowing them to veer away from the difficulty of talking about racial conditions.[213]

- *Redemptive and retributive violence*: Look no further than the most recent mass shooting or state-sanctioned violence to understand the link between patriarchy, white supremacy, and violence to uphold both.[214]

John McClendon argues that whiteness cannot be separated from conversations about race, nor can we negate race as foundational to one's experience even though there is no scientific, biological difference between the races.[215] In the context of this country, it is delusional to insist that race does not exist, as doing so negates our varying sociopolitical experiences. Often, a culture of whiteness seeks to affirm the value of a colorblind society so that it need not address the fact of race nor the impacts of racism. Simultaneously, colorblindness supports fantasies about individualistic meritocracies and enables blaming the disenfranchised for their

---

[213] Paraphrased from powell, *Racing to Justice*, 32–33.

[214] At the time of the first draft, the most recent mass shooting was in, New York, on May 14, 2022, by a 19-year-old with white supremacist views. This could well be replaced tenfold by the time this document is complete. At the time of completion, there have been more mass shootings than days passed in 2023. See Collins, "Buffalo Supermarket Shooting Suspect Allegedly Posted an Apparent Manifesto Repeatedly Citing 'Great Replacement' Theory," *NBC News*. See also "A Partial List of U.S. Mass Shootings in 2023," in *The New York Times*, 2023.

[215] McClendon, "On the Nature of Whiteness," 289.

disenfranchisement. It is a limited constructionist view that suggests that the social world is an illusion and that a "real world" awaits, thus permitting the minimization of one's experience in societies and systems.[216] Adopting colorblindness seduces us into thinking we have a racist system with no racists. If we completely depersonalize racism by denying race and ignoring inherited or adopted beliefs, then no responsibility for changing systems will be taken.

Furthermore, recasting colorblindness from a liberal humanist position to a neoconservative one has increased the Right's control over the political spectrum. Racist policy continues even as the Right claims "racelessness" because race is a social construct unsupported by biological fact. The argument for removing racial references and categories when examining law and policies does not allow us to adequately understand how it still informs programs like affirmative action, redrawing voting districts, school funding, and housing.[217] Such a stance protects White innocence while simultaneously exposing the harm we know "being raced" does.[218] Very few of us would trade places with a Black woman, a migrant child from Honduras, or a Pakistani man precisely because on some level we know the cost of being raced by dominant groups. In the unconscious White psyche, acknowledging race surfaces the uncomfortable assumptions we have made or learned about it.

…

---

[216] powell, *Racing to Justice*, chap. 2.

[217] powell, 58–59.

[218] hooks, *Killing Rage*, 270.

We never talked about race as kids. Therefore, we could believe it did not apply to us and that racism wasn't our problem. My internalized understanding is that to be White is to be lucky. The only lesson I got about my race and class growing up was that I was "a member of the lucky sperm club," which is a sexist trope implying the connection between patriarchy and racial hierarchies. I understood that my family and ancestors had done everything right, played by the rules, and been appropriately rewarded for it. We deserved our good fortune. Although not explicit, the unspoken assumption was that "other people" did not. The presumption of White as normal and good was so pervasive that I did not even realize I had a race until adolescence.

Felicia, a Black friend on my track team, pointed out that I had characteristics of a Black girl—full lips, speed, and a sizable enough backside so as not to be flat nor perceived as White if you were not looking at any other part of me. I knew I was not Black, but I had not exactly known I was White either. I also had not consciously equated full lips and a round derrière with being Black. From an early age, however, my sister teased me by calling me "monkey lips." My mother would rhetorically ask how I got "Black man arm muscles." These are so obviously racialized comments, though I did not explicitly know it at the time. I knew they were not intended as compliments but used to "other" me. The body, one's whole being, gets raced, whether one knows it or not. My mouth, my arms, and my backside evidently have a different race than the rest of me. How absurd.

I remember announcing Joel Kelley's arrival in my fourth-grade class. He was one of a handful of Black children to get bussed to my otherwise White school in the mid-1980s—thirty years after Brown v. Board. I told my mother I thought he was cute and that I might like to "go" with him—the term we used at the time for coupling up, as much as a fourth-grader can. When I told her this, she got her funny, tight smile, tilted her head, and said, "Oh?" Nothing dramatic, just "oh." I knew immediately I had done something wrong, but it was unclear what. Was a memo circulated among the White moms that a Black boy was in our class? Did they talk about these things and whisper "Black" like it was a bad word? Did they warn each other not to let their daughters near him? And gosh, he had a haircut just like the rapper Kid 'n Play, whose antics and sassy style all the White kids wanted to emulate. This is what Thandeka names the toxic shame of learning to be White, this unnamable ignominy that blooms inside when we step outside the acceptable box. She claims (and I agree!) that a child's natural temperament is open, curious, empathetic, and longs for connection.[219] *But we feel the direct heat of disapproval when the connection sought is not "White-approved." I could not and did not choose Joel in order to maintain my mother's approval. My own forbidden desires rendered me different, and to remain in the fold I had to suppress them. To remain in community, I had to split off from myself.*[220] *This split self fuels a toxic culture of whiteness. My mother did not have to say explicitly, "You cannot 'go' with a Black boy." The words hung between us, and I knew to say no when he finally asked me.*

The memory of my crush on Joel Kelley flooded my being when I told my parents I was marrying my husband, Josh. It is the moment I knew being White meant something more to my parents than they had ever intimated, despite their insistence that they did not see color. When their bargaining chips of "Dating was okay, but I never thought you'd marry one of them" and "Think of your children and how you will complicate their lives" and "He is not our people" did not work, my mother escalated to "race traitor," and "ni**er lover." Wait, weren't we "colorblind?" How can I betray something I was not trained to see, or value something I was taught not to mention?

Other comments trickled in over the years: exception to his race, sounds so Black, unsophisticated, loud. With each comment, a thin skin of internalized supremacy peeled away. Oh

---

[219] Thandeka, *Learning to be White*, 18–19.

[220] Thandeka, *Learning to be White*, 12.

yes, I would think, I was raised to believe that Black equated with incorrect and White with correct. Black quintessentially meant race or minority—a notion challenged by critical race theorists Delgado and Stefanic—whereas White represented normal, the standard-bearer.[221] It is work to undo such thinking. When these things are said about someone so close and so loved, the absurdity becomes glaringly obvious. I am not sure I would have recognized the toxicity and commonality of such thinking if I were not so intimately connected to a Black man. My maternal grandmother, already addled with dementia, once looked at Josh, clutched her purse to her chest and demanded, "Who is the colored boy?"

My mother and her mother were created in specific contexts, and their thinking was not at all unusual to their time. Because we have lost a historical sense of how cultures shift and have few rituals to honor change as it happens, we mistakenly made our mothers gods and expected them to be right, to be infallible. Forever and ever, daughters have felt outraged that our mothers, our gods, did not raise us according to the progressing standards of our own time, but by the values of theirs.[222] I am no different. Part of mothering the world more whole is to attempt to acknowledge and integrate intergenerational rifts, missteps, and misunderstandings.

To be fair, my parents grew to respect and admire Josh. They see him as a great father, an unflappable rock, a good man—all true. If I were to remind them of their words, they might claim to have never said them. Even at the time, my father had the decency to say he felt embarrassed by some of his feelings, and I had the audacity to suggest that maybe they were his to deal with. I am not sure if their changed perspective about my husband has facilitated a broader examination of their ideas about race or if Josh remains, to them, an exception. Nursed on the myth of colorblindness and

---

[221] Delgado and Stefanic, *Critical Race Theory*, chap. 5.

[222] Lowinsky, *Motherline*, xvi.

White as just-human, I was ill-prepared to consider Josh's race fully. I realize now how little I understood about my own racialized experience, what I absorbed and how that inclined me toward innocence about racial dynamics. I still had so much to learn and unlearn. Yes, I had the proverbial diverse friend group growing up, but no real insight into the impact of my internalized white supremacy on the relationships.

I remember how my mother responded when I gave birth to my third son, lighter-skinned than my other two. "You finally got your White baby!" she said.

You finally got your White baby.

As if "the White baby" was the one I was holding my breath for.

The primacy of whiteness, the way it believes so fundamentally in itself, assumes everyone else desires it, and maintains the right to determine who belongs to whiteness is astounding.

An enormous tension blooms in me, one I have only recently understood. I recall again James Baldwin's words, that we do not know ourselves, that non-white people do not need to be loved or pitied or accepted by us, but that White people "will have quite enough to do in learning how to accept and love [ourselves] and each other."[223] When we can do this, look at and love ourselves; there will be no need to desecrate the "other." What might love from a place of freedom look like? Loving the self and the other as transcendent and sacred does not negate our differences but includes and celebrates them. It was certainly not out of love that my parents could make the statements they did, but out of fear, the opposite of love. And yet they are "the innocents" who inherited benignly passed-down beliefs that became accepted truths.

There is a distinct difference between being White and adopting whiteness. We cannot trade our White skin, but we can trade a culture of whiteness for something more humane. If I conclude

---

[223] Baldwin, *Fire Next Time*, 20.

one thing about a culture of whiteness, it is that it does not uphold one of the holiest commandments to love another as yourself. It is a stance, a philosophy focused on "Me" and the other as "It," that values the independent individual over communally embedded personhood at every turn. While I will never be not White, I can unlearn whiteness. The shadows of whiteness precede me and hang over me like a cloud, but the clouds are not immovable. White-identified people need to ask the following questions: When did I first learn that I am White? What do I understand about whiteness as a culture? What could it look like to choose the margins as a site of resistance to it?

…

White Innocence

It is necessary to explore how choosing to abide by a culture of whiteness is a commitment to hyper-individualism, shame, and denial that protect "innocence" and ontological expansiveness. Abiding in the shadows of whiteness perpetuates the assumption of belonging, consumption, and ownership, especially of non-white worlds. This often results in an unrealized ignorance of how the habits of whiteness oppress others. Very often they are dismissed as expressions of individuality."[224] Consider the consumption of Native American practices and spiritualities without the ancestral collateral. It is my White right to dabble in other cultures, which simultaneously seeks to distance the actor from whiteness and limits the ability to see it operating. Also consider an intentional choice to live in a "diverse" neighborhood that both interrupts the ubiquitousness of interacting with an all-White world but betrays racial and economic privilege simply because the choice of where to live

---

[224] Sullivan, *Revealing Whiteness*, loc. 309, 338.

exists at all.[225] Neighborhoods with economic and racial diversity are important places that increase the potential for rich intersections, but it is important to recognize who has the power of choice.

White innocence of our shadows and insistence that we belong wherever we are is not a childlike, sweet naïveté. James Baldwin explained it as a betrayal of a deep-rooted fear of the other, a fear that, if faced, reveals truths about us and, if upheld, affords continual opportunities to avoid reality and remain ignorant.[226] In a state of innocence we continue to claim, "But I don't see color!" Or "We are all just human!" Both are harmful sentiments to the type of conversion I propose. White people in the United States must push past discomfort, denial, and the seductive innocence of White as "normal" or "just human." We need to allow ourselves to feel lost, disoriented, and imperfect. We need to unbelong from whiteness, which requires a recognizing continued participation in perpetuating socially unjust systems and taking responsibility for the oppressive impact of whiteness.[227]

If I am to imagine different possibilities for the "human element," I must presume that a dominator construct can be challenged and changed. If we choose to talk openly about racism in the United States, it helps to begin with the understanding that "white supremacist thinking" is the foundation that upholds and

---

[225] Sullivan, loc. 171.

[226] Baldwin, *Fire Next Time*, 23.

[227] Dei, Karumanchery, and Karumanchery-Luik, "White Power, White Privilege," 82.

maintains our culture of domination and tends to function unconsciously.[228] Whiteness has tentacles in every institution with which we interact, which is why it feels normal and intractable. We are not all white supremacists, but we all need to be mindful of how white supremacist *thinking* informs conscious and unconscious beliefs and behaviors about race. Insisting upon innocence perpetuates the problem.

A genuinely free society is impossible until we understand and address the hegemonic culture of whiteness in which we live and move and have our being. I cannot assume that embracing a multicultural, pluralistic society is a universal desire, but as the success of pluralism begins with a basic tolerance for diversity, it would behoove us to engage ethically and authentically with one another. To be clear, whiteness is not a monolith, but it is essential to address it as a culture that developed habits of harm and behaviors of entitlement at the expense of non-white others. Though it is vital to denounce individual acts of racism and groups that perpetuate it, it is just as crucial to look beyond them to understand how White people have been indoctrinated into a culture of whiteness that perpetuates perceptions of superiority. I am no more innocent of whiteness than another. I am also not "guilty" of whiteness. It is an inherited condition continuously validated by our society.

White innocence seeks to disguise and minimize the impacts of race on lived experience in some of the following ways:

- Calling attention to one's ethnic roots even if they present as White. "My grandparents are Hungarian."

---

[228] hooks, *Writing Beyond Race*, 11.

- Minimizing the salience of skin color, either by denying it or saying it doesn't matter.
- Listing hierarchies of oppression, that is, calling the "real problem" class, not race.
- Fantastical thinking. "Well, if Africans were colonizers, White people would be oppressed." Or "White people are oppressed because we do not have special laws or holidays."
- Geographic relativism. "It could be worse. You could be a woman in Afghanistan."[229]

I do not list these to invalidate the many experiences of oppression because of immigration status, gender, class, sexuality, religion, and so on, but in our country, skin color is the most obvious marker for who is historically oppressed or empowered. Racial injustice flourishes when we refuse to interrogate the construction and persistence of oppression. It is a "privilege" to continually obfuscate or downplay the realities of historically marginalized populations and to construct our own histories as noble and heroic. It is much more complicated than that, however. Our histories, both personal and collective, have elements of heroism and elements of shame. It is a tension we must be willing to hold to imagine unbelonging from whiteness and evolving the "human element."

Part of decolonizing whiteness is examining how dominator culture teaches us to think about race and difference as unfavorable. Partaking in cultural critique

---

[229] Dei, Karumanchery, and Karumanchery-Luik, "White Power, White Privilege," 82.

and taking personal inventory offers freedom for the "colonized" and the "colonizer."[230] Decolonization challenges disunion and the myth of separateness without insisting on simplistic solutions or sameness for peace and harmony. Liberation from a culture of whiteness seeks to disaggregate White from oppressor and Black from oppressed and to eliminate the oppressor–oppressed duality from society. It seeks to restore us to one another in ways that dignify differences rather than exploit them. My ancestry is complicit with the formation of a culture of whiteness in both conscious and unconscious ways. As a result, I inherited false "truths" about whiteness as heroic, normal, and American. I suspect these truths have been taking shape for hundreds of years as sketched below.

…

England, circa February 1610. I try to picture the scene. An announcement arrives from Jamestown, Virginia: "Help. The situation is dire. Send food supply and men." Lord de la Warr, the de facto but distant governor of the colony, stocked three ships, among them the Hercules, *and gathered a crew. There were to be no women and children except for the one, nine-year-old John Chandler, parentage not listed. It is possible he was sold as collateral to ensure the later passage of his family or as debt relief. It is possible that his family worked as servants for the nobleman. It is possible Lord de la Warr (for whom Delaware would be named) took a shine to little John and wanted him for his own personal cabin boy, a thought that makes my stomach churn. In any case, he was not nobility and relatively unremarkable until later in his life. His departure from London and arrival in Jamestown are almost mythical. We don't know a lot about Chandler's life before*

---

[230] hooks, *Teaching Critical Thinking*, 24–25.

Virginia.[231] *Like Zeus's children erupted from his head, John Chandler's life seems to have risen right out of the loamy Jamestown soil.*

He arrived during the starving time, the winter of 1610 when seventy-five percent or more of the colonists died by disease or battle or returned to England.[232] *Given his age and absence of guardians, his survival is remarkable. Was he frightened? Was he cared for? Did he cry out at night? Was it an Odyssean adventure, a larger-than-life tale that grew ever more heroic and horrific as he aged? My body pulls inward as I have an almost maternal ache for his nine-year-old self. I want to hold him close. Would the trajectory of this country, of which he was a significant early part, have turned out differently if he had been mothered? His is a remarkable story when told from the singular perspective of his arrival and survival. However, there are significant holes in the re-telling, especially regarding upon whose suffering his success was dependent. Told from the perspective of whiteness, this nation's history was there for the making, a lump of clay to be formed. Very little in my ancestral story mentions conflict with Native Americans or others, unless to call them "revolts," "attacks," or "massacres," all initiated by the Native or non-white population. As my father once quipped: "The victor writes the story."*

John Chandler, who survived out of the ashes of a dying colony, is my earliest known ancestor to arrive here. He would come to embody the lore of the self-made man, a myth my father handed me that persists today. The self-made man, of course, secures the financial well-being of his women and children but does not empower the independent capacity of females to make it on their own. Stories about the Chandler families are almost exclusively drawn from the male line.

---

[231] All personal ancestry comes directly from my late aunt, Karen Lewis Dale, who was an avid genealogist. It is supplemented by information from The Chandler Family Association.

[232] Chandler Family Association, "Genetic Chandler Family 7A," par. 9.

Unmarried women are marked by an asterisk, unconfirmed as kin unless tied directly to a man. So many institutions were closed to women that their power usually came from having their husbands' respect. When I got married, I overheard a family friend say to my father, "At least she is someone else's (meaning my husband's) problem now." Cultural beliefs are powerful and sustaining.

Chandler eventually received a land grant of twenty-five acres in 1618 just for surviving the starving time and early conflicts with Native Americans. The designation of "Ancient Planter" was later bestowed upon him for surviving the "Indian Massacre" of 1622, an ironic title at a young age with so little history. The land he received was possessed and redistributed from battles with Native Americans, never purchased, given, or earned outright. I often wonder what he thought of what transpired. Had he ever played with a Powhatan boy his age? At what point was he pulled away from him, told not to play with the savages? Who parented him into thinking this way? Just one year after receiving a land grant, he must have witnessed "20 and odd" Africans step ashore in Jamestown.[233] With only 700 inhabitants, word surely traveled quickly of this strange cargo. Surely a crowd gathered. What did he think, then? I want to hope that in the base of his belly, he was at least uneasy about trading people for corn and "victuals" that fed the hungry seamen. But I know in the base of my belly that uneasiness is not enough to rectify all that would follow. I do not come from a lineage of people who speak out, but from those who bow their heads and claim innocence.

---

[233] The passage in the middle of a letter from John Rolfe to Sir Edwin Sandys (1619) reads:

> About the latter end of August, a Dutch man of Warr of the burden of a 160 tunnes arrived at Point-Comfort, the Comandors name Capt Jope, his Pilott for the West Indies one Mr. Marmaduke an Englishman. They mett with the Treasurer in the West Indyes, and determined to hold consort shipp heterward, but in their passage lost one the other. He brought not any thing but 20. And odd Negroes, which the Governor and Cape Marchant bought for victualls (whereof he was in greate need as he pretended) at the best and easyest rates they could." (243)

I often wonder if my husband's earliest ancestor here was among the "20 and odd" Africans who were likely put to work in tobacco fields at the time alongside European and Indigenous indentured servants trying to earn their way to freedom. There is no way to know. Nonetheless, Josh's and my futures were sketched that day, fated together by ocean voyages, land, and survival.

A few years later, Chandler married a young widow, Elizabeth Lupo, with some 950 acres of her late husband's "right of conquest" from battles with Native Americans or granted outright for paying his passage. Chandler eventually owned the Newport News, several thousand acres, was twice elected to the House of Burgesses, and became a County Court Justice.[234] Survival was his highest qualification. Remember that Black people who survived 250-plus years of enslavement were never rewarded with so much as an acre and a shared mule. Unless he was a different kind of man, John's wife had no more than a passing say over what happened to her property, also likely begotten by nefarious means! The presumption of entitlement astounds me, and yet it is not so different from my conditioning that privilege is earned, not a given.

Chandler grew a sprawling cattle plantation and tobacco farm, most assuredly with the use of some combination of indentured servants, Native Americans, and Africans, any ache in his belly about the wrongness of it long dissipated. The planter elite did not work their land. The servants and Native Americans could eventually purchase their freedom, the latter by converting to Christianity and disavowing tribal affiliations. Enslaved Africans and even the rare free Blacks could not buy social mobility. This was true even when another ancestor, descended from John and settled in Barbados, fathered an "outside child" with his mistress, the daughter of a formerly enslaved woman. His son, William Edward Chandler, could not inherit land, money, or goods. He

---

[234] Chandler Family Association, "Genetic Chandler Family 7A."

could, however, live in the house, perhaps as a favorite servant of sorts, and receive an education. Cut off from his family for an unspecified misdeed, listed only as "behaving rashly to a sister," he eventually migrated to Australia with no means, just the mark of an anchor and a star on his left arm to mark his years at sea. After twenty years in prison for a bank robbery, he became a saddler and landowner. The contradictions between the Black and White Chandler family stories are laid bare. Who is truly the "self-made man?" Who is more the thief?

My paternal lineage signifies the entangled creation of a culture of whiteness in the United States with anti-blackness. It is a passed-down fact, though documents are sparse, and slavery was dismissed as "a financial necessity," that every generation owned or inherited enslaved people until emancipation. They were nearly all farmers in Virginia, Tennessee, and Georgia. The "nice ones" freed their slaves upon their deaths.

Here's the thing that strikes me. My family got to live. We get to know our names and our histories dating back more than 400 years. Yes, many of the women who did not marry are erased, cut short somewhere, a broken branch of the family tree. But we got to live and live free. We got to define freedom, who had it, who didn't, and how it got distributed. We got to choose to be abolitionists, enslavers, or disinterested. We got to write history, decide what got left in or out. We got to define belonging and humanity in the context of the United States. We got to decide who lived and who did not. That is an enormous responsibility to bear, one that was not handled with the utmost care. We got to live when life and family is such a precarious thing for Black people in this country. In the sense of domination and the assumption of belonging, whiteness is universal. How can we move forward with humility, compassion, and enough grace even for ourselves to unbelong and create something new?

My earliest ancestors came here with hope, but they carried with them the shadows of religious trauma and burgeoning ideas of white supremacy. They helped create a culture of whiteness *and, given the many branches of the Chandler family line, had quite a wide reach in establishing it. I am fascinated that the name Chandler means "candle maker," maker of light. Though I do not bear his last name, I choose to shed light on the aspects of our legacy that need to be reconciled and repaired.*

...

Emergence of Anti-blackness

To unbelong from a culture of whiteness, we need to unlearn erroneous associations with the dark and therefore Blackness. Color archetypes influenced the hardening of racial categories. Early Christian writers aligned the color white with purity, lightness, and salvation. In contrast, the color black got associated with evil, sin, and fear, seducing even an enlightened thinkers like Goethe into believing "that the colour of the skin and hair has relation with the differences of character . . . that the White man . . . is the most beautiful."[235] Light was synonymous with Divinity; dark equated with Evil. Black was inferior and of the body; White was superior and of the mind.

In the deep folds of the Christian and Hebraic mystical traditions, dark relates to mystery, wisdom, and creation, symbolizing something archetypically feminine. Mystically speaking, the dark is the cosmic memory that dwells within, and the light reveals its multitudes.[236] Mainline Christianity has strayed far from its mystical and inclusive roots. The Christian obsession with darkness as "bad" was transposed onto ideas about skin color and degrees of humanity that influenced race

---

[235] Goethe, *Theory of Colours*, 265.

[236] C. Keller, *Face of the Deep*, 200–12.

construction. Fear of the dark directly correlates with establishing a racial hierarchy. Further, anti-blackness is anti-feminine. According to hooks, anti-Black racism "created an aesthetic that wounds us, a way of thinking about beauty [and blackness] that hurts."[237] Imperative to deconstructing White racism is unknowing our associations with the dark and, therefore, blackness. Ignorance is not a sin, as it can be unlearned. Rather, the sin is to deny the very existence of the darkness, to convince ourselves we have nothing to learn.[238]

Concepts of a racial hierarchy emerged as early as the fifteenth century when the Portuguese added the capture and trade of Africans to an existing enterprise between European nations vying for imperial domination and westward expansion. Despite the presence of some powerful African kingdoms and a robust existing slave trade between European, African, and Muslim kingdoms, ultimately Pope Nicholas V granted the king of Portugal the exclusive right among European kingdoms to invade, plunder, and reduce West Africans to generational, hereditary slavery in Europe and eventually the so-called New World.[239] As such, White Christianity aligned itself with slavery and was often used to justify it. The Portuguese already had a practice of capturing North African Moorish people as part of gaining access to their vast riches, namely gold. Gradually, the difference in skin color and religion between Europeans and Africans solidified two things: (1) Enslavement became

---

[237] hooks, "Aesthetics of Blackness," 113.

[238] C. Keller, *Face of the Deep*, 205.

[239] C. Keller, "Crusade, Capital, and Cosmopolis," 248.

aligned with race. (2) Enslavers became aligned with Christianity and justified it as "missionary work" to civilize the "savages."[240]

As I interpret it, the pope's move also placed Europe into a powerful position in a saturated market that would dictate the sadism of a race-based trans-Atlantic slave trade and ultimately create the domestic slave industry in the "New World." While the master–slave paradigm and the practice of human capture resulting from conflict long predates European colonialism, by the sixteenth century, European colonizers participated in the exclusive practice of capturing Black Africans to advance European settler colonialism, imperialism, and ultimately capitalism.[241]

Spain authorized the shipment of captive Africans to Florida as early as 1492.[242] However, it was conditional compared to the more horrific version of domestically bred, inherited chattel slavery that arose as British colonization persisted and the Southern states were settled. The Spanish and French at first offered freedom to Africans brought to the "New World" in exchange for conversion or taking up arms against competing colonizers. France's and Spain's willingness to free Africans for loyalty to their causes designated religious and imperial allegiance rather

---

[240] Reynolds and Kendi, *Stamped*, 6.

[241] Horne, *Dawning of the Apocalypse*, 37.

[242] Horne, *Dawning of the Apocalypse*, 8.

than race as a primary mark of belonging.[243] Theirs was a religious, not a "whiteness," project.

It was the English, unwavering in their policy of racial separation, who ultimately won the competition to colonize what would become the United States. Horne asserts that England, based on its persecution of their Jewish population, easily converted their bigoted practices to Blacks in the burgeoning North American colonies, similarly stigmatizing them as "criminals," an attitude that persists today.[244] The British prevailed, as did their model of anti-blackness. Even future settlers who thought slavery morally wrong could be taught to comply if convinced of the subhuman myth or of the social, political, and economic benefits of being subsumed into "whiteness." Such thinking constitutes an ethical distortion and fragmentation of consciousness. By the late 1600s, a shift occurred in which race, not religion, designated one's social position and access to freedom.

The trans-Atlantic slave trade that contributed to developing the United States introduced a commercialized, racialized, and inherited system of dehumanization. Enslaved people were commodities to be bought, sold, and exploited to further the upward mobility of the European colonial settler.[245] They were used as human chattel upon whose backs a robust agricultural and industrial economy was built in the "New World." The slave trade and subsequent abuses of

---

[243] Horne, *Dawning of the Apocalypse*, 14.

[244] Adapted from Horne, *Dawning of the Apocalypse*; and Reynolds and Kendi, *Stamped*.

[245] Elliott and Hughes, "Four Hundred Years."

Black bodies and souls and the extermination and expulsion of Native Americans wove concepts of race and racism into the fabric of a developing society that persist today. The most lasting outcome about enslavement is the historical and continued denial of liberal rights and subjectivity to African Americans, a denial that Edward Baptist claims ranks among the greatest in modern history.[246] He furthers that it not only killed large numbers of people, but it also stole everything from them, including emotional and spiritual safety, health, a sense of place, and personhood. This was all to advance an economy while fueling modern ideas about race that maintained the powerful illusion of White unity and power.[247]

Attitudes toward difference fortified a cornerstone of a culture of whiteness: hegemony and homogeneity. Today those values express themselves through White privilege, expecting assimilation to a culture of whiteness and casting White as "normal." As racial lines were more rigidly drawn, whiteness continued to articulate itself as more fair skinned colonizers arrived in the Americas and assumed control over Indigenous land and participated in taking advantage of free labor. Like Africans, Indigenous Americans were perceived as non-Christian savages in need of controlling and taming, often referred to as *chichimecas* or "uncivilized dogs," and their freedoms were quickly restricted.[248] Various theories of White superiority surfaced that paved the way for a culture of whiteness to dominate in Europe and

---

[246] Baptist, *The Half Has Never Been Told*, 23.

[247] Baptist, 23.

[248] Horne, *Dawning of the Apocalypse*, 85.

the so-called New World.[249] A righteous colonial-settler ethic, which ultimately expressed itself as violent White male superiority, cast itself culturally and religiously above Indigenous people, non-Christians, women of every race, and Africans.

The arrival of twenty Africans on a wayward Portuguese ship in 1619 solidified the British colonies' adoption of extreme racism whose conditions were inherited, reverberations of which are felt today. The first trans-Atlantic slave ship and the ensuing slave trade furthered a fierce commitment to anti-blackness in what would become the United States. As colonization continued, the Caribbean was rife with revolt and insurrection of enslaved and Indigenous populations, owing to their disproportionately large numbers compared to White Europeans. Colonists in forming the United States cried that "nothing is so much wanted in [the Carolinas] as White inhabitants"[250] to avoid a similar large-scale revolt. Thus, more Europeans were encouraged to make the perilous trip across the Atlantic with the promise of great reward: land, the right to participate in a developing economy with free labor, and ultimate assumption into the White race.

A White racial identity ultimately arose from suppressing ethnic immigrant populations previously in conflict. The Irish, Italian, Slavic, German, Catholic, Jewish, and Russian were olive, sallow, cream, peach, and freckled. The aggregation

---

[249] The Climate Theory emerged from Aristotle's rationalizing of the need for an enslaved class and posited that Africans were inferior and darkened because of the African heat. Further, this absurd theory suggested that a colder climate could eventually make Africans White, therefore, more civilized. The Curse Theory justifies White superiority as Biblical truth. It states that Africans were the cursed sons of Ham, disliked even by God. See Reynolds and Kendi, *Stamped*, 12–13.

[250] Horne, *Counter-Revolution of 1776*, 67.

of diverse ethnicities into a more monolithic "White" race could train the collective attention on anti-blackness. They were not born but *bred* White. Horne observes that "whiteness has been enormously, often terrifyingly effective in unifying coalitions of disparate groups of people."[251]

No one wanted to be enslaved, so they learned to mask cultural and ethnic expressions in favor of economic participation and political representation. In so doing, many publicly hid their cultural identity and narrowed the scope of pluralism. The concept of pan-Europeanism was an essential aspect of the transition from religion as the animating force of society to race.[252] Those subsumed into a growing culture of whiteness could engage to varying degrees in an economy intended to expand the British empire and ultimately build an independent nation. Whiteness represented imperialism, colonialism, and capitalism; blackness represented indentured servitude at best, generational enslavement at worst. This kind of race-based hierarchy has serious implications for generational life expectancy and wealth accumulation.

If still unconvinced of anti-blackness as a galvanizing force to create some semblance of "culture" in the colonies, one can be sure that white supremacy and anti-blackness were written into the law by the early 1700s. The colonies began to explicitly distinguish Black people from White people mainly because of Bacon's

---

[251] Dyer, *White*, 57.

[252] Horne, *Dawning of the Apocalypse*, 13.

Rebellion in Jamestown, 1676.[253] The line between settlers and Indigenous tribes was solidifying, and there were extreme efforts to exterminate or drive Native Americans away. Wealthy property owner Nathaniel Bacon wanted them removed, while his cousin, Governor William Berkeley, feared that doing so would unite nearby tribes against the colony. Even though a small population of Blacks bought their freedom, most were indentured or enslaved. Their numbers grew in tandem with the ascension of whiteness. In a revolt against his cousin, Bacon organized a militia of White and Black indentured servants and enslaved Black people, who joined in exchange for freedom. Ultimately Bacon's militia captured and burned Jamestown to the ground.[254]

What resulted was an intense fear among the planter elite of future multiracial, intra-class alliances that could displace the wealthy from a seat of power.[255] It also brought further dehumanization of both Black enslaved people and Native Americans to the forefront. That Black people and the Indigenous population would have feelings about their oppression astonished the elite because they were perceived as inhuman, another species entirely incapable of genuine emotion who needed to be ruled.[256] Bacon died shortly after his famed rebellion, and the enslaved who fought with him were not freed. Subsequently, Virginia lawmakers began to

---

[253] Information gathered from Kendi, *Stamped from the Begining*; and Horne, *The Counter-Revolution of 1776*.

[254] Horne, *The Counter-Revolution of 1776*, 40–41.

[255] Kendi, *Stamped from the Beginning*, 53–54.

[256] Kendi, 56.

distinguish between poor White and Black inhabitants in the language of the law, giving poor White indentured servants new rights and status and enacting laws relegating people of African descent to hereditary enslavement whose souls could potentially be saved while their bodies were treated as beasts.[257] Securing Whites' freedom and Blacks' enslavement was simultaneous, enacting a divide and conquer strategy that continues today. White supremacy seems inevitable, but it is not intractable.

White, Black, and Brown are abstracted versions of colonizer, slave, and colonized, respectively. Continued oppression, enslavement, and denial of personhood created a wide berth for anti-blackness to swell. A strengthening culture of white supremacy rationalized brutality by pointing to the deficits of Black people rather than the actions of White people for generations to come.[258] Anti-blackness and assumptions of inferiority justified centuries of enslavement that built a robust economy based on unpaid labor; continued throughout the Three-Fifths Compromise, emancipation, and failed Reconstruction; and remained relentless during the reign of terror, Jim Crow, and segregation. Poor Whites do not thrive in a system that favors wealth and elitism, but their allegiance to whiteness as a symbol of power remained more potent than the actuality of sharing that power equally.

…

In an assignment from a unit on Westward Expansion, my son was invited to take the perspective of anyone involved in the Oregon Trail. He chose the perspective of a bird flying above the

---

[257] Kendi, *Stamped from the Beginning* and Reynolds and Kendi, *Stamped*

[258] McGhee, *The Sum of Us*, 71–72.

fray. How prophetic. He wrote, "I follow them everywhere. I see some of them die of disease, some die of accidents, and some are caught in storms. They harm Native Americans, and I manage to open an escape route so they can escape without the settlers noticing. I free the slaves they have brought, discover landmarks I'd thought I'd never see, and make friends with animals I have never seen before.

"We arrive at a place called Oregon city. Apparently, this is what the journey was all about. I am not sure what to think. I have seen what these humans do to each other. They destroy each other. They enslave each other. They declare war on each other, and they just simply push animals out of their habitat so they can make room for themselves. All I can say is I hope that one day, humans will realize the consequence of their actions."

Oh, my sweet boy. This seems to be your persistent inquiry: what does it mean to be human? Are we even good? I wonder if we, you and I, can imagine us 500 years from now and build ourselves a ladder in the sky long enough to hold the time and space between. Westward expansion is an illustration of ontological expansiveness that reinforced the idea that White settlers were deserving and the rightful inhabitants of whatever land they sought. Whiteness manifests as conquering energy. My son, nine at the time, named, challenged, and lamented this fact in his seemingly simple story.

…

The most powerful outcome of an economy and social order founded on enslaved labor from Africa cemented in this country's psyche that one race of people is superior to another. Any person who arrived here had an immediate sense of the racial hierarchy. If one was not Black, there was hope for freedom and upward mobility. Before 1865, Blacks were synonymous with slaves. After 1865, Blacks continued to be abused, denied, lynched, burned, imprisoned, and kept from participating in every facet of a "free, democratic" society. Emancipation from enslavement did not mean freedom. Even with changes in laws brought about by the Civil Rights era, "Black Lives Matter" remains a contemporary plea for equity. As we become a more interracial, intersectional society, the absurdity of a system based on preferencing whiteness is thrown into sharp relief. How do we navigate this with the reality that the United States still feels like an inherently "white" country, in character, structure, and in culture?[259]

Today, most people consciously disavow racist beliefs. Still, the establishment of a racial hierarchy that runs through our nation's veins impacts everything from implicit bias in social interactions to dynamics in law enforcement to hiring practices to curriculum, resulting in profound anti-blackness. Out of our shame, our original sin of classifying one's humanity according to skin color, we have continually scapegoated "the darker brother,"[260] made him un-American, criticized his resistance and resilience without transforming our attitudes toward him, and minimized his pain and struggle to remove ourselves from complicity or responsibility. We've done all this while equating a culture of whiteness with power and being White with human. In this country, whiteness has come to depend on anti-blackness.

Whiteness allowed blackness to become its shadow for no other reason than it could not face the darkness within. Our psycho-spiritual conversion is incomplete

---

[259] Guess, "Social Construction of Whiteness."

[260] Hughes, "I, Too." I persist in using 'him' to align with Hughes' poem but want to be clear that the continual scapegoating and criticizing of Black resistance applies to both men and women.

without interrogating why whiteness needs to denigrate the "other" to elevate itself. James Baldwin's challenge remains relevant.

> It is entirely up to the [White] American people, whether or not they're going to face and deal with and embrace this stranger whose they maligned so long. What White people have to do is try to find out, in their own hearts, why it was necessary to have a "ni**er" in the first place, because I am not a ni**er; I'm a man. But if you think I am [one], it means you need him. . . . You the White people invented him. Then you've got to find out why. And the future of the country depends on that, whether it's able to ask [and answer] that question.[261]

How might one disaggregate the "White American" in a modern context? I recognize that a second-generation, white-skinned, Eastern European immigrant may not feel tied to our racialized history and therefore may not feel compelled to participate in acts of repair, just as the second-generation, British-educated Nigerian American may not directly benefit from such actions. The complication is that based on the optics of skin color alone, the Eastern European will inevitably receive preferential treatment *in our current state* over the Nigerian. Both get subsumed into this country's narrative about race. Nigerian-born writer Chimamanda Ngozi Adiche speaks to this phenomenon.

> In Nigeria, I had often thought about who I was—writer, dreamer, thinker—but only in America did I consider *what* I was. I became Black in America. It was not a choice—my chocolate colored skin saw to that—but a

---

[261] Peck, *I Am Not Your Negro*. ** mine.

revelation. . . . To be Black in America was to feel bulldozed by the weight of history and stereotypes, to know that race was always a possible reason, or cause, or explanation for the big and small interactions that make up our fragile lives. To be Black was to realize that it was impossible for people to approach one another with the simple wonder of being human, without the specter of race lying somewhere in the shadows. To be Black was to feel, in different circumstances, frustration, anger, irritation, and wry amusement.[262]

Adiche, Baldwin, many others, and I observe that to be White in America is to be willfully and sometimes blissfully ignorant of this dynamic. Adiche often hears from her White readers, and I hear in many predominately White circles I inhabit, "I had no idea."[263] Repairing the damage done by our racial hierarchies and ignorance about them is not only about paying our past debts but investing in a more equitable present and future by transforming racial attitudes and racist systems.

As previously mentioned, accepted research confirms that race is not a meaningful biological concept, but a social and cultural construction that continues to provide or deny privilege. Anti-Black racism is a construction of our capitalist system that grew alongside an individualistic socio-religious framework. Our dependence on a race, class, and gender-based order supports competition and capitalism. If White people cannot become free of the pervasive systems that privilege a culture of whiteness, there is little hope for justice for Black and other

---

[262] Adiche, *Americanah*, 14–18.

[263] Adiche, 18.

non-white people without the use of force.[264] I argue that if White people remain wedded to maintaining privilege at the expense of another's oppression and inequity, we lack integrity in espousing freedom as this nation's highest value. At the very least, it is unstable freedom based on maintaining it by limiting the freedoms of others. Because it is socially constructed, anti-Black racism is not irrevocable, but we must face how a culture of whiteness perpetuates it. Baldwin warned, "To accept one's past—one's history—is not the same thing as drowning in it; it is learning how to use it. An invented past can never be used; it cracks and crumbles under the pressures of life like clay in a season of drought."[265] The invention of White superiority at the expense of anti-blackness is a history to acknowledge and dismantle.

Dr. King's statement still applies: "Whites, it must frankly be said, are not putting in a similar mass effort to reeducate themselves out of their racial ignorance. It is an aspect of their sense of superiority that the [White] people of America believe they have so little to learn."[266] I propose that White people challenge and redefine whiteness—and therefore our understandings of humanity—based on principles of interdependence and love. To do this requires submitting to unbelonging from current systems of power and privilege that have long benefitted White people. We cannot do this by denying a racialized past and present, only by telling the truth

---

[264] hooks, *Teaching Community*, 37.

[265] Baldwin, *Fire Next Time*, 39.

[266] King, *Where Do We Go from Here?*, 27.

about it and doing the work to untangle it. Love and truth are a step toward freedom.

CHAPTER 3 | IMPACTS OF WHITE RACISM TODAY

Robust scholarship exists around the long-term economic impacts of White racism on historically marginalized communities. While economic reform is not the central purpose of my work, it is important grounding to understand how racism has very tangible impacts on who belongs and has access in our economic systems. We cannot meaningfully shift economic systems without also shifting the deeper psychological and spiritual layers of White racism. This chapter intends to name the tangible and intangible impacts of racism on the white psyche, how racism has become necessary to sustain myths of superiority and deservedness. However, what we have come to accept as normal is detrimental to our psychological and spiritual formation.

Economic Impact

The practice of seizing land without compensation and creating an economy based on unpaid slave labor laid the groundwork for a modern caste system. Caste renders inevitable a rigid and pervasive hierarchical system of inclusion and exclusion based on class, race, and gender. The US caste system is shapeshifting, unspoken, and race-based. An invisible but ever-present human pyramid affects who has access to power and resources.[267] When colonists first arrived, Native Americans were thrust into a marginal space of unbelonging on their own land unless they agreed to participate in privatized property ownership, capitalism, and Christianity—essentially to "become White."

---

[267] Wilkerson, "America's 'Untouchables.'"

Stripping the Indigenous population of resources, identity, and sovereignty caused generational poverty at twice the national rate, high rates of alcoholism, and low rates of economic and educational attainment, as they neither benefitted consistently from social programs and economic inclusion nor were they permitted to freely practice traditional ways of life. Many suffered both physical and soul deaths. The wound deepened, and the caste system strengthened when Indian Removal policies forced Native American tribes to new parts of the country about whose cyclical farming they knew nothing. Their regional indigeneity was lost, tribal affinity blurred, and their invisibility grew.[268] Reservations were eventually granted some independence; those who live on them today can neither borrow against, sell, nor develop the land. Because of archaic titling rules, participation in the global and national economy remains limited.

Further, reservations do not have the economic infrastructure to support local entrepreneurship. Lands were unlawfully "purchased," and some nations negotiated land for cash or casinos in an effort to relieve poverty.[269] Money earned ultimately leaves the community, and widespread poverty remains. Among themselves, tribes do not share equally in resource development or retention, creating an internal caste system based on scarcity and competition.[270] Colonial values, established by a White ruling class, equated land ownership with political

---

[268] Delgado and Stefanic, *Critical Race Theory*, 179 and Wall Kimmerer, *Braiding Sweetgrass*, 26.

[269] Wall Kimmerer, 282.

[270] Snipp, "The Changing Political and Economic Status of the American Indians," 147.

representation, from which Native Americans were excluded. Tribes face an impossible binary dilemma—integrate into White, capitalist society or preserve identity and potentially flounder.

The devastation of Indigenous Americans, including colonial possession of land, erasure of traditions, and destruction of resources, and the enslavement of Black Americans became a necessary condition for corporate capitalism.[271] We have a system based on theft and entitlement and must come to grips with the fact that capitalism has functioned in support of spiritual and physical exploitation, ghettoization, and genocide. The principle of "kill the Indian and save the man" had a single mission: assimilate them into a burgeoning colonial culture based on individualism or isolate and annihilate them.[272] This was not dissimilar to the misguided justification of enslavement as a Christian missionary project. While their skin could never be White, African souls could perhaps "become White" if converted to Christianity.[273] Their bodies were damned while their souls might be saved by becoming white in the next life. Here, Christianity gets conflated with whiteness in the colonization of the "New World." Such misguided ideas about both Christianity and white purity ignore embodiment, a fundamental flaw of whiteness.

Colonialism continues to negatively impact Native American and Black American well-being. Both are disproportionately ill-served by inequitable economic policies that impact everything from annual income to home equity loans to

---

[271] Pratt, "'So Much Has Been Destroyed,'" 2.

[272] Pratt, 5.

[273] Reynolds and Kendi, *Stamped*, 13.

mortgage rates.[274] Even Blacks freed from slavery were conscripted into indentured servitude as sharecroppers. They were often forced to buy goods from the landowners at higher prices and daily wages were garnished to pay inflated debts. Often, they owed more than they made. As freed Blacks moved west, hoping to gain more autonomy and land, they too were conscripted into the complexities of racial exploitation in that any purchase of property was complicit with the theft of Native American land. White colonists continued to gain the most wealth via racial exploitation, going so far as to charge a head tax for non-white immigrants entering the United States.[275]

Exclusion ran much deeper than economic, as Blacks and other non-white groups were prohibited from participating in and co-creating systems of commerce and education. In fact, efforts made toward their own edification were often destroyed or driven out of town. Such was the case with the 1921 Tulsa Race Massacre.[276] Every effort seems to have been made to keep the non-white "other" from accruing wealth and social mobility. The accumulation of generational wealth for some Whites is morbidly dependent on the generational poverty of most Blacks. Racial justice, which is also tied to economic justice, would entail the equitable redistribution of wealth whose absence perpetuates racial exploitation today.[277] It is a

---

[274] McGhee, *The Sum of Us*, chap. 2.

[275] Birt, "Racial Exploitation," 67.

[276] Parshina-Kottas et al., "What the Tulsa Race Massacre Destroyed."

[277] Birt, "Racial Exploitation," 73.

hugely complicated task, and in almost every aspect of our sociopolitical system, White people benefit from a system of racial domination, regardless of whether we have ill-will toward non-white people and immigrants.

The modern wealth and resource gap is vast, and we must question economic policies that continue to invest in upholding White supremacy over the collective good. In a transactional economy based on competition and commodification, relationships deteriorate. We become anesthetized to human suffering and focus on who is deserving or undeserving. As a culture, we tend to ask, "Why is poverty endemic among Black, Latino, and Native populations?" Instead, we should ask, "What are the conditions that made it so? Have I personally benefitted from those conditions?" Wrestling with these questions is a moral dilemma. For example, I am keenly aware that my ancestors' land and monetary wealth directly resulted from the exploitation of Native Americans and enslaved Black people. I must consider how to participate in repair. Typically, poverty among immigrant Whites, apart from rural areas, lasts only a generation or two. This was the case for my mother's Irish immigrant ancestors and remains so for other White immigrants today. On the contrary, Black and Brown poverty tends to last for generations and their middle-class status is less secure.[278]

Our current economic system is morally indefensible. Our love affair with economic power, both personal and global, continues without adequate attention to signs of ecological and social breakdown.[279] The ten wealthiest people in the world,

---

[278] Delgado and Stefanic, *Critical Race Theory*, 115–16.

[279] Bellah, "Birth of New American Myths," 148.

eight of whom are from the United States, White, and male, own more wealth combined than the bottom forty percent of the world's population. In the United States, the two wealthiest people—currently Elon Musk and Jeff Bezos—own more wealth than the bottom forty-two percent of our country's population combined.[280] I would be remiss not to note that the 2020 census found that Black Americans "represent 13.2% of the total population in the United States but 23.8% of the poverty population."[281] Uncorrected historical racism impacts generational wealth earning potential, who has access to land and resource allocation. Du Bois aptly called White imperialism and capitalism "the ownership of the earth forever and ever, Amen!"[282]

…

I can trace my paternal ancestral acquisition of property and wealth to 1618 in this country. While I am sure that some individuals and generations struggled more than others, there seems to be a legacy of solid middle-class achievement with supporting documents to show steady possession of land and assets. My mother's family were poor Irish immigrants who arrived in the late 1700s. Their plight was not easy. They were despised and mistreated for being Irish, considered dirty and diseased, barred from many jobs, and given menial, dangerous work. They encountered signs that read: "No Irish. No Blacks. No Dogs." Though they initially struggled, the Irish were

---

[280] Michelle Alexander reported this information at a March 31, 2022, symposium with the Rothko Chapel in Houston, TX: "Beyond the Rhetoric: Civil Rights and Our Shared Responsibility." Michelle Alexander is a credible source, and a quick Google search backs up her statements with supporting articles and links.

[281] Creamer, "Poverty Rates for Blacks and Hispanics," par. 17.

[282] Du Bois, "Souls of White Folks," 45.

absorbed into the White race by colluding with Black oppression. Within two generations, they owned land, and my great-grandmother had a small farm. It is no small irony that inscribed beneath the feet of the Statue of Liberty are the words "Give me your tired, your poor, / Your huddled masses yearning to breathe free, / The wretched refuse of your teeming shore."[283] Some strange promise that this country turns trash into treasure if the trash is White.

My husband's earliest recorded ancestors here were born circa 1862: Simon Lewis and Cecelia Charles. Ironically, my connection to the surname Chandler eventually became Lewis through marriage. Lewis is a common name, but still . . . I can't help but wonder. Simon and Cecelia were born enslaved just before the end of the Civil War but counted as "free Negroes" in the 1870 census. Before their births, family history is speculative. Amazingly, a single name can give the impression of an entire lineage spun from smoke, as if existence is contingent upon freedom. Unlike John Chandler, they were never rewarded for their survival. Unlike my maternal ancestors, they were not absorbed into whiteness.

His first relative to own land was his Great Aunt Tee, who bought a small shotgun house in New Orleans's Lower 9th Ward in 1972, more than 100 years after Emancipation. Ownership seems uniquely tied to our sense of Americanness, our participation in a society that values assets over ethics, things over people. Ownership is agency that provides leverage in the marketplace and wealth to pass down to future generations. Neither capitalism nor this country would have thrived without slavery, yet those who physically built the economy—cotton, tobacco, sugar, and rice plantations—did not benefit from it. Almost every aspect of our infrastructure and business has ties to the slave trade, but neither the enslaved nor their descendants saw reparations.

---

[283] Lazarus, "New Colossus."

I grew up inhaling intoxicating stories about the innovation and invention of my predecessors. Edward Baptist confirms these "stories about industrialization [that] emphasize white immigrants and clever inventors, [my father is the latter] but they leave out cotton fields and slave labor."[284] *Both my genealogy-obsessed aunt and my financially-driven father passed off enslavement as an economic necessity to the building of this country as a world superpower, to what it is today. In their minds, enslavement is peripheral, not integral to the family success and therefore permissible, or at least ignorable. Surely, we can recognize the cognitive dissonance, the absurd insistence that America's entrepreneurial, self-made modernization was incongruent with chattel slavery, thus the two had nothing do with one another. That the commodification, suffering, forced labor, and killing of African Americans made the United States powerful and rich is not a happy idea, but it is a truth we must learn to hold.*[285]

My husband has known this story, sometimes through quiet whispers and tongue clucks calling him to attention. He also knows it in his body, through generations of working hands that birthed and raised him. He is aware that his ancestors' impoverishment made my ancestors' wealth. There is a sense in many generationally poor Black families of "paying it backward" or at least in two directions. In contrast, my family has only ever paid land and wealth forward. My husband is the first person in his maternal lineage to break the cycle of financial insecurity. We continue to budget a certain amount of money to give to his mother every year. His situation is not uncommon. Braided together, our stories are an apt illustration of class and race in this country.

…

---

[284] Baptist, *The Half Has Never Been Told*, 22.

[285] Baptist, 25.

Though the intersecting issues of race and class are countless, there are two primary economic impacts of a culture of whiteness I examine: the "zero-sum paradigm" and universal programming. I intend to demonstrate how our thinking and policy around race persist in keeping it alive.

Zero-Sum Paradigm

Heather McGhee set out across the United States to research the question, "What keeps us from uniting across differences for mutual benefit in a post-segregation era?" Along with analysis done by Kinder and Sanders, she collected narratives that supported their findings that racial resentment drives modern manifestations of anti-Black hostility even as laws changed to support greater social equality.[286] Resentment is anger that results from real or perceived unfairness, and in the case of whiteness, it evolved from biological racism to cultural disapproval and fear. McGhee argues that if politics stoke fear and resentment that challenges equality and inclusion, racism will persist.[287]

The zero-sum paradigm operates under the erroneous and baffling assumption that progress for one group of people equals an automatic threat to another.[288] Granted, as whiteness evolved, it did amount to a threat to other people's well-being and myths about who is more deserving became more concrete. As integration spread and public spaces and resources were shared, some White communities resisted policies that could benefit them simply because they also

---

[286] McGhee, *The Sum of Us*, chap. 2.

[287] McGhee, 57.

[288] McGhee, introduction.

benefitted non-white people. What is evident to me is that White communities feared backlash from historically marginalized populations, so many sabotaged efforts toward inclusion. The extension of the illogical zero-sum story is that a future without racial hierarchy is a source of fear for White people.

The same illogic drove Virginia lawmakers to "divide and conquer" a rainbow coalition after Bacon's rebellion. Upholding whiteness depends on supremacy. A zero-sum relationship existed between the colonizer and Indigenous population and master and enslaved. Both shaped the economy at an unforgivable cost. Early settlers could equate their success and freedom with conquest and bondage in both situations. At that time, their gain was in direct proportion to the immiseration of others.[289] The narrative that domination was necessary to maintain freedom felt true. Today as non-white people rise to prominent positions, cries of "reverse racism" and "replacement theory" attempt to undermine their achievement and opportunities for solidarity are lost. I conclude that a scarcity mindset is a form of jealousy or resentment that results from the subjugated feminine.

One of the most startling illustrations of the self-defeating zero-sum paradigm is the public swimming pool.[290] As a kid, I spent whole days and weeks of summer at our community pool. Founded in the 1940s, the park and its amenities were initially funded by residents, some public money, and upkeep by membership dues. Today, the neighborhood parks maintain steady income through a healthy "friends of the parks" fund whose donors give up to a million dollars each. It was

---

[289] McGhee, 26.

[290] McGhee, chap. 2.

indeed "our pool." My skin darkened to a rich olive as my hair and swimsuit lightened and faded. I remember, once, that a Black family showed up to swim. This was strange because of the nearly homogeneous White, upper-class neighborhood I grew up in and because you had to prove residency to get in or pay exorbitantly for a day pass, for which one had to be accompanied by a resident. I cannot recall a single Black family from my neighborhood in the 1980s.

That day, two tall girls and a more petite, skinny boy were there. The girls carefully tucked their hair into swim caps before getting in the water. I remember not taking my eyes off them and vaguely wondering if they would dirty our pool or if we would have to get out so they could get in or if they wore sunscreen. Did they even know how to swim? Were they someone's maid's children? I had never seen swim caps used before except for the older White ladies who swam laps like elegant, slow-moving fish. I knew some Mexican nannies sometimes brought their children to the homes of the ones they minded when school was out, so I supposed the same could be true if your nanny were Black.

Where had I gotten these unconscious ideas strung together like beads without gaps? I do not remember learning them overtly, but the morphogenic field of whiteness would have passed such cumulative thoughts down, learnings absorbed and exchanged like oxygen. No White person needed to come directly in contact with a racist act; the energy and influence of white supremacy are pervasively felt. Whiteness organized itself around dominance, and those who inhabit it absorbed it, too. Just as blue tits in Holland almost ubiquitously learned to open the cardboard cap and dip their beaks into the layer of cream that rose to the top of milk bottles without ever being taught, whiteness also learned superiority from the breast of our nation.[291]

I was not alive during the time of legal segregation or enslavement, but I inherited the vestiges of its justification. Sometimes, it is a subtle learning, but just as beliefs are learned, they can also be unlearned. When the blue tit learned to uncap and sip from the milk bottle, the solution was not to remove the milk but to allow adaptations to flourish. When we remove or diminish the stimulus for cultural change that is more inclusive, we restrict possibilities for moral evolution. What is remarkable about human consciousness is that we can choose to change our minds at any given point. Without examination, learned behaviors and thoughts are upheld like facts. Thoughts manifest as spoken and unspoken rules that govern systems. I do not remember overtly *un*learning my seemingly automatic beliefs except by gradual exposure and the dawning awareness that my world was not the whole.

Pools like ours dotted the landscape as towns and cities outdid each other with resplendent features that could hold thousands of swimmers. Local officials ran campaigns on improving quality of life, calling pools "social melting pots." Still, notions of classlessness did not extend to differences in skin color.[292] Two things happened post-segregation. Public pools were privatized, the direction my childhood pool took, or they were drained and put out of use. White and Black families lost access to a coveted amenity, especially in the sweltering Southern summers. The

---

[291] The example of the blue tit as indicative of the subtlety of morphogenic fields comes from Judy Cannato, *Field of Compassion*, 28, who cites Rupert Sheldrake, *The Presence of the Past*.

[292] McGhee, *The Sum of Us*, chap. 2.

closure was not limited to pools. It extended to zoos, community centers, and recreational spaces.[293] The willingness to close public spaces to resist integration points to something so strange and sinister in the White imagination. Everyone lost.

The notion of who participates in programs for the public good says more about whom we deem as "good" rather than expanding programs for the entire public. Long-held assumptions about the "makers" (hardworking, often perceived as White taxpayers) and the "takers" (lazy, often perceived as Black welfare recipients) became part of the zero-sum story.[294] The White populace preferred removing resources over sharing with the "takers." Presumably based on racial allegiance, many Whites, both rich and poor, voted against their best interests. The resulting policy and the (mis)direction of public funds disproportionately affected poor White communities, too. It's the kind of unchecked thinking that needs disruption. In all aspects, be it student loans, public benefits like healthcare and the GI Bill, the zero-sum paradigm is based on the exclusive emphasis upon competition and scarcity, both myths of a dominator construct. The narrative that one race or group is more deserving than another fuels zero-sum thinking and tears apart the web that supports everyone.[295]

Perhaps a less concrete example of the zero-sum paradigm that creates an opening for a critique of universal programming is the racist pushback to "Black Lives Matter" of "All Lives Matter." "All Lives" is an abstraction that does not give

---

[293] McGhee, chap. 2.

[294] McGhee, 41.

[295] McGhee, 55.

special attention to any specific marginalized group. Yes, philosophically and actually, all lives matter, but there are specific, concrete (Black) lives that do not fit into the paradigm of All. If "all lives matter" were actual and not theoretical, Tamir Rice, Trayvon Martin, Elijah McClain, and countless others would still be alive. There would never have been slavery or violent backlash to Emancipation, integration, and resistance to teaching accurate history. "All Lives Matter" is a euphemism for "White Lives Matter" and insinuates who is considered a "life" or more human. It is a racist concept that assumes White lives don't matter because Black lives do. This kind of zero-sum thinking that we can't amplify the voices of those who have been historically marginalized without upsetting the dominant group impacts where we steer money, resources, and policy. It ensures that racism persists.

Much energy is invested in the need for race not to matter to White people, with exception to resurgent numbers of white supremacists to whom whiteness is right. The rationale for "All Lives Matter" or "I don't see color" only amplifies our ignorance that White is also a racialized experience. Ironically, the energy spent indicates the opposite: race does matter, and we know it, or we would not defend against it. A culture of whiteness is haunted by scarcity thinking, and it has built an entire economic and social system around it. Part of unbelonging from whiteness is challenging scarcity and the misguided idea that if things improve for non-white people, it must be at the expense of White people.[296]

---

[296] McGhee, 20.

Universal Programming

Universal programs attempt to apply ubiquitous solutions to specific problems. Efforts that minimize the needs of particular communities in favor of a universal approach uphold color blindness and false neutrality on the issues of race. We cannot afford neutrality because the race assignment in this country has been anything but.[297] Fairness in terms of access to resources and programs is not sameness, for each racial group and region is differently situated. For example, Houston, Texas, will never need to invest federal funds into a fleet of snowplows. We have specific needs around protections for watersheds and from hurricanes and flooding. Similarly, poor air quality in Houston due to chemical plants is concentrated in low income, mostly Black, Latinx, and Indigenous communities. They need specific interventions with targeted outcomes to drastically reduce incidents of asthma and related diseases.[298]

Universal solutions ignore dynamic, constantly changing sociopolitical conditions that impact identity and racialization. To borrow from john a. powell, racialization is described as

> the set of practices, cultural norms, and institutional arrangements that both reflect and help create and maintain race-based outcomes in society. Because racialization is a set of historical and cultural processes, it does not have one

---

[297] powell, *Racing to Justice*, 42.

[298] See Texas Environmental Justice Advocacy Services for more information.

particular meaning . . . [but varies] from location to location as well as throughout different periods in history.[299]

Dynamic approaches to racialized experiences do not necessarily break reflexive habits around race and racism but can ensure that we can think about them with more creativity and nuance. Racism is a universal problem, but short of a global transformation of consciousness that awakens the depths of human compassion and appreciation for the necessity and beauty of diversity, the consequences of systemic racism require specifically located solutions that are dynamic in nature.

When supposedly colorblind policies govern systems, as in the case of school desegregation, the impact is twofold. It fails to directly address the effects of a hostile environment that is unprepared and unwilling to engage or intervene on the issues of race and racism. The fact that armed guards accompanied Black school children to White schools in the wake of Brown v. Board across the South, as well as the fact that many Black students today report feeling unwelcome in predominately White institutions, proves that federal integration mandates did not successfully attend to the specific needs of Black students in particular communities.[300] Instead, the universality of legal integration primarily advanced the self-interests of White people. To be clear, I am not against integration. Quite the contrary. However, the way it was done was neither holistic nor considerate of the well-being of Black

---

[299] powell, *Racing to Justice*, 35.

[300] There is a movement called "Black At . . ." that provides a platform for Black students at predominately White institutions to share their experiences. It is both validating and eye-opening. Their words indicate that implicit bias, microaggressions, and explicit racism are still alive.

communities and individuals. It did not adequately prepare White communities for navigating the complex reality of intercultural, interracial spaces, nor did it shore up the strength of primarily Black schools. Even still, by every social indicator, White racism continues to blight the lives of non-whites at all levels of the social and economic stratosphere.[301]

The feeling of having lost something, whether it was power, control, or simply predictability, led to waves of backlash, the consequences we are witnessing in the rise of Trumpism. White supremacist propaganda and white nationalist hate groups reached an all-time high in 2021.[302] We want to believe the kids are different, that race doesn't matter to them, but children are sitting at the feet of hate groups, still breathing in the stale air of racism, and it is difficult to leave the field without Promethean effort. It is also challenging to develop a positive White identity when whiteness is often associated with supremacy.

There are few examples of White children struggling to attend Black schools whereas Black students were on the front lines of integration. Thus, the message is clear and persists today. "We will tolerate you if you do not disrupt the status quo or demand that we change to suit your belonging." Just recently, a White educator I know reflected that she preferred teaching "inner-city" (read: non-white) students because the "parents were so grateful to us." Often when Black students attend predominately White or White-led institutions, they are expected to feel grateful to

---

[301] Delgado and Stefanic, *Critical Race Theory*, 28.

[302] See Anti-Defamation League, "U.S. White Supremacist Propaganda."

be there. There is little leeway for even minor failures and little shared struggle outside of individual acts of solidarity.

One-directional "universal" integration does not address the root problem that many non-white schools, communities, and programs are underfunded, under-resourced, and suffer from historical patterns of unequal distribution. Funding for public schools is partially dependent on property tax brackets and the disposable income allocated by families via fundraisers and donations. The breakdown of wealth along racial lines in a still-segregated society strongly correlates with how well-resourced schools are. The concept of universally funded programs such as public schools are, in fact, *not* universal and often benefit wealthier, mostly White communities and individuals while ignoring the plights of mostly non-white, poorer, urban areas. Herein lies the Catch-22 of universal programming. In theory, it is a good idea, but in practice, rarely disseminated equitably.

Such was the case when government programs like the GI Bill and the Interstate Highway Act of 1956 were implemented. The GI Bill afforded more home loans, higher-education degrees, and entrepreneurial opportunities than any other effort in history. However, because it was overseen at the state level by White, mostly Southern congress members without just oversight, no bill did more to widen the racial wealth and education gap, a problem our country still reels from today. Blacks were excluded from partaking in one of the most generous federal programs in history even as it was billed as "universal."[303] A specific intervention like

---

[303] powell, *Racing to Justice*, 49.

affirmative action, while imperfect, continues to help right some of the inherited in equity.

Similarly, the Highway Act created infrastructure presumably for all. It expanded the suburbs, inseparable from "White flight," while simultaneously destroying urban housing occupied mainly by working class non-whites. The money generated from developing highways and wealthy suburban neighborhoods did not get reinvested in urban neighborhoods, churches, or schools that were destroyed to make way for highways that thread through many modern cities.[304] Again, the development affected mostly non-white communities. As government practices like eminent domain and condemnation continue to acquire private land for public use, they impact poor, often non-white families and communities.

Even as wealth transfers back into cities, many are seeing the reversal of "white flight." Those who had to forge their way despite lack of major public investment now cannot afford city living and are being pushed beyond city-limits, further away from jobs. In my home city of Houston, labeled the most diverse in the country, a title about which it feels very smug, wealth remains mostly in the hands of Whites, and historically Black neighborhoods are being overrun by developers and investors. There is very little safety net protecting them from losing their homes, and the cash offered by developers is enticing and often needed. A targeted approach to working with specific communities to preserve affordable land and housing could help preserve livelihoods, culture, and businesses while also promoting mutually sustainable, integrated, and mixed income communities.

---

[304] powell, 48.

Many critical race theorists argue that civil rights advances universal in scope coincide with changing economic conditions of White elites, who feared backlash from marginalized domestic minorities and losing previously enjoyed access to widespread privilege.[305] In such cases, zero-sum thinking and universal programming coincide. A documentary about integration in my hometown recounts that it was primarily an economic effort. It was negotiated behind the scenes between moderate business owners and Black and White community leaders to mitigate threats of violence that would paint Houston in a negative light in the national media as well as threaten local White stakeholders. Over the course of a few days, news coverage was censored, protests were kept at bay, and nearly overnight public spaces were integrated.[306]

While this seems like a peaceful strategy, it was driven by the concerns of mostly White, male financiers who ran the city. It also completely quieted voices of outrage and opposition to injustice that swelled across the South. Wheelers and dealers called leaders of the city's historically Black university and threatened financial losses if planned student protests should proceed. The move was not altruistic, but pragmatic and based on avoiding financial loss and public unrest. The conclusion is that for universal programming to occur at all, it needs to appeal to the economic interest of White people, even down to considering bringing our now-beloved baseball team to the city and needing the financial support of Black fans. Interestingly, baseball teams today are almost 100% White-owned and -managed,

---

[305] Delgado and Stefanic, *Critical Race Theory*, 72.

[306] Berman, *Strange Demise of Jim Crow*.

even though many cities have diverse fan bases. Referred to as "interest convergence," universal gains in civil rights that presumably benefit historically excluded groups kept the interests of the dominant group in the foreground.[307]

Another example of universal programming coinciding with zero-sum thinking is in resistance to beneficial approaches like universal health care. Because it could disproportionately benefit non-white, first-generation, and generationally poor people, there is much resistance to implementation among elites.[308] Universal health care could address specific impacts of racism by providing community-identified health interventions in affected localities. In mostly White communities, we might be served by having chapters of organizations like SURJ (Showing Up for Racial Justice) in each community so that we might educate ourselves about local systemic inequities and work to change them. In mostly Black communities, it may look like having a team of community mental health practitioners at no cost. Both communities need spaces for grieving and undoing, but not always in the same space.

Systemic racism is a factor that precludes us from making the often ethical and generous choice. The long-term economic impact of universal social programs or initiatives have largely advantaged White people when we consider resource allocation, neighborhood gentrification, home ownership, property values, social

---

[307] "Interest convergence" was coined by the lawyer Derrick Bell, who stipulated that civil rights victories occur only when White and Black interests converge. It is hard to battle with this concept when considering the need for a deeper, psychological, and spiritual transformation is needed to impact human division and racism. Delgado and Stefanic, *Critical Race Theory*, 26.

[308] powell, *Racing to Justice*, 68.

security, and the like.[309] Watching the documentary about integration in Houston, I ascertain that control of the narrative about remained in White hands.[310]

Despite our hopes, we are not a post-racial society. Universal programs begin with the assumption that people have the same experiences, and are often based on White normativity; thus, the strategies tend to be formulaic rather than innovative. In some cases, such an approach continues to worsen existing inequities. Similarly, *not* focusing on a universal problem like poverty or disease, which primarily impacts historically marginalized or colonized populations, highlights White fears that programs will disproportionately benefit them at the expense of Whites.[311] In addition, the over-reliance on programs without localizing implementation "can be used as a sophisticated device to evade action."[312] They can lull us into ignoring the root causes of social problems and operate under the assumption that the government is inherently benevolent, awaiting only the presentation of brilliant ideas and enthusiastic participants. In this case, the burden of success is placed on historically oppressed populations.[313]

How we talk about and implement policy for issues of race and racism matters. Our mixed intentions in implementing universal programs have the

---

[309] powell, Ch. 1

[310] Berman, *Strange Demise of Jim Crow*.

[311] powell, 48–49.

[312] King, *Where Do We Go from Here?*, 154.

[313] King, *Where Do We Go from Here?*, chap. 5.

unmixed consequence of perpetuating systemic racism. Inattention to policies and programs sensitive to racialized experiences has severe consequences for social good. There are many valid arguments for universal healthcare, strengthening Social Security, and state-funded education all the way through. In theory I support all of these, but in practice they are not implemented equitably or according to specific needs or social locations. Ideally, social programs uphold universal goals (like ending poverty) but have targeted implementation in hard-hit communities. While universalism has benefits such as lower overall costs, avoiding paternalism between benefactors and recipients, and lessening tensions between those excluded and included in programs, a targeted approach benefits not just the most marginalized people but also many other intersectional groups, such as people living in rural areas, people with disabilities, the elderly, homeless youth . . . the list goes on.[314] Imagining specific solutions underscored by shared values that are, at least in part, informed by community members place trust in their hands and have a higher likelihood that funds will be used as needed.

Psychological Impact

According to sociologist Michael Emerson, our society "allocates differential economic, political, social, and even psychological rewards to groups along racial lines; lines that are socially constructed."[315] Even though we might logically agree that race is a construct with changing definitions, it has become one of the most powerful ideas in our country that permeates our psyches, cements thoughts about

---

[314] powell, *Racing to Justice*, 270–72.

[315] Emerson and Yancey, *Transcending Racial Barriers*, 10.

worth and value, affects behavior, and organizes our neighborhoods. Data reveals the social determinants of the effects of racism on non-white people, from anxiety to depression to life expectancy and outcomes for success. It is widely considered a public health crisis and correlates with other issues like health equity, stable housing, and employment prospects.[316] These are the outcomes we can measure, but how can we begin to understand the psychological impact of racism on *White* people when so many declare they are not racist or do not see color?

White superiority and resulting racism are part of this country's neurosis, and the harms done by it are decidedly less as we become aware of what we are repressing and projecting. A neurosis is sustained when we cannot recognize its power over us as it takes on a kind of separate existence and belongs in the realm of shadows.[317] I believe the neurosis that sustains a culture of whiteness in this country has four major characteristics. There are, of course, nuances, subtleties, and advances among individuals and groups, but the pervasive ethos of our culture has been affected by myopia, narcissism, denial, and shame.

Myopia

When bacteria first developed the precursor to the eyeball some 500 million years ago, it was a crude light-sensitive spot that couldn't detect shapes or color but were able to distinguish between light and dark and use photosynthesis for food. Over several millennia, that spot developed into the complex, water-based eyeball

---

[316] See American Public Health Association, *Analysis: Declarations of Racism*.

[317] Jung, "Problems of Modern Psychotherapy," par. 125.

humans have today, but at first, it only detected black and white.[318] It would be some time until the eyeball could distinguish color and hue. Today, only seven to eight percent of the population are colorblind, limited in their ability to distinguish color, and it affects primarily men. In contrast, only twelve percent of women and one percent of men are tetrachromats, able to perceive up to 100 million colors through four distinct channels. I fall into this category, as do many artists. Between the tails of the bell curve, most people are trichromatic and see the basic spectrum of colors yielded by the three primaries.[319] Symbolically, how we experience color affects our mood and how we interpret the world. Ironically, though it has many shades, white is considered a non-color that reflects all hues on the visible spectrum. This fact reinforces the idea that the White race affords itself invisibility and transparency.

My point is that most of us see color but are narrow in perspective and imagination about *how* we see it. Psychological myopia insists on colorblindness or personal innocence where race and racism are concerned. We often say, "Race doesn't matter," yet a culture of whiteness has worked hard to keep the racial "other" out of schools, neighborhoods, and public systems over the years—an indication that race matters very much.[320] Most people remain myopic unless they make deliberate efforts to get proximate to divergent experiences and points of view as well as practice continual self-examination.

---

[318] Swimme and Tucker, *Journey of the Universe*, 56.

[319] Jewell, "Tetrachromacy."

[320] powell, *Racing to Justice*, 47.

One of the most challenging psychological tasks is to individuate from one's family or community of origin. Individuation is neither rejection nor an embrace of individualism, but a willingness to develop the lens of the inner observer and integrate various layers of experience to amass a complete sense of self.[321] In a White dominant society, psychological myopia impacts how we think, act, and relate to communities, most of which is unconscious but accepted as true. The single-sightedness of whiteness influences every level of the system, from news outlets, education, entertainment, healthcare, and what we learn in families and schools. It has become a kind of cultural archetype that influences our character and behavior. I distinguish whiteness from the archetypes of the collective unconscious because it is not a universal image that has existed since the beginning of time.[322] However, concepts of light as pure or good are ancient and have fueled the idealization of whiteness in culture. Only recently has whiteness been submitted to conscious evaluation, which is necessary to deconstructing its influence.[323] Phenomenal properties assigned to the color white influence how we experience it as a race: ubiquitous, normal, invisible, pure. I assert that we cannot fully individuate from a culture of whiteness if we do not critically examine it. The radically imaginative skill to imagine ourselves as we'd like to be, not just as individuals but as whole societies, is our ladder in the sky that can further the cause of transformation and liberation. I believe we are at a critical crossroads of examination and growth.

---

[321] Jung, *Archetypes and the Collective Unconscious*, 275, par. 490.

[322] Jung, *Archetypes and the Collective Unconscious*, 4, par.5.

[323] Jung, *Archetypes and the Collective Unconscious*, 6, par. 6.

A culture of whiteness is a complex system. One person cannot encompass the whole of it, just as a single water molecule is not the ocean, and a single neuron cannot think. Because whiteness is centralized and identified with the seats of power in this country, it has implications for the psychology of our whole system. Systemic properties like discrimination and hierarchy do not reside discreetly in individuals, though they emerge and express through them because the properties are already pervasive at the macro level. Individuals mirror and reproduce the values of the system, creating what feels like an endless feedback loop. As impossible and idealistic as it sounds, whiteness can undergo a reckoning with itself, a self-examination that re-teaches us how to *see*. If we can inherit psychological myopia, we can also inherit thoughtful, wise sensibilities that appreciate the millions of colors that make up our glorious reality.

I cannot recall a better example of myopia than Baldwin's "Going to Meet the Man." In this horrific but compelling story, a White male is introduced to us at two critical moments in his life. The scene opens with his adult self ruthlessly beating a Black man lying on the floor of a jail cell. The man is bleeding from his mouth and nose but still insists on singing, *"I stepped in the river at Jordan."* The singing triggers a memory and takes us to the White man's childhood when he attends a lynching picnic, absorbed by the disturbing zeal of his community as they prepare to murder a Black man. The prisoner's present singing contrasts with the strange and eerie silence of that long ago day. As a boy he sensed the trembling, uneasy excitement, more pronounced because of the absence of the usual Black laborers and town folk singing.

He is caught up in the almost ecstatic fervor of a community that lacked an inner observer, a voice of doubt. The boy knows "somethin' ain't right"[324] but lacks the agency to name it. He is only seven. Though he senses the competing feelings of disgust and anticipation mingled with belonging, he is taken by the raw power of the White men around him, able to take a man's life and openly mutilate his body without consequence.[325] The reader is drawn into compassion for the little boy even as we feel his inner turmoil, even as his adult self never reckons with it and does not leave the field of whiteness. He never learns personal responsibility.

As a grown man facing a similar battle of his conscience, he hurts "all over with that peculiar excitement which refused to be released."[326] He remains myopic, fearful of wrestling with the tension within, and projects it by beating the Black man at his feet. Baldwin uses startling imagery to elicit an ethical and emotional response from the reader, paint a clear picture of the dangers of an unexamined inheritance of racism, and illustrate the difficulty of individuating from it. He is our social conscience and mirror. His story is not pure fiction, but a parable based on true events that alert the reader to the psychosocial effects of unexamined racism on White people. The psychological work of "othering" has convinced us of a natural and unquestionable delineation between the slaver and enslaved, White and Black,

---

[324] Hafiz, "Damn Thirsty," 168.

[325] Baldwin, "Going to Meet the Man."

[326] Baldwin, "Going to Meet the Man," 232.

self and other.[327] No such line exists, and it is a habit of separation and single-mindedness we must work to overcome.

…

When I announced my engagement to my parents, I mentioned they had a host of reasons as to why I should not go through with it. Nothing in their world had prepared them for this. My mother recruited her friends to convince me away from Josh with polished, White businessmen who also liked art. After a conversation with my parents, I returned to my home, where Josh was waiting for me on the sofa, and I cried. I did not know what to do, whether my parents would disown me (no one said that outright, but the threat felt real) or whether my unborn biracial children would receive educational trusts as my blonde, blue-eyed nieces had. I am ashamed that this thought crossed my mind, but I wondered how far they would go. I questioned whether I should marry Josh and what it could cost him to have to sit at a table with my parents someday or if there would ever be a shared table. I wondered what I could risk if any of these fears were to materialize.

Though I had always been marked the rebellious child who went against the grain, I did not have an immediate answer in my grasp. The right answer hung loosely before me but seemed elusive. In his unflappable grace and equanimity, Josh just held me. I had what I call a periscope moment, able to look ever so slightly beyond what was right in front of me through an unfogged lens, and I went back to my parent's home the next day. I told them with more courage than I felt and with a tremendous quiver in my voice that I was not marrying for them, that I could not live the remainder of my life meeting their expectations, and that they had a choice as to whether they wanted to do their work and get on board.

---

[327] Morrison, *Origin of Others*, xii.

If I were to recall this story to my parents today, seventeen years later, they might deny their judgments and minimize their reaction. They are still in my life, my kids have trust funds, and they respect Josh. My mother has called him "an exception to his race." I recount this story not to echo my heroism or sacrifice (I am not heroic and have had to sacrifice less than feared) but to illustrate the difficulty of challenging and leaving what is familiar. No matter how acrid the soil we are grown in, most of us long for acceptance from our community or family. It is incredibly lonely to leave it, even when it is the right thing.

The gift, however, is that I found something in myself capable of growth and change, however scary. Perhaps my parents feel the same way about themselves as they have come to respect Josh. Baldwin's character could not face that perhaps his whole community had been wrong, even as he sensed it; thus, individuation from it remained elusive.[328] *I know there are plenty of White parents who would not bat an eye if their adult child were to partner with a non-white person, someone of the same sex, or a different faith, but they are the ones who have at least begun to challenge the psychological myopia of whiteness.*

…

Primitive Narcissism

Myopic tendencies, characterized by a lack of imagination and intellectual insight, cause a culture of whiteness to prioritize itself and remain cloaked in overt and subtle racist attitudes, such as the belief that institutions pay disproportionate attention to non-white populations. It may provoke a response such as, "Does it always have to be about race?" Well, no, but also, yes. We live in a racialized society. Denial of this fact contributes to zero-sum thinking and the inability to think

---

[328] Baldwin, "Going to Meet the Man."

creatively about solutions to complex social problems. It contributes to ontological expansiveness and epistemologies of ignorance. Finally, it contributes to primitive narcissistic tendencies in the underdeveloped White racial identity.[329]

On the one hand, narcissism is a self-protective adaptation that guards a person against vulnerability. On the other, it is triggered by excessive over- or undervaluation in childhood, so a person craves abnormal amounts of validation. In any case, the narcissist has fragile self-esteem in the face of frustration and fears separation between the self and others even as they create it. The narcissist values the "other" only in their quiescence to the ego's demands. Infants undergo a healthy and normal narcissistic phase on the road to adulthood. Infants cannot separate themselves from others, and their world revolves around attention from caregivers. According to Jean Piaget, during the sensorimotor stage of development, the infant shapes her world through the eyes, touch, and voice of her caregivers as well as through interaction with objects, including her own body.[330] It is a self-focused,

---

[329] Hinshaw, "Pale Narcissus." Hinshaw's is a working theory that distinguishes between narcissistic personality disorder as listed in the *DSM-V* and "primitive narcissism" as a key aspect of white privilege and those White persons who cannot tolerate tension and difference that threatens their immature racial identity. His theory is clear, concise, and merits further consideration, and his definition of "primitive narcissism" is based on Freud's theory of infants passing through a stage of "primary narcissism" in which they cannot understand other people as fully separate beings. His participatory research also stages White racial identity into three primary categories: pseudo independence, immersion/emersion, and autonomy.

[330] Jean Piaget is the initiator of the psycho-social stages of cognitive development that I first learned of in my early studies of psychology. His theories are sound and contribute to understandings of developmental stages, but they are limited by looking at the child as strictly independent, and very often his subjects were male babies of European descent. While further critique of his theories is needed, for these purposes a simple explanation of the sensorimotor stage can be found in McCleod, "Piaget's Sensoriomotor Stage."

relational, and pleasure-seeking phase not to be confused with the development of narcissistic personality disorder.

However, in an immature or rigid White identity, one could say that childhood need to experience oneself as the center of the universe never matured. Our culture reinforces the centrality of whiteness at every turn, so it would be logical to assume that we maintain at least a degree of primitive narcissism. A non-racist, non-rigid White racial identity develops self-awareness and unfixed perceptions of non-white people; remains critically aware of the proliferation of institutional racism and White privilege; and open to the prevalence of white supremacist thinking.[331] According to Hinshaw, White people rarely achieve complete individuation from whiteness and deep, sustaining commitment to anti-racism. I discuss this in later chapters, but we have an opportunity to cast our ladders in the sky and ask, "What is the world we want to imagine, and who do we want to be in it?" We may not get there in our lifetime, but we can help build it. Through increased awareness, we can sever ourselves from ancestral trauma, abuse, and ignorance and create possibilities for future generations.

When we remain in a phase of primitive narcissism, we have an underdeveloped relationship to conflict, which furthers our inability to simultaneously hold several feelings and perspectives. We tend to need rescuing from conflict and make appeals about why it should not exist. In inter-racial spaces, it can show up as difficulty taking personal responsibility for feelings and actions or minimizing the impact of racialized experiences. Fritz Künkel called this the

---

[331] Hinshaw, "Pale Narcissus," 20.

"Embalmed-We," in which an individuated identity cannot develop in a community that preserves old habits and opinions, defers to public opinion, and longs for "the good ol' days."[332] Communities that remain enmeshed in essentialist identity politics cannot make space for selves to emerge and group behaviors do not transform.

When individuals and groups deny the tension necessary for birthing new layers of empathy, conscience, and relatedness, there tend to be several responses that continue to center the White self as opposed to deconstructing and decentering hegemonic whiteness.

1. Racial heroism: Offering proof that "I am not like the others" with a "social justice resume."
2. Helplessness: "What am I supposed to do?" followed by a plea to be seen as a good person with good intentions. It places the burden of undoing whiteness on non-white people.
3. Self-victimization: This can look like claims of reverse racism or "They don't like me, so I'm not going to keep showing up." "They" usually implies Black or non-white people after someone has asserted themselves, set a boundary, or shared an experience in an interracial space.
4. Defensiveness: "Well, *I'm* not racist," "I didn't own slaves," or "Maybe you are overreacting." Another tendency is to blame non-white people or institutions (depersonalization) to resolve their own anxiety about racism.

---

[332] Sanford, *Fritz Künkel*, 97.

Defensiveness lacks empathy, openness, and the ability to listen because it is rooted in fear of losing power, comfort, and privilege.[333]

All these responses center the experiences of whiteness and reinforce primitive narcissism. Certainly, racism impacts Whites but very differently than non-whites. The impacts should never be equated or compared except that when racism or domination prevails, it affects the health of the whole system. Whites must address the effects of racism and white supremacy on our psychosocial and spiritual development to shift systems based on new understandings rather than popular, perfunctory trends. A black square on Instagram only goes so far. An overemphasis on "I," a lack of stamina for discomfort, and an inability to address conflict that challenges identity shapes a culture of whiteness. However, sustaining and engaging in conflict can lead to greater intimacy, empathy, and understanding. Learning to hold tensions aids in the process of individuation, liberation, and ultimately unbelonging from whiteness.

Anti-racist identity development depends on the degree to which one can tolerate negative racial representations while maintaining a positive, growth-oriented sense of self. It requires going through the following stages: (1) pseudo-independence—understanding racism intellectually in which White people see it as their duty to "help" Black people; (2) immersion/emersion—a deeper, emotional understanding of White racism and building alliances with like-minded White people; and (3) autonomy—examining and letting go of acquired racist attitudes and

---

[333] Matias, "Not I."

committing to anti-racist action.[334] I discuss this in Chapter 6, but achieving autonomy is necessary to unbelonging. I further it by asking us to imagine deeper belonging in ways that can forge the creation of Beloved Communities.

Shame and Denial

Narcissism that persists individually and systemically is fueled by and produces shame and denial in the system. The immature White racial identity claims innocence about racism and remains disconnected from the vulnerable or unconscious self (denial). Difficult emotions that arise and challenge the vulnerable or grandiose sense of self are often disowned (shame).[335] Denial is the life blood of racism. Denying a history constructed by race-based division and hierarchy perpetuates an insidious narrative of racial difference and the ideology of white supremacy that renders White lives more valuable than others.[336] Such ideology undergirds our habits and systems like education, health care, and banking, from which White people have never been excluded.[337] Because they are deeply ingrained, it is hard to imagine disengaging with them and perhaps even harder to recognize

---

[334] Hinshaw, "Pale Narcissus," 21.

[335] Hinshaw, 28.

[336] Bryan Stevenson and Eddie Glaude both express this, albeit differently. Both speak to the impact of racism on our psyche, how certain things feel true even when no longer supported by the law. Each of us is born into certain circumstances that influence at best, dictate at worst, the ways in which we learn to operate in the world. "Growing up," personally and nationally, is learning to tell the truth about how these circumstances that raised us came to be. Stevenson, *Just Mercy*; and Glaude, *Democracy in Black*.

[337] Glaude, *Democracy in Black*; and Tim Wise, *Dear White America*, both explicate these issues. Glaude calls it "the value gap" whereas Wise mostly uses the more ubiquitous term "White privilege."

how racism operates inside them, furthering denial and fueling a shame that is difficult to name. It is a vicious cycle.

A particular bodily phenomenon that White people often encounter when confronted with issues of race and racism is a kind of resistance or brace that fuels disconnection. Menakem suggests it indicates long-held racialized trauma.[338] The resistance in our bodies wants us to believe that things can't be as bad as "they" say or that we are not complicit. It also points to long-buried truths. Noticing such responses interrupts habits of denial. Denying them affords one the right to remain distant and claim innocence. Even if we insist that we have never had a racist thought nor performed a racist act, we inherited a society that is neither genuinely free nor equal. The trauma of it embeds in the body and causes denial to become a standard response to difficulty. As a result, we are left to deal with a legacy of racism that makes most of us wince but continues to persist.

The Sisyphean effort of toiling with the impact of the past feels prohibitive to forward movement. Liberation from policies that prioritize control over belonging comes through struggle, which challenges White stamina around racially sensitive topics. To struggle with something is to love it; to love is to grow up; to grow up is to take responsibility for repair. We simply cannot afford to be in denial if we wish to usher forth a psycho-spiritual process of unbelonging from whiteness. If the US government is the parent, those who identify as White in this country who favor a more equitable society need to individuate from the ideology that keeps us dependent and cared for while denying that protection to non-whites. It is deeply de-

---

[338] Menakem, *My Grandmother's Hands*, 28.

centering, depending on the level of clinging to the "parent." Our instinct is self-protection, but at what cost to the well-being, freedom, and safety of others? At what cost to our own awareness and ability to act on it?

Often born of shame, denial contributes to defensiveness and violence. The twin shadows of denial and shame grow in tandem and morph into normalcy if left unaddressed and unnamed. Guilt motivates one to take personal responsibility for a concrete action, whereas shame results when the whole self is perceived as wrong. Race-based shame blooms because as young White children, we were often encouraged to alienate ourselves from feelings of empathy, compassion, and love for the non-white "other."[339] When we do not learn how to acknowledge, process, and integrate shame, it embeds in our unconscious, leading to two general strategies: attacking the self or attacking others. Some part of us exiles a perceived unacceptable aspect of the self that does not resonate with White racial values.[340] Rather than investigate the origins of shame, it is often easier to identify with the dominant narrative instead of subverting learned social norms. I felt an unnamable shame when I announced my crush on Joel Kelley. I did not equate his being Black as problematic, but when my mother held me with a quizzical look, my desire for her approval led to a split between myself and my White mother that fueled shame. There were unspoken racial rules at play that I had not overtly learned. I experienced

---

[339] Thandeka, *Learning to Be White*, 19.

[340] Thandeka, *Learning to Be White*, 18.

them again when I announced my engagement. Both times I feared rejection, which I now understand as a feeling of not being at home within my White community.[341]

According to Reverend Thandeka, "Shame is the death of an unloved part of the self . . . an emotional display of a hidden civil war."[342] Shame exposes difference, which in my White community equated with *bad*. As with the little boy-turned-grown man in Baldwin's "Going to Meet the Man," I did not want to be abandoned by my people. As I grew up, I learned I did not want to abandon myself. Herein lies the conflict that needs revolving when individuating from hegemonic whiteness. Where shame drives behaviors, transformation is impossible, and resentment arises. There is inevitable suffering when we encounter internal conflict or when the inner world is at odds with the external world. A culture of whiteness has taught us that we do not deserve suffering or discomfort, yet so many have suffered because of it. Baldwin warned that "people who cannot suffer can never grow up, can never discover who they are."[343] If we remain innocent, driven by shame and denial, we suffer from the disintegration of the more complex self.

Regarding our racial history, our first great denial was personhood. Denial is the pulse, the lifeblood of racism. A White-dominant society denied personhood to Black and Native Americans unless it benefitted White people economically, as with

---

[341] Thandeka, *Learning to Be White*, 13.

[342] Thandeka, *Learning to Be White*, 12.

[343] Baldwin, *Fire Next Time*, 70.

the Three-Fifths Compromise. Like the little boy in Baldwin's story,[344] White denial was adaptive. It provided belonging and made us feel deserving, even powerful. Many of us have never left the field. If we objectify, dehumanize, and criminalize the "other" as savage, chattel, or undeserving, we need not feel guilt or regret for their mistreatment. Instead, we find ways to justify it. Notice how the media engages in character assassination of the victim when a Black male is shot by police versus compassion for mental health issues when an armed White male assaults a Black church.[345] Similarly, a society that denies and therefore tolerates racial injustice makes little of projections predicting that one-third of Black males born in the twenty-first century will go to jail or prison in their lifetime.[346] This should be a national crisis that demands attention toward prevention. Shame and denial contribute to normalizing abnormal behaviors and circumstances.

If we choose to remain in denial of our earliest ways of knowing about race, the unspoken and spoken rules we learned, then we indicate that we are beyond thinking about race and therefore beyond *being* raced. We take on a posture of learned helplessness that may foster defensiveness and further the acceptance of racism as normal. Becoming conscious of race privilege and the ways it informs our social mobility allows for more meaningful discussions and resulting changes to take place. As we move from denial to awareness, White people may suddenly realize that

---

[344] Baldwin, "Going to Meet the Man."

[345] For a comprehensive overview of the racial differences in media portrayal, see Bjornstrom et al., "Race and Ethnic Representations of Lawbreakers and Victims in Crime News."

[346] Stevenson, foreword to *America's Original Sin*.

a culture of whiteness encourages us to deny our understandings of race and racism.[347]

When we cannot internalize the human impact of racism, not just on those who are most often the victims but also on those willing to tolerate it, we maintain the illusion of separation. Such a stance enables denial and rejection of the "different other" and inhibits the ability to empathize and connect across differences. Pure autonomy is an impossible state of being because our selves, any concept of I is defined in relationships with others.[348] Shame papers over a more profound sense of relatedness, allowing indifference to fill the void.

I believe White people in the United States experience a degree of collective shame because there is no explicit, concrete action, like reparations or truth and reconciliation, in which communities can participate to remedy past events. There are many opportunities for education and awareness but fewer for reconciliation. We tend to deny the prevalence of racism, dismiss it as unintentional, limit our imagination around learning, and prohibit creating a restorative, reparative society. Our debt, though, is so large and feels insurmountable because no amount of money will heal the inner conflict of the privileged majority. Repair takes time, generations even, and a willingness to excavate the past and carve a new way forward. Carl Jung warns that if an internal situation is not made conscious, in the case of an individual, it happens in the outer world as fate.[349] Such a paradigm operates in a culture of

---

[347] hooks, *Teaching Community*, 26.

[348] Thandeka, *Learning to Be White*; and Birt, "Quest for Freedom as Community."

[349] Jung, *Part II: Aion*, 70–71.

whiteness too. If it remains unconscious of its inner contradictions, as in the damaging impacts of systemic racism in contrast to a supposedly free and equal society, the conflict plays out by castigating the "separate other" relegating them to shadowlands of society. The unresolved conflict is stored as cultural shame and continues tearing the world into opposite halves.[350] Part of healing racism involves reconstituting the halves, integrating the opposites, bringing our collective shame and denial into the light, and regathering society's detached and denied aspects. It is a psychology and spirituality of "We," that includes a healthy, relational sense of "I."

Shame and denial are erasure, prohibitive to love, which is creative, integrative, and transformative. To echo Baldwin again, "I use the word 'love' here not merely in the personal sense but as a state of being, or a state of grace—not in the infantile American sense of being made happy but in the tough and universal sense of quest and daring and growth."[351] As long as we commit to a separate "other," to whom we owe nothing and are not connected, we deny something essential in ourselves. If I erase the other, I erase my own "otherness" and reduce love to a narcissistic projection. A radical, transpersonal love discussed in Parts II and III honors the distinction between self and other as well as interconnectedness.

When we fail to interrogate both the privileged and subjugated aspects of the self and remain attached to dominant positions, it is difficult to adopt a multicultural, multiracial, integrative perspective.[352] Often, our socialization focuses on the

---

[350] Jung, "Christ, a Symbol of the Self."

[351] Baldwin, *Fire Next Time*, 44.

[352] TCE Media Review, "Privileged Self vs. Subjugated Self."

perceived shortcomings of the "other" at the exclusion of the self. We remain trapped, unable to thoroughly look at the self because we fear that we might encounter the "strange other" within. Empathizing with the "strange other" challenges one's racialized ranking and puts one's enshrined and more valued difference at risk.[353] It is incumbent upon White people, especially those who identify as allies, to develop an awareness of the multidimensional self, lest we perpetuate estrangement from one another.

Denial cloaks anguish and thwarts a healthy response to change. Once we begin to awaken to it and release it from the body, Wendell Berry suggests that we are "subject to staggering recognitions of [our] complicity in history and in the events of [our] own life."[354] It is an overwhelming experience to say the least. With more information about race and racism available than ever, we have an enormous opportunity to consciously adapt to changing circumstances rather than remain protected by what we refuse to see. When we feel helpless, overwhelmed, or confused by social norms changing, it is easy to cling to familiarity. However, disturbance creates growth opportunities. Part of our psychological work is to sit with our anxieties and fears about change and establish contemplative practices to address them.

"Quest and daring and growth"[355] might well begin with learning to love ourselves, to stay present in discomfort and open our eyes to another so that we will

---

[353] Morrison, *Origin of Others*, 30.

[354] Berry, *Hidden Wound*, 7.

[355] Baldwin, *Fire Next Time*, 44.

no longer need to invalidate them as "other." Thus begins the process of reconciling the opposites.[356] Internally, I must recognize that I am both dominator and liberator, capable of denial and change. Externally or socially, we need to learn to narrate our story in light of our contradictions *and* aspirations. Menakem suggests that the trauma of our country's racialized history lives in our bodies in various ways and impacts how we move through the world.[357]

…

Borderline traits run through my maternal lineage, in part due to untransformed trauma that results in a fractured sense of self. The description that often resonates with children of borderline parents is that it feels like "walking on eggshells," so named because it teeters on the border of psychosis and neurosis.[358] *Behaviors are unpredictable, and the borderline person is not usually aware of their confusing patterns. One day a child could do no wrong, another only wrong with no significant change in her behavior. The child learns to adapt to the parent's moods and learns how to make herself scarce. The push/pull dichotomy is exhausting and confusing. My mother might say, "I love you more than anything in the world," but her eyes were hard, her body stiff, and her grip on my shoulder too hard. As a child, I could not leave the field. I learned to retract from my mother at a very early, likely preconscious age. My body still retracts in her presence,*

---

[356] In Jungian Analysis, reconciling the opposites represents the full integration of the human psyche, what is often referred to as individuation. See also Edward Edinger, *The Christian Archetype* (1987) for a concise description of the process.

[357] Resmaa Menakem specifically explores the impact of racism on White, Black, and police bodies but concedes that anyone who has spent time living in the United States is, consciously or not, impacted by "White-body supremacy." Menakem, *My Grandmother's Hands*, 14–18.

[358] Lawson, *Understanding the Borderline Mother*, xi.

really whenever I feel unsafe. It is reflexive, habitual. The cycle of relationship can be summarized as follows.

The child's relationship with the mother is one of vital dependency, thereby making it critical for the child to assess communications from the mother accurately.

The child receives contradictory or incompatible information from the mother at different levels, whereby, for example, her explicit verbal communication is fundamentally denied by the metacommunication, the nonverbal context in which the explicit message is conveyed (thus the mother who says to her child with hardened eyes and a rigid body, "Darling, you know I love you so much."). The two sets of signals cannot be understood as coherent.

The child is not allowed to ask questions of the mother that would clarify the communication or resolve the contradiction.

The child cannot leave the field, that is, the relationship.[359]

Borderline mothers often negate the child's perspective or painful experiences, thus building trust is incredibly difficult.[360] *This is not unlike White people negating another's experience of racism. Other traits relevant between the borderline personality and a culture of whiteness may include the following: an inability to apologize, the expectation of being coddled or cared for when difficulty arises because of the mother's behavior, punishment of independence, diminishment of or ignoring accomplishments, undermining self-esteem, expecting accommodation (or in racial terms, assimilation), threatening abandonment or carrying out overly harsh punishments, and not believing in another's basic goodness.*[361]

---

[359] Tarnas, epilogue to *Passion of the Western Mind*.

[360] Lawson, *Understanding the Borderline Mother*, 11.

[361] Lawson, 35.

Strangely, borderline personality disorder (BPD) is the single most common personality disorder in the United States, and women outnumber men two-to-one in clinical populations.[362] *There is no way to prove this, but I wonder if it doesn't have something to do with the sublimation and minimization of the feminine in our culture, that so many of us live with a part of ourselves cut off. When one lives with a part of themselves hidden or in shadow, it gets dangerously projected onto others, making them the targets of our unwanted emotions.*

Like children of borderline parents, I surmise that Black and other non-white people feel confusion and tension in their bodies in the presence of whiteness. The metacommunication and consequent restriction are so strongly conditioned that they feel immutable. From one side of its mouth, White society speaks of desires for freedom and justice, but it conveys scorn and criticism if Black and other non-white people do not fit into their parameters. "We support your cause but disapprove of your methods. Try again." The effect minimizes longstanding oppression. Out of the other side of White mouths, "Do you know how much you matter to me? I covet your culture, music, style, and hair, but not enough to fight for your liberation."

I imagine a culture of whiteness feels like a borderline mother. We have projected our shame and denial of our dark and painful past onto non-white bodies for generations. As long as it remains unacknowledged, the shame of this inheritance causes us to continue to live in the shadows.

…

Optimism possesses America, which prohibits telling harder, darker truths about our history and the effects of generational trauma inflicted and experienced. The stories we tell and our posture toward "who and what we choose to exclude

---

[362] Lawson, xv.

exposes the limits of our ideas of justice."[363] When we refuse to see that we have inherited a system of violence and domination, we continue to inflict it upon others. As we learn to love courageously, to recognize and shed the inheritance of white supremacist thinking that keeps us bound to denial, we create possibilities for future generations to thrive within the matrix of a multicultural, democratic community. We create pathways toward wholeness.

Spiritual and Religious Impact

All ontological arguments about the existence of God aside, whether the God in question is immanent, preeminent, or transcendent, involved or disinterested in human affairs, we are a species that craves meaning and purpose. Religions, myths, and rituals are cultural practices emergent from the pursuit of meaning. They are our cosmologies that help us make sense of the "human element" as well as mystery. While distinctions between religion and spirituality can be vague, in general religion involves commitment to communal practices and shared beliefs or customs whereas spirituality is typically rooted in independent experience and oriented toward something sacred or mysterious larger than the self.

Robert Bellah quotes Durkheim in defining religion as "a system of beliefs and practices relative to the sacred *which unites those who adhere to them in a moral community*"[364] as he calls for the remaking of the church and religion, which I understand to be a critique of the integrity of our "moral communities." In another

---

[363] Glaude, *Begin Again*, 207.

[364] Bellah, "Religion and Evolution," 47.

publication, he states that religion creates and is the key to understanding culture.[365] Inasmuch as White Christianity has shaped our spiritual and moral culture, it is necessary to understand its connection with anti-Black racism. Paradoxically, the liberatory roots of Christianity can also be the key to liberating and transforming a culture of whiteness, a topic I discuss further in Chapter 5. We cannot achieve a lasting social and political revolution without also appealing to the soul and inspiring a new sense of human possibility.[366]

William James wrote that both science and religion attempt to answer the question, "What is the character of this universe in which we dwell?" And "Do we accept it if only in part and grudgingly, or heartily and altogether?"[367] A robust spirituality helps us to accept both pain and joy, difficulty, and ease "heartily and altogether." Carl Jung once named God "all things which cross my willful path violently and recklessly, all things which upset my subjective views, plans and intentions, and change the course of my life for better or for worse."[368] This more inclusive idea about God seems to be a course correction of an earlier quote that God is "the prototype of all light."[369] I conclude that ideas about God must include both the dark and light. As it pertains to understanding a culture of whiteness, we

---

[365] Bellah, "Birth of New American Myths," 162.

[366] Bellah, "Birth of New American Myths," 162.

[367] James, *Varieties of Religious Experience*, 53.

[368] Quote originally said by Carl Jung in a 1961 interview and featured in Edward Edinger, *Ego and Archetype*, 101.

[369] Jung, *Archetypes and the Collective Unconscious*, 102, par. 149.

must examine how ideas about God as light inform anti-blackness. Our religious and spiritual redemption entails accepting the *all* of it and maintaining a willingness to be disrupted by embracing the both/and of life characterized by embodied transcendence. To get there, however, it is also necessary to investigate the shadow side of religion and spirituality, which I attempt to do from within my experience of the White Christian church.

Spiritual experiences ideally create awareness and acceptance, allowing seekers to hold tensions adeptly rather than bypass difficulty and discomfort. The "spiritual bypass" seems particularly common in White religious and spiritual spaces when suggestions for growth around investigating the effects of race and racism occur. It is particularly tempting to rationalize and reinforce old defenses and avoidance of personal and systemic issues.[370] It may look like believing in your own superiority to hide from difficult conversations, claim colorblindness, or insist that "we are all just human."[371]

Even though we live in a nation that claims to value religious freedom and pluralism, nearly two thirds of the country, regardless of race, identify as Christian, among which exist many subgroups such as mainline Protestant or Catholic,

---

[370] Buddhist, transpersonal psychologist John Welwood coined the term "spiritual bypass" in 1984. It is the tendency to use spiritual ideas and practices to sidestep or avoid facing unresolved, complex emotional issues, psychological wounds, and unfinished developmental tasks. This defense mechanism impacts the personal, interpersonal, and systemic levels of being. For further information, see Welwood, *Toward a Psychology of Awakening*.

[371] Tochluk, *Living in the Tension*, 23.

Evangelical, or Progressive.[372] Of those identifying as White and Christian regardless of the denomination who were polled regarding their perceptions of race and racism, nearly two thirds deny the existence of historical structural barriers to Black thriving as well as current structural injustices that impact their treatment by law enforcement, workplaces, schools, and other institutions in this country.[373] Religiously unaffiliated Whites align more closely with Black Christians in their perceptions of racism, but there is still too large of a gap (nearly twenty percentage points) between how non-religious Whites perceive the cultural prevalence of racism as prohibitive to safety and well-being compared to Blacks.[374]

On the one hand, I assert that racism is explicitly un-Christian, and on the other I acknowledge that anti-Black racism was nurtured in the White Christian church. What are we left with when assessing Christianity through a cultural lens? I draw the conclusion that a culture of whiteness is un-Christian because it runs counter to the liberatory, inclusive nature of Jesus's teachings. Predominately White churches, many of which have not reckoned with their complicity with the domestic slave trade and ensuing race-based terror, continue to shape and uphold an exclusive, racist, patriarchal narrative. Whether one is religiously affiliated or not, the broader culture is influenced by White Christianity as it bleeds into social and political institutions. We are seeing this phenomenon in the rise of Christian Nationalism as it

---

[372] Jones, *White Too Long*, chap. 5. Statistics in his book taken from Jones' organization, Public Religion Research Institute (PRRI) in a 2018 American Values Survey.

[373] Jones, 181.

[374] Jones, 182.

conflates with current expressions of white supremacy.[375] Christian Nationalism is a view that claims the United States is a White, Christian nation whose laws should be rooted in narrowly interpreted, white-washed renderings of Christian values. Du Mez indicates that such views are a reaction to changing demographics that reject pluralism as well as cultural and generational shifts as the country becomes less White and Christian.[376] In addition to anti-Black sentiments, Christian nationalists tend to also support anti-immigrant, antisemitic, anti-Muslim, and patriarchal views. It echoes Manifest Destiny in which European colonist believed they had dominion over the land and its people.[377] It is possible that more White people are choosing religious unaffiliation because of the ethical incongruence between the intent of Christianity and current iterations of it.

I argue that wise spiritualities, including those influenced by or aligned with Christianity, support anti-racism and inclusion, a stance that needs reclaiming. However, the allegiance between Christianity, white supremacy, hyper-individualism, and personal salvation inadvertently contributes to denial of personal responsibility for one's behavior and capacity for changing systems. I aim to disaggregate the liberatory, inclusive roots of Christianity from the way it is expressed in a culture of whiteness. There are White Christians actively engaged in liberation, but overall,

---

[375] Many recent articles and studies discuss the relationship between white supremacy and Christianity, specifically Evangelical Christianity. Kristin Kobes Du Mez explicates the rise of this relationship in *Jesus and Josh Wayne: How White Evangelicals Corrupted a Faith and Fractured a Nation*; whereas Robert P. Jones found racist attitudes to be more generalized among those who identify as White and Christian.

[376] Kobes Du Mez, *Jesus and John Wayne*, introduction.

[377] A. Lopez, "More than Half of Republicans."

predominately White Christian churches remain untransformed. Robert P. Jones wonders whether white supremacist attitudes are so woven into the DNA of mainline Christianity in the United States that the two are synonymous and inseparable.[378] Further, in seeking to understand the role of racial attitudes on White Christian identity, he finds that they are directly and independently linked.[379] Given the influence of Christianity on this country's formation, it becomes difficult to tease our general spiritual, religious, and moral ethos apart from white supremacy.

Psychological development informs spiritual maturity, thus the tendency for White Americans to overly focus on "me" instead of "we" informs our spiritual development. In this section I explain how the spiritual impact of racism on a culture of whiteness a hyper focus on individualism is, resulting in spiritual shame, and a longing for disembodied transcendence—all of which hinder the type of embodied psycho-spiritual transformation I propose. Unbelonging from whiteness will entail that we work to disaggregate religions, specifically Christianity, from white supremacy and restore it to its liberatory, communal roots.

Individualism

The result of a culture overly identified with the separate self is a spiritual ethos that disconnects from the natural world, severs the ties that bind us to others, and reiterates themes of self-confidence and personal happiness.[380] Further, the false, often-grandiose notion of the separate self fuels hyper-individualism that is

---

[378] Jones, *White Too Long*, 169.

[379] Jones, 168.

[380] Bellah, "Religion and Evolution," 159.

detrimental to our spiritual becoming.[381] There is nothing wrong with a spirituality that focuses on self-improvement and awareness if it is also rooted in relatedness and how the individual may contribute to the betterment of the world. What we lose by practicing a completely personalized spirituality are shared visions about reality and how we should act in relation to it. I do not advocate for a return to orthodoxy or blind commitment to doctrine but the institution of shared public covenants that inform personal practice and communal action. I do not intend public covenants thinly disguised as nationalism or American Exceptionalism. I do intend covenants that recognize the brokenness within the United States project, its failures in executing equitable human rights, and the need to reappropriate traditions and ideas such as "liberty and justice for all" as catalysts for rebirth. We need authentic engagement with the spiritual and political traditions of liberty and justice such that we do not lean toward nostalgia, sentimentality, and non-critical thinking.[382]

The Christian context I grew up within emphasizes a "personal relationship with Jesus" and individual salvation through baptism, confession, or conversion. It has somehow lost its connection to the earth, concepts of kinship, and the possibilities for transformation through relatedness. What began as an empowered, inclusive community of misfits who resisted the dominant Roman Empire has, over time, inverted its sense of hospitality.[383] In the colonization of the Americas, a new institutionalized Christianity proliferated that demanded allegiance and assimilation

---

[381] Thandeka, *Learning to Be White*, 53.

[382] Thandeka, *Learning to Be White*, 144.

[383] Jennings, *The Christian Imagination*, 22.

and prohibited Indigenous populations from practicing earth-based, embodied, communal traditions. There is something to be gained, however, from the marrow of the Christian tradition that points toward the formation of a multicultural, multiracial, interfaith Beloved Community responsive to the meaning of divine incarnation.

…

It was a sweltering August night in the Ozark mountains.

We had just come down from the cross at Vesper point, where we heard a testimonial about giving our lives over to Christ, moving from a life of sin into a grace-filled life of purity, and the promise of eternal life in God's heavenly kingdom. In our cabins we were invited to ponder the message and accept Jesus as our personal Lord and Savior. The counselors, all college-aged and fresh-faced, wearing various Greek-lettered t-shirts, waited for us on the porch to receive our conversion.

I cried out to this Jesus who died for me, "Am I bad? Will I really go to Hell if I don't do this?"

I received no answer.

In this moment, my individual soul felt in peril and anxiety consumed me. For a long time, I obsessed over what God wanted for my life, from attending the right college to living in the right city to marrying the right person. I worried I was doing it all wrong or that I would look the other way and miss the signs. I worried I was going to Hell. Instead of decreased shame I felt overwhelmed by it. There was so much focus on the self that I lost a sense of connectedness. Later I learned the words "spiritual abuse" and understood how a theology based on individual salvation that feeds upon anxiety, shame, and guilt warped my sense of sovereignty and personal responsibility. I would later hear my mentor call substitutionary atonement theology "divine child abuse," which I felt guilty laughing about for a long time. It is a confusing ball of thread to untangle, to say the least.

The religious obsession with individual salvation is fueled by the same sense of rugged individualism, puritan culture, and "White specialness" that drove colonialism in the United States.

My mentor once gave me an article for anxious Christians titled "No Secret Plan." It admonishes the church for fueling anxious individualism rather than a broader, more creative, and prosocial path of "walking humbly, loving kindness, and doing justice."[384] *There is no hidden agenda. Regardless of our religious path, any spiritual practice that focuses on these three (humility, kindness, and justice) makes good stewards of us all. We might begin to conceive that an individual practice can awaken a deep sense of awareness that we can care for ourselves, others, and the world around us in a way that increases the potential for change for generations to come.*[385] *We begin to answer to ourselves and to society at large. My camp, however, seemed much more concerned with my individual salvation through "good" behavior, especially as it pertained to sex and sexuality, rather than my participation in ushering forth a more just world, rather than protecting the beauty of the Ozarks and experiencing myself as part of them. What became endemic to my experience of "White" religion is an intense focus on my intangible soul rather than the condition or action of my body in the world. It is this anxious, individualistic, scarcity-minded culture I seek to challenge.*

…

The contemporary rise of "spiritual, but not religious" identification tends to inspire a private spirituality constructed from many sources and popular among

---

[384] Cary, "No Secret Plan," par. 5.

[385] Lipsky and Burk, *Trauma Stewardship*, 39.

those who seek faith and community outside of organized religion.[386] On the one hand, this creates potential space for inter-religious dialogue that may surface similarities in traditions, beliefs, or sacred texts. It also provides license for creativity and invites new words for the divine. Certainly, it exposes a desire for something different than what orthodox traditions offer. On the other hand, it prohibits community agreements and rituals because of an intense turning toward the self and may inadvertently trigger appropriation of cultural practices and moral relativism. Anecdotally, it is interesting to note the increased fascination with Native American traditions or the presence of Negro Spirituals in White churches without accreditation or humility. Similarly, language and consumer practices develop around spiritual individualism. "The Universe told me . . ." is no different than claiming to hear a private message from God that suits the needs of the ego. This kind of spiritual individualism is problematic if neither the Universe nor God work for the well-being of one at the expense of the whole. An individualized spirituality can lack accountability and shared social covenants, increasing moral relativism and atomism. We ought to take very personally the task of finding our place in the mysterious cosmic unfolding, but not at the expense of the well-being of the whole.

Surely our spiritual practices can focus on self-improvement and self-awareness. However, we also need interfaith agreements that champion collective liberation and transcend individualism. We need a spiritual orientation that honors our autonomy and embeddedness and does not divorce individual action from collective good. Shelly Tochluk asserts that White people who seek spiritual healing

---

[386] Kitchner, "What It Means to Be Spiritual."

to decrease personal pain are often unaware of the pain caused by a lack of understanding of the embodied experience of racism.[387] In many ways we are permitted to ignore race and racism as factors that shape our spiritual lives and bodies. Thus, the pain remains ambiguous and manifests as shame. It also results in a disconnection from experiencing incarnation as transcendence. Spiritual shame inhibits empathy. Similarly, ignoring race and racism and the body allows White individuals to separate from a culture of whiteness. The distance between the self and others prohibits engaging in meaningful repair. Individualized spiritualities may undermine the suffering in the world in favor of the self.

Instead of aligning more deeply with Jesus's teachings of radical inclusion as foundational to Christianity, a percentage of White Christians align their religion with a "religion of whiteness" and thinly veiled nationalism whose totems are money, the flag, and the cross.[388] This is especially overt in White evangelical traditions, though it pervades other predominately White religious spaces, too.[389] It is not uncommon to see the national flag and semiautomatic weapons proximate to representations of White Patriarchal Christianity in the United States. Note the number of local and national politicians representing the religious Right who sent Christmas cards of their

---

[387] Tochluk, *Living in the Tension*, 57

[388] Emerson, "Divided by Race."

[389] Jones, *White Too Long*, 161.

families flaunting semiautomatic weapons in front of brightly decorated trees.[390] A White pastor–friend of mine shared that their church fundraisers frequently involved the sale of guns at the welcome table just outside the sanctuary. This strange and unsavory variety of "Muscular Christianity" is an outgrowth of violent colonialism that sublimates the feminine aspect of interconnectedness in favor of rugged individualism. In the 1940s and '50s, a potent mix of traditional gender roles, militarism, and Christian nationalism formed the basis of a revitalizes evangelical identity.[391] More than forty percent of White Evangelicals own firearms, a number that outpaces other religious groups and gun owners in the general population.[392] Reinforcing patriarchy, submission, violence, and power run parallel to "the bad faith of whiteness."[393] Contrast this with the nonviolent, liberatory resistance of Black-led churches in the 1950s and '60s[394] or with Quaker abolitionists who worked furiously to end enslavement and abetted the Underground Railroad.[395]

If freedom is realized in and supported by loving communities, then individualism restricts it. Freedom is relative to one's social location that includes an

---

[390] A quick Google search reveals several politicians' family photos inspired by Lauren Boebert (R-CO) and Thomas Massie (R-KY), who posted otherwise congenial images of their families smiling while cradling menacing firearms. See Manseau, "Why So Many Guns?" for reference.

[391] Kobes Du Mez, *Jesus and John Wayne*, 15.

[392] Kobes Du Mez, 284.

[393] Birt, "Bad Faith of Whiteness"; phrase borrowed from the title of the article.

[394] See Cone, *A Black Theology of Liberation*.

[395] Martin and Jordan, "Quakers Helped Abolish Slavery in the U.S."

ensemble of intersecting identities: class, race, ability, gender, culture, religion, history, and so on. Though we can transcend challenging aspects of our situations, our lived realities and senses of self form in relation to experiences in the world. Spiritual freedom is not separate from the facticity of the situated self which is always embedded in community. We cannot abdicate responsibility for becoming our best selves, nor does it serve to become solely interested in the self such that we abdicate responsibility for the whole.

Spiritual Shame and Misguided Transcendence

Puritan ideology was instrumental in developing a culture of whiteness. Before racial categories solidified, the color white symbolized purity and otherworldliness, qualities of the mind or spirit. In contrast, the color black represented impurity and sin, qualities of the body. The closer one was to the color white, the more likely one was perceived as "good." Unacceptable qualities about the self, about the body in general, got projected onto others. For example, Black men are historically characterized as aggressive and Black women as hyper-sexualized, even as White people deny these characteristics in themselves.[396] White people may feel challenged to stay engaged in conversations about race and racism because it requires engagement with the very thing we have been taught to deny and even hate: the body.

Part of our cultural learning and an outcome of ontological expansiveness is to avoid discomfort; thus, we seek ways out of uncomfortable situations. One impact of White Protestant Christianity is a tendency to disconnect from the body by

---

[396] Menakem, *My Grandmother's Hands*, 97.

focusing on the afterlife to escape the challenges and pain of an embodied experience. Seeking peak spiritual experiences and the ultimate physical transcendence of getting beyond the body in an Eternal Heaven can foster avoidance of embodied pain and suffering, which contradict the work of racial justice. A spiritually informed racial justice practice requires that we attend to the ways race impacts people's bodies differently.[397] Growth and transformation occur when one is grounded in the body. Menakem suggest that the body's response to discomfort is the soul nerve at work, cautioning us to attend to inherited soul wounds that challenge a sense of safety and belonging.[398] His suggestion resonates with Tochluk's definition of the soul as the connecting principle between body and spirit.[399] If we desire to heal the soul wounds, we need to attend to disturbances felt in the body that are likely activated when we attempt to distance ourselves from the fact that White belonging and comfort often comes at the expense of others.

Apart from avowed white supremacists who capitalize on racial superiority and belonging by offering quasi-community, manufactured history, and cohesive symbolism, whiteness in general tends to deny the social privileges afforded by its racial facticity.[400] Insofar as whiteness refuses to see the truth about its privilege and subsequent proximity to power, then it is incapable of spiritual freedom. On the one

---

[397] Tochluk, *Living in the Tension*, 23–25.

[398] Menakem, *My Grandmother's Hands*, chap. 10.

[399] Tochluk, *Living in the Tension*, 17.

[400] Menakem, *My Grandmother's Hands*, 143.

hand, Robert E. Birt questions whether White people can experience transcendence at all if we believe ourselves beyond the socially located body. On the other hand, a commitment to *exclusive transcendence* believes whiteness represents the essence of the mind and blackness exists in the realm of the lowlier body. As Birt puts it, "whiteness is predicated upon the denial of transcendence to the Other."[401] We may experience redemption from the "bad faith of whiteness" if we honor embodiment, refuse an us/them paradigm, and embrace interdependence.

Ultimately spiritual and religious traditions ought to teach us to become more human, and part of being human is embracing incarnation. The avoidance of psychic and psychical pain prohibits entrance into the "initiatory fire of transformation"[402] and may inadvertently collude with colorblindness, dismissal of another's racialized experience, or minimizing the privilege of whiteness. An embodied spirituality allows us to be more present to "all things which cross [our] willful path violently and recklessly."[403] It is usually disruption that gets our fullest attention. Part of psycho-spiritual unbelonging requires allowing for the disruption.

Our spiritual task is to experience divine mystery incarnate *in* the world, not separate from it. Separation from the embodied self leads to shame, even if we cannot name it as such. In our shame we remain untransformed, unable to take personal responsibility for our lives, and unable to fully individuate, or unbelong, from that which we mistake for identity. Whiteness is not our truest identity but a

---

[401] Birt, "Bad Faith of Whiteness," 87.

[402] Tochluk, *Living in the Tension*, 25.

[403] Jung, as quoted in Edinger, *Ego and Archetype*, 101.

shield that keeps us in a state of disunion and denial while upholding power dynamics of who belongs and who does not. In the process of acknowledging our embodied reality, transcendence becomes possible.

In protest of Nazi Germany, Lutheran theologian Dietrich Bonhoeffer suggests that our shame arouses "grief for this estrangement, and the powerless longing to return to unity with the origin. [Humans are] ashamed because [we] have lost something essential to [our] character, to [ourselves] as a whole."[404] Abstract grief increases spiritual and psychological shame. Spiritually, it references "the lost wholeness of life"[405] and interpersonally prohibits us from really seeing one another, from gazing into the eyes of the "other" and recognizing something both fundamentally shared and distinct.

Spiritual shame is embedded in the Christian narrative. In the fourth century, Augustine concluded that the expulsion from the Garden of Eden related to something essentially wrong with humans. His conclusion that we are unable to control sexual arousal even during moments of religious contemplation profoundly affected the direction of Christianity. There are many historians and theologians who offered nuanced interpretations of the Genesis story, but Augustine's would have a lasting impact that shaped much of Western Christianity, generating the focus on personal salvation. Although a brilliant and introspective mind, he wrestled with his own urges, and if I may, an undifferentiated relationship with his mother. His quest for Wisdom, the feminine face of God, was eroticized, and his wrestling resulted in

---

[404] Bonhoeffer, *Ethics*, 22.

[405] Bonhoeffer, 22.

an interior split. He saw the flesh as a wicked force, limiting one's ability to discover the hiddenness within. The result deepened a wedge between Christianity and its tehomic, mysterious, ultimately feminine depths.[406] He concluded that our ability to know the soul must be mediated because of the limitation of the flesh.

Because Eve's temptation was blamed for our fallen nature, shame retained a particularly feminine face, further deepening the divide between our masculine and feminine aspects. The shame of separateness seeped into our spiritual marrow, effectively removing ourselves as actors in recovering our lost parts. What Augustine's struggle exposed what Reverend Thandeka names a "pitched battle by a self against the self in order to stop feeling what it is not supposed to feel."[407] In turning against the self, the interior world of the deep, it became that much easier to turn against the other.

Catherine Keller challenges Augustine's presupposition that we are inherently sinful and dismantles the flawed notion that Eve is the cause of our fall. She suggests that Augustine's misconstruction of original sin resulted from profound and pre-existing "tehomophobia," a fear of our own depths. Beyond simple fear, a phobia obsessively repeats itself, making it ever more difficult to face the origins of it.[408] Tehom is not the birthplace of evil, as concepts of original sin might suggest, but

---

[406] Keller, *Face of the Deep*, 65–83. In these pages Keller simultaneously uplifts Augustine's profound struggle evident in *Confessions* and challenges his mind/body dualism. Her reader, then, is encouraged to enter their own wrestling, to go beyond dualism and into the depths.

[407] Thandeka, *Learning to Be White*, 12.

[408] C. Keller, *Face of the Deep*, 26–27.

"the active potentiality *for both good and evil*."[409] It is, in essence, the fertile but morally demanding ground of freedom.

I must explain what I mean by sin. In the Christian context, it has come to mean disobedience to the will of God, indicating our separateness from the divine. Once the Augustinian doctrine of human sinfulness took hold, it became the dominant interpretation of the fall in the Garden of Eden. Here we are not agents of our own "salvation" but dependent on the grace of an external deity, or in Christian theology Jesus Christ, to catalyze metanoia or spiritual conversion. Grace is certainly part of conversion, but the greater part of a co-created theology of becoming is finding grace within.[410]

I subscribe to the understanding of sin less as disobedience and more as desecration or separation and resulting estrangement from the self, one another, and "the Ground of Being."[411] By our choices we deny and exploit our fundamental relatedness, to the self and the sacred other.[412] This type of sin is redeemable, albeit along an arduous path. Here we are "saved" by taking personal responsibility and committing to growth, so we are spared from ignorance. Metanoia is an intrinsic change that births new perspective of the self, others, and the world. It is a

---

[409] C. Keller, *Face of the Deep*, 91.

[410] C. Keller, *Face of the Deep*, 79.

[411] Paul Tillich wrote that sin is separation in *Systematic Theology*. He also references God as "the Ground of Being," which I interpret as reality itself. Many in Tillich's orbit, including Dietrich Bonhoeffer, repeated the concept of sin as separation.

[412] C. Keller, *Face of the Deep*, 80.

conversion of sorts, but we are agents and co-creators in our becoming. In a theological sense, our wholeness is recovered, and we are restored to the knowledge that "God is in each thing, and each thing in God."[413] In a philosophical and cosmological sense, it is restoration to the fact of profound relationality, that "each thing is in each thing."[414] In a psychological sense, it is integration or individuation. Racism is a sin against the inherent relatedness of reality as it affects our theologies, philosophies, and psychologies.

It is necessary to unloose ourselves from spiritual shame, as it prohibits the kind of psycho-spiritual transformation I am proposing. Seen another way, Eve, a symbol of the Biblical feminine, could be the great revealer of our deeper nature, our longing for insight, and the potentiality for wisdom. She represents our ability to realize, grieve, and resolve our disunion. She leaves the garden and goes into the world with a new consciousness that is both exhilarating and terrifying, as change often is. This is not unlike the ascent from Plato's cave into the light. Birthing something new is indeed painful. That Eve can bear it is a mark of her strength and essential humanity. What the feminine can teach us in relation to peeling away the layers of White racism is how to be with inevitable pain as we "see what is really going on"[415] and how deeply it operates.

---

[413] C. Keller, *Face of the Deep*, 206.

[414] C. Keller, *Face of the Deep*, 206.

[415] Peterson, *The Message*, Genesis 3:7. Interpretations of the passage are mine, but generally represented in feminist theology.

Bonhoeffer suggests that disunion with our inherent depths is the fundamental cause of human evil. His name for the deep is God who incarnated love in Jesus Christ.[416] His is an embodied notion of spiritual truth in that we come to love God through the flesh, by loving each other's bodies. But Jesus was not the last word. Love was in the world before and after him. If we are to steward the great teachings of love, it should continually manifest in the world through and between us. To fundamentally eradicate racism, we must allow ourselves and our entire existence to be transformed by transpersonal love, whatever faith tradition encompasses it.

Racialized violence—Native American Genocide, the Holocaust, enslavement, lynching, apartheid, and continued police violence against Black individuals and communities—is an evil fueled by a disregard for the body because certain bodies are deemed less worthy. Bonhoeffer believed that violence carried out by warped beliefs about separation and domination, produces shame that conceals us from one another and deceives us with the false notion that we are somehow safer if we, too, cannot be seen, for if we are truly seen, we are reminded of our lost wholeness.[417] In Bonhoeffer's words, "Beneath the mask there is the longing for the restoration of the lost unity."[418]

From spiritual shame, profound grief arises that our culture can hardly feel, much less name. I suspect White people in this country have deep grief around the

---

[416] Bonhoeffer, *Ethics*, 48.

[417] Bonhoeffer, *Ethics*, 22.

[418] Bonhoeffer, 23.

unnamed shame of disunion from feminine principles, physical embodiment, and the sacred, non-white other. In our messiness and denial, we continue to hurt ourselves and others. As Keller laments, "[We] hurt. . . . [We] hurt all over . . . but [we] don't know where to begin to cry."[419] Neither religions nor spiritualities embedded in a culture of whiteness seem driven by understanding the hurt of a hurting world.[420] If we bypass the hurt, the grief, and even the buried shame in favor of easy transcendence that separates from the body, we cannot grow.

If faced, shame and grief are excellent teachers. They prompt movement from covering to discovering, from self-concealment to self-revelation, and from solitude to fellowship.[421] But first, it is necessary to recognize the shame, to honor it with integrity, humility, and honesty so that we may begin to find our way toward one another. If we project sub-humanity and abuse onto others we also dehumanize the self. Embodied spirituality provides tools and practices to engage with profound grief, whereas an abstract and escapist transcendent spirituality bypasses, minimizes, or intellectualizes it and insists on a way out without suffering and without ever truly seeing.

"Thinking Black"

Despite the prevalence of White male patriarchal religion, a second melody operates just below the first. "The telling is so soft. . . . I set my ear to it as I would

---

[419] C. Keller, *Face of the Deep*, 66.

[420] Jennings, *Christian Imagination*, 11.

[421] Bonhoeffer, *Ethics*, 23.

to a heart."[422] Pulsing beneath our dominant paradigms is a vision of Beloved Community and collective liberation. The invitation is to align with expressions of spirituality allied with those historically rendered invisible and disposable. To "think Black," is to cease relying upon a White theology of individualism, toward liberating the sufferings of the historically oppressed, and freeing ourselves from the values of an unjust society that protects whiteness. It is to pay specific attention to bodies that suffer.

Directed toward White theologians, James Cone suggests that "thinking Black" is the only pathway for liberation. He further suggests that White clergy must completely divest from white supremacy within the church and openly criticize it. He asserts that "creative theological revelation about God and God's movement in the world is possible only when one frees oneself from the powers that be. The mind must be freed from the values of an oppressive society."[423] I do not disagree, and I suggest that White theologians and clergy must also learn to "think White," which is a kind of inside-out experience because inevitably, "condemnation of [this country] entails their own condemnation."[424] Thinking White entails becoming more

---

[422] Lighthart, "Second Music," 3.

[423] Cone, *Black Theology of Liberation*, 21.

[424] Cone, 21.

conscious about their own racialized experience and how religious institutions have protected white-body supremacy.[425]

Without engaging with a personal hermeneutic process, they cannot learn to speak from the assumption of common humanity. Whiteness needs to be examined, questioned, and transformed in spiritual and religious spaces. Whites need to know ourselves in the context of a racialized body, not as an absent and unmarked neutrality. Liberation is not a disconnection from the physical world, but an enriched experience of it through interrelatedness, achieved in part by attempts to stand where the oppressed person has stood.[426] Liberation restores the relational imagination and fosters connection and belonging beyond our particular "tribe."

As Cone suggests, "God cannot be both for [Black liberation] and white oppressors at the same time."[427] Who or what we perceive God to be is bound up with liberation from whiteness and domination of any kind. White theology and spirituality must cease being *White* and become Black such that whiteness is denied as the most acceptable form of human existence, and total liberation is the intention for humanity.[428] I don't intend to imply that White congregations should co-opt Black religious traditions and start forming gospel choirs. Rather we need to investigate

---

[425] Menakem uses white-body supremacy "because every white-skinned body, no matter who inhabits it—and no matter what they think, believe, do, or say—automatically benefits from it." See Menakem, *My Grandmother's Hands*, 13.

[426] Cone, *Black Theology of Liberation*, 21.

[427] Cone, *Black Theology of Liberation*, 8.

[428] Cone, *Black Theology of Liberation*, 9–10.

how White churches have protected individualism, racism, or remained neutral on issues of justice.

In the context of Christianity, it is to understand that Jesus is not neutral; he is not *for all*, but for whoever seeks liberation from mental, physical, and spiritual oppression. The Christian scriptures remind us that "whatever you did not do for the least of these, you did not do for me."[429] Concrete freedom at the societal level is possible when White people not only participate in such a move but lead the charge in their own communities rather than wait for a Black "voice of reason" to teach them how. Black people are not to be pitied nor seen as needing our help, but we must come to see that in practicing or complying with dehumanization of the other, we deprave them as well as ourselves. We become just like those we perceive "the least of these." If Cone asserts that letting whiteness define the limits of Black existence equates with their death,[430] then I assert the same for White existence. If whiteness governs our moral, spiritual, and social selves, we are not spiritually alive. The degree to which we experience spiritual aliveness increases parallel to the degree we embody genuine liberation for all.

Cone is not nuanced in his use of White and Black in that he aligns whiteness with oppression and blackness with the oppressed, though he concedes that not only Black people are oppressed. Poor Whites who have suffered at the hands of oppressors fall under his definition of blackness if they are not also in collusion with Black oppression. God, however, is not colorblind, for to render God such is to

---

[429] Peterson, *The Message*, Matthew 25:45.

[430] Cone, *Black Theology of Liberation*, 12.

assume God is also blind to injustice.[431] Of course, this is an anthropomorphic idea of a God directly involved in human activity but suffice to say that if we take spiritual and religious premises seriously, we must also take justice and liberation seriously. Learning to think outside of the constrictions a culture of whiteness represents is predicated upon the full acceptance of the "transcendent other."[432] We can embrace a God who loves the uniqueness of every being and asks that we do not merely tolerate but celebrate that uniqueness in our efforts to repair the world.

An embodied and transcendent spirituality is fundamentally rooted in an I–Thou relatedness defined by holistic interdependence, authenticity, and awareness of an essential but relationally differentiated unity. It is based on concepts of shared realities and seeing others as sacred.[433] To ground it in the Christian tradition, Jesus's teachings were fundamentally rooted in such a spirituality. He was not a theologian per say, but a religious radical and Jewish mystic who upended the social order in favor of inclusivity, liberation, and transpersonal love.[434] I agree with Willie James Jennings that Christianity in the Western world operates within a "diseased social imagination"[435] in that it concerns itself with who is right rather than tend to those

---

[431] Cone, *Black Theology of Liberation*, 6.

[432] Birt, "Bad Faith of Whiteness," 87.

[433] Buber, *I and Thou*.

[434] There are many credible sources for this statement, including the Jesus Seminar, founded by Robert Funk in 1985. My own spiritual teacher hails from this lineage and teaches from the perspective of the historical Jesus rather than the divine being immaculately conceived.

[435] Jennings, *Christian Imagination*, 19.

who are excluded. We do not have a cohesive understanding of Christianity in the United States. To that end, we must challenge spiritualities that deny or minimize our bodies and seek wisdom from those that want us to be more deeply human, not beyond human.[436] If the goal of a personal spiritual practice is to relate to our humanness, then the social outcome is to treat one another more humanely. Spiritual depravity grows where racism thrives because it allows us to conceive of "the other" as less human.

The fractured soul of our nation upholds division and domination, and perhaps that realization is just beginning to come clear in the mainstream. A culture of whiteness is awakening to its missing, lost, invisible, and unhealed facets even as it writhes in discomfort. At times we stand incredulous as we protest, "But this is not who we are," paralyzed by the dawning awareness that the United States is not the land of the free. Race-based violence and dehumanization persists. We suffer from a complex and hard to name spiritual sickness with a sustained addiction to violence that infiltrates every layer of our society.

Many writers, social critics, and modern-day abolitionists feel hopeless about the willingness for a culture of whiteness to change, that if our self-interests are protected, we lack the motivation. I suggest that our Self interests are at stake, that our True Selves will remain captive if we do not disentangle from white supremacist thinking and "the bad faith of whiteness."[437] It is a journey toward greater belonging. Belonging does not require uniformity or uphold scarcity, as a culture of whiteness

---

[436] Benner, *Human Being and Becoming*, 12.

[437] Birt, "Bad Faith of Whiteness."

would have us believe. It is a set of conditions that support an individual's right to fully express themselves within a supportive community without fear of harm or exclusion. Telling truths about failures to create belonging will help us release the hold a culture of domination has on us economically, psychologically, and spiritually. Strong storytelling and embodied spiritualities recall, as mystic Henri Nouwen does, that "the most personal is the most universal, the most hidden is the most public, and the most solitary is the most communal. What we live in the most intimate places of our beings is not just for us but for all people."[438] Spiritual healing is social healing.

…

Unbelonging to create greater belonging is both deconstructive and reconstructive, the spiritual path of the via negativa *and* positiva. *It is destabilizing because of the human's innate social nature to want to belong, to be in community, to feel safe. Discomfort is unfamiliar to White people, socially speaking, and I notice that many want to move at lightning-speed from apocalypse to transformation without education and elucidation. On the opposite side of that quickening is a dangerous reactivity to a world diversifying before our very eyes. The notion of a "great replacement theory" has taken hold of the reactionary American imagination.*[439] *Even though we have more language than ever to understand identity and privilege and construct better worlds, to some, diversity and inclusion is terrifying. Some seem to be in a war with reality.*

In 1972, Baldwin wrote,

---

[438] Nouwen, *Bread for the Journey*, 80.

[439] Wilson and Flanagan, "The Racist 'Great Replacement' Theory Explained."

An old world is dying, and a new one, kicking in the belly of its mother, time, announces that it is ready to be born. This birth will not be easy, and many of us are doomed to discover that we are exceedingly clumsy midwives. No matter, so long as we accept that our responsibility is to the newborn: the acceptance of responsibility contains the key to the necessarily evolving skill.[440]

By all accounts, we are between the old world and the new. In some sense, this in-betweenness is a perpetual state of becoming, but it can be pushed toward greater belonging every moment we choose humility, justice, and mercy. Will we choose to participate in the birthing process, cast our ladders in the sky despite not knowing what awaits? Will we participate in love?

Unbelonging is a liminal space, a threshold of sorts. I often feel I have one foot steeped in a 400-plus-year-old ancestry of White land and wealth acquisition, the other in realizing that none of that was designed to benefit my husband or my children. And yet, they are here. The persistence of blackness in this country is a guiding light. May I commit to recovering my humanity in a way that honors that light.

Liminality is creative, a space of examination and reflection, of widening the view. I am not alone in this space, and a prerequisite to entering is not interracial marriage or having the proverbial Black best friend, but a willingness to see and be with what is. Situated there, we can serve as keepers of memory, transformers of a scarred past into a healed future. The Talmud cautions us not to be daunted by the enormity of the world's grief but to do justice now. Love mercy now. Walk humbly now. We are not obliged to complete the work, nor are we free to abandon it.[441] Reimagining America is not just an economic and political issue but a spiritual one that will beget

---

[440] Baldwin, *No Name in the Street*, 221.

[441] J. Jacobs, "Pirkei Avot."

new economic and political structures. Inhabiting the liminal spaces can break into the numinous. The clouds part. The sun shines. A ladder awaits that leads to new and unknown worlds. new economic and political structures. Inhabiting the liminal spaces can break into the numinous. The clouds part. The sun shines. A ladder awaits that leads to new and unknown worlds.

PART II:

ELUCIDATION

Elucidation furthers awareness and plants seeds for imagining a world where racism is challenged and eradicated. We are aware of the light, and although our eyes are still adjusting, there is a path of greater clarity and belonging. In this section I intend to show that adopting anti-racism broadens the "human element." I also define liberation as a necessary philosophy and praxis for White people to adopt to facilitate unbelonging from a culture of whiteness. Finally, I propose an antidote to the problems discussed in Chapter 3 by offering ways to embrace and practice liberatory philosophy, psychology, and spirituality.

> At first, when any [one of us] is liberated and compelled suddenly to stand up and turn [our] neck round and walk and look towards the light, [we] will suffer sharp pains . . . unable to see the realities of which in [our] former state [we] had seen the shadows . . . [our] eye is turned towards more real existence . . . what will be [our] reply? . . . [Our] eyes will be dazzled, and [we] will not be able to see anything at all of what are now called realities. [We] will gaze upon the light of the moon and the stars and the spangled heaven; and [we] will see the sky and the stars by night better than the sun or the light of the sun by day. . . . And [we] will contemplate [ourselves] as [we] are . . . having turned from darkness to the day.[442]

"The shadow elements in a personality [are] those repressed or unlived sides of a person's total potential. Through lack of attention and development,

---

[442] Plato, *Allegory of the Cave*, 12.

these unlived and repressed qualities remain archaic or turn dark and threatening. . . . The demand for growth in consciousness often comes from the shadow."[443]

The quality of light by which we scrutinize our lives has direct bearing upon the product which we live, and upon the changes which we hope to bring about through those lives. It is within this light that we form those ideas by which we pursue our magic and make it realized. . . . These places of possibility within ourselves are dark because they are ancient and hidden; they have survived and grown strong through that darkness. Within these deep places, each one of us holds an incredible reserve of creativity and power, of unexamined and unrecorded emotion and feeling. "The woman's place of power within each of us is neither white nor surface; it is dark, it is ancient, and it is deep."[444]

---

[443] Johnson, *She*, 29–30.

[444] Lorde, *Selected Works*, 19–20.

CHAPTER 4 | LIBERATION

In this chapter I define liberation as a communal process that frees both the oppressed and the oppressor, albeit in different ways. In some sense we must divest from fight language so that we move from thinking about liberation *from* or *to* and toward conceptualizing freedom *with*. Ultimately, I conclude that practicing public, transpersonal love as a liberatory action creates the conditions for concrete, relational freedom and facilitates unbelonging from whiteness. Participating in cultivating inclusive and equitable freedom ushers forth the kind of greater belonging I dare to imagine. The type of freedom I propose entails forging a different, more ethical, and inclusive path that is unknown to us, which can provoke anxiety. Every time we avoid the anxiety of affirming inclusive freedom, we reduce freedoms in both the present and future.[445]

Defining Liberation

To imagine and participate in creating a more whole, inclusive, and loving society, White Americans need to expand our ideas about freedom. Robert Birt asserts that we are human by virtue of our freedom, that it constitutes the *being* of the human. However, it is more than a property that we have, more than a state to achieve, more than a contract between people. It is, as he said, "the peculiar mode of being which we *are*."[446]

Freedom is intrinsic to human nature but remains unfulfilled in our society. American ideals about freedom were born out of oppression. Early settler-colonists

---

[445] Benner, *Human Being and Becoming*, 34.

[446] Birt, "Quest for Freedom as Community," 87.

on this continent chased dreams of religious and political liberty that they did not have under the rule of monarchy. Despite the rhetoric threaded through our documents, anthems, and monuments, freedom never applied to all. It applied to wealthy, White males primarily, and today it applies inconsistently to non-whites and women. If whiteness were representative of freedom—defined by negation as *not slavery*—then our very concepts of freedom have been erroneously created alongside concepts of domination that included enslavement and racial hierarchies. An extreme form of enslavement is foundational to the United States, and one could say an equally extreme, even unhealthy view of freedom that relied upon another's captivity.[447] It was almost as if the White person could not conceive of themselves as free without direct juxtaposition to its opposite.

For my purposes, I interchange freedom and liberation but use "liberation" as the modifier to philosophy, spirituality, and psychology. I define freedom in the following ways.

- Following john powell, "Freedom is found not in autonomy but in embeddedness."[448] Freedom arises out of interdependent relationships and communities, as it is synonymous with widespread inclusivity and belonging. Implied in freedom as interdependence are the ideals of the Beloved Community in which adherents are asked to stand for loyalty to a thoroughly communitarian love that is unified by an active, indwelling

---

[447] powell, *Racing to Justice*, xviii.

[448] powell, 20.

purpose that supersedes the isolated self.[449] Here again I assert that if White people to participate in liberation, they must resist whiteness as the highest ideal and adopt a stance of differentiated unity. Movements for liberation are always communal. Therefore, loyalty to the individualized White self is antithetical to genuine freedom.

- Freedom disrupts real and perceived barriers to belonging and inclusivity and challenges attachments that hold our minds captive.
- Freedom is holistic, and it includes pedagogies, psychologies, and spiritualities.
- Freedom honors struggle. Paradoxically, it is important to note that one of the problems with liberation movements is their dependence on struggle, which I address later.
- Freedom upholds and honors pluralism.

To further expand on the relationship between pluralism and freedom, the qualities of a pluralistic society are as follows:

- A willingness to energetically pursue and engage with diversity.
- The active seeking of understanding across lines of difference rather than mere tolerance. Tolerance is a basic premise of democracy in that we must first permit and tolerate differences. We do not have to like or agree with one another, but we do need to honor each other's intrinsic dignity and first do no harm. On that fundamental supposition, the United States has not achieved its democratic ideals.

---

[449] Herstein, "Roycean Roots of the Beloved Community," 98.

- A willingness to hold our deepest differences in sacred relationship with one another.
- A commitment to open, constructive dialogue.[450]
- An acknowledgment of trans-religious wisdom. Each "river of faith" that flows through the national landscape has its own internal complexity. However, each one is also made richer by its dialogue and interaction with others. Pluralism accepts that religious traditions are dynamic and mutable, not static.[451]

Ultimately liberation is neither a result of occupation nor bestowed upon one group by another. It is neither "help" nor missionary work, both upheld by inequalities of power. It is not done *for* another, nor is it what is frequently called "nation building," which often involves imposing one country's way of governing onto another. It cannot reduce to oppressed and oppressor binaries because, at different moments, one might be on either side of this fence. Genuine liberation addresses the various wounds to our humanity and involves insight, restoration, and possibilities for a healed society for victims and perpetrators, bystanders, and witnesses alike.[452] True liberation is transformation.

An obvious question is whether liberation theories can apply to dominant groups, what Enrique Dussel calls the center, as they were explicitly conceived as

---

[450] Definitions of pluralism adapted from The Pluralism Project at Harvard University. See Pluralism Project, "About."

[451] Pluralism Project, "Rivers of Faith."

[452] Watkins and Shulman, *Toward Psychologies of Liberation*, 59.

methods to gain sovereignty for historically marginalized and oppressed groups from the center.[453] Dussel defines the periphery as a forced result of the unjust center, whereas hooks pushes readers to reorient the margins as space of chosen participation and collaborative empowerment. Redefining the periphery, or margin, as more than the subjugated aspects of colonialist powers allows for recognizing it as a site of resistance and coalition building. Used insightfully, liberatory philosophies provide frameworks for creating freedom from structures and systems designed and upheld by imperialist, capitalist interests.

Dussel defines liberation as the action of the oppressed to express or realize themselves.[454] However, the kind of liberation I propose also demands action from the oppressor. It is a decisive stance of solidarity with historically marginalized people that unravels internalized, systemic white supremacist ideology. Genuine liberation requires White people to examine, deconstruct, and redefine a culture of whiteness and acknowledge how it has been weaponized to perpetuate oppression. Liberation theories should not create pathways for assimilation of marginalized groups nor appropriation by dominant groups. Rather, I suggest they inform resistance, solidarity, and self-awareness. In standing with oppressed people, the dominator is better situated to recognize their own lost or repressed aspects. While oppression comes from an external source and repression is an internal psychological phenomenon, the relationship between the two needs examination. According to

---

[453] Dussel, *Philosophy of Liberation*, 2–9.

[454] Dussel, 62.

Dussel, "the domination of the oppressed becomes repression."[455] What the oppressor does not know about themselves is projected—often violently—onto the oppressed.

Ideally, the whole project of liberation is guided by a shared commitments to justice, freedom, and love within community. Liberative justice is not the same as legal justice, be it distributive or commutative, but rather genuine justice that subverts the established unjust order upheld by the center.[456] Genuine justice happens in the margins where dialectical processes and proximity to pressing social issues are the norm. We gain a kind of exteriority, or what Dussel names an "unfathomable spring of wisdom"[457] that allows us to criticize the system in which we operate without fetishizing the experiences of those who are historically oppressed. Here, liberation is more than mere ideology but a function of everyday experience. Genuine liberation exposes the fundamental interconnectedness of reality.

Types of Freedom

Definitions of freedom put forth by Erich Fromm classify the two types as *freedom from* (or negative) and *freedom to* (or positive). *Freedom from* is underdeveloped without *freedom to*. Simply put, *from* is the absence of obstacles or constraints and *to* is

---

[455] Dussel, 78.

[456] Dussel, 65.

[457] Dussel, 180.

the possibility of personal agency to realize one's purpose.[458] These definitions, while helpful, are also limited. Freedom from is easier to measure objectively than freedom to in political and social institutions. Defined by negation, it is absent of tyranny, domination, enslavement, and injustice. By these standards, the United States has neither achieved genuine democracy nor freedom. I argue that a genuine democracy does not oppress or exclude any of its inhabitants, regardless of citizenship status. The story of freedom in the United States is inseparable from the eradication of the indigenous population and enslavement of Africans, even as patriots fought relentlessly against the British crown to achieve *freedom from* their oppressors. One of the great contradictions of this country is that even with a rallying cry of "Liberty!" it never applied to all. At some point, everyone outside of White men of European descent had to fight for their liberty. From the early stages of colonization, freedom aligned with violence and struggle, tools of the oppressor.

We cannot defend negative freedom while ignoring massive injustices, poverty, despair, and inequity. Negative freedom defends against totalitarianism and incursions while positive freedom intends to create the conditions for full participation of all citizens.[459] Problems in upholding positive freedom arise when only certain people are considered citizens and treated as such. Who is granted full rights of citizenship in this country seems to be in perpetual debate and continues to be determined by White Patriarchal values.

---

[458] Working definitions adapted from two sources: Ian Carter, "Positive and Negative Liberty" and Adam Okuliez-Kozaryn, "'Freedom From' and 'Freedom To.'"

[459] Bellah, "Birth of New American Myths," 152.

The United States mostly upholds republican liberty, a status bestowed upon individuals who enjoy relative noninterference from the government or ruling entity.[460] Essentially, you are free if you are not a slave. This type of freedom often comes at the expense of others who may not enjoy the same access as those privileged by the "republic." Freedom often gets confused with nationalism and isolationism, and problems arise when ideas about individual versus communal freedom clash. Current divisions call for a rethinking of the entire freedom project. We cannot afford to uphold sectarian freedom by pitting identity groups against one another. We affirm our humanity by the degree to which we develop a broad sense of community and belonging based on *freedom with*.

It is necessary to distinguish between nominal freedom and realized freedom. I use nominal freedom to mean freedom in name or idea that doesn't always apply. "With liberty and justice for all" and "Life, Liberty, and the pursuit of Happiness" indicate nominal freedom because the structures that support them never applied to the whole population. Nominal freedoms are great ideas, but we have yet to fulfill our best ones. Realized freedom is autonomous and embedded, in that individuals receive support to become themselves in their intimate communities who enjoy nominal freedoms like access to health care, accessible and equitable education, a livable wage, access to food, and resources that support a positive quality of life. Realized freedom honors individual agency and choice without causing harm to others. It aligns with the belief that no individual is free until everyone is free.

---

[460] Carter, "Positive and Negative Liberty," 5.

Everyone has degrees of nominal and realized freedom and degrees of freedom from and freedom to, but in a real sense, they do not apply equitably to all. Degrees of freedom apply differently in specific situations. I think of how enslaved people often formed subversive communities, underground churches, and spaces for laughter and music, even in the most oppressive conditions. I think of how White allies fought for abolition at the risk of belonging. Even my earliest ancestors, though eventual enslavers and protectors of the status quo, cast their lot for the idea of freedom in the "New World." Without romanticizing these examples, I intend to highlight that positive freedom can be ephemeral, momentary, and hard to sustain without realized freedom because it requires immunity from outside forces.[461] It must be upheld by an ethical ruling class, which is a fragile trust. This inability of the self or selves to disconnect entirely from outside forces is a clear indicator that freedom is not autonomous; it cannot happen in isolation from one's circumstances. *Freedom to* is more a mindset than a set of circumstances. However, the ability to find contentment with one's situation should not be confused with happiness or justice. People like Nelson Mandela, imprisoned on Robben Island for thirty years, or Buddhist Jarvis Jay Masters, currently on death row in San Quentin Prison,[462] seem to have achieved it. Still, I assert that it is exceedingly difficult to develop a whole self when one's bodily autonomy is restricted.

...

---

[461] Carter, 3.

[462] Egelko, "Death Penalty Upheld."

Black people in the United States are free from chattel slavery, but not free from the tyranny of racism. It follows that White Americans are not free from the tyranny of racist thinking. It is a poison that infiltrates the very air we breathe. Many White people say, "Oh, but the kids. They seem to get it. I mean, my kids don't care what color your kids are." It may be true, in some sense, that this generation of kids is more comfortable with fluidity of all kinds, but my youngest son and another Black-biracial boy he was playing with were recently called the N-word on a group camping trip. This happened to my youngest son, who my mother called "my White baby." No one, not a single kid or parent, most of them White, came to their defense, and those who knew displayed disbelief that it happened at all. My son chose to get out of the lake and quietly walk away. He later said he felt ashamed for not knowing what to say.

Freedom from *the tyranny of racism would allow for the White kids, some of whom later whispered to their mothers that they felt uncomfortable by the language used, would have the* freedom to *speak against it without fear or shame. My child, his White friends, and the White teens who issued the slur were imprisoned by a culture of whiteness. None were truly free, yet there is a fundamental difference in how each can behave in an incident like this.*

We can whisper all the kindnesses we want to my son, hold his face in our hands, pour love into him, and tell him this ugly word is not about him but the person saying it, some sickness in his mind. But let me tell you, my boys know the crudeness of that word in the mouth of a White teenager, how it drips with power and the ghosts of America's crueler history of lynch mobs and White terror. No matter what we say to him, it leaves a tear in the fabric of his being. He will always recall the first time he was called the N-word.

Some weeks after that, we were traveling, staying at a hotel with a pool carved into the side of Utah's brick red canyons. Kids love hotels with pools; mine are no exception. It was splendid, complete with a small slide and a waterfall. They'd often rather be swimming than exploring the novelty of a new place. At some point, four White teenagers arrived and cannonballed in from the edge, laughing carelessly. My son was suddenly at my side, his wet body huddled up against me, knees pulled to his chest, and said, "I don't think I want to swim anymore. They remind me of that time . . . you know . . . camping."

Freedom from/freedom to. Technically my son exercised his freedom to exit the pool, to care for his spirit. And even though freedom is not always synonymous with happiness, shouldn't my child have the fundamental right to splash, laugh, and play in a pool without fear of incident, without sacrificing his right to fun? As it is, public-use pools have a strange history. I would never have thought to get out, but my child is perhaps more trained than I by generational wisdom and self-preservation. As parents of Black and biracial children, we must shore them up against this kind of tyranny and help them to believe in their rights to freedom, however precarious, despite the world and that which we cannot control in it. I realize every parent has this task to a degree. Who is free, though, when White kids still wield power by uttering the N-word, reducing Black kids to something ugly on the bottom of your shoe?

No, neither Black people nor White people are free from the tyranny of racism.

…

Ideally, positive freedom is a mutual set of values supported by the community so that the potential for shared, genuine freedom is ever-present. For positive freedom to be successfully systematized, the conception of self must extend beyond the isolated individual. The genuine interests of the individual ideally conflate with the genuine interests of the whole and vice versa.[463] I believe this is possible at the small scale and repeatable in rippling patterns at the large scale. It requires

---

[463] Carter, 2–3.

creating community agreements and continually engaging to uphold them. If *freedom to* is partly about personal agency and actualization, it is necessary to realize that personhood is only ever known in proximity to our relationships. Personhood reflects the quality of one's relatedness within community.

My background in psychology, both as a teacher of the subject and mental health practitioner, has afforded me ample opportunities to engage with Maslow's hierarchy of needs, first published in 1943. It is so ubiquitous, it is considered true. However, I recently learned that his pyramid, based on individual evolution over a single lifetime, is an interpretation of observations from his stay with the Siksiká (Blackfoot) people in 1938. To be fair, Maslow's hierarchy has been adjusted by others over time, as most ideas are. What initially had five tiers eventually grew to seven and eight by the 1960s and '70s, and he originally used "self-transcendence" rather than the more commonly known "self-actualization," implying a metaphysical transformation as the highest need, thus entangling freedom with spirituality and psychology.[464] Regardless, his progression is linear and based on individual potential rather than communal and generational potential. To my knowledge, he never publicly credited the Blackfoot Nation for his elaboration on what he observed. He later critiqued his own implication that self-actualization happens in isolation or linear fashion.

Blackfoot philosophy presupposes that the duty of community is to meet the basic needs for nourishment, shelter, and support for each person's process of becoming. Everyone is encouraged to participate meaningfully in the community

---

[464] Bray, "Maslow's Hierarchy."

whose ultimate hope is cultural perpetuity. The Blackfoot Nation understood self-actualization to be innate, not something earned over a lifetime. Elders understood their role as drawing forth the sacred being of the young without presumption or force. The purpose of becoming an actualized self is to be of service to the community that ensures the safety and meeting of basic needs for all individuals. The "wealthy" community members were those who provided abundantly to those in greater need. There is no word for poverty unless defined as "without community." A "deviant" person could restore themselves to the community if they take responsibility and gave up miscreant behaviors.[465]

Cultural perpetuity is "the breath of life"[466] sustained by promoting communal values of generosity, trust, forgiveness, and cooperation across time and space. The individual is immersed in the cultural milieu, aware of their place in ensuring future generations' well-being and drawing from their ancestors' wisdom. The relationship between the individual and the community is symbiotic. Blackfoot community structure is the ultimate example of autonomous and embedded freedom whose baseline is the expectation that the community meets every person's basic needs and honors their innate worth and dignity.

It would be contradictory for a society to mandate *freedom to*, as such mandates slide toward authoritarianism. It is, rather, an agreement made, a shared cultural value. This is a third space that I name *freedom with*, also inspired by the Blackfoot Nation's perspective. *Free from* and *free to* maintain binary, either/or

---

[465] Ravilochan, "Could the Blackfoot Wisdom?," par. 7.

[466] Michel, "Maslow's Hierarchy Connected to Blackfoot Beliefs," par. 11.

thinking that certifies only two ways of being free. One is either moving against a system or toward agency. *From* is either granted (one was never enslaved) or fought for (one struggled against oppression). *To* is primarily contingent upon *from* being in place, or it requires great spiritual fortitude. *Freedom with* deconstructs systems of power and does not depend on historically marginalized people to lead the way. It is mutually empowering with a particular impetus on those who hold power to critically examine it. Genuine freedom is triadic in that it combines negative and positive, individual and communal liberty to achieve *freedom with*.

Freedom with abides by the values of pluralism and, as hooks puts it, "accepts the interlocking, interdependent nature of systems of domination"[467] and liberation. It recognizes that domination and liberation exist in a delicate loop but asserts that the presence of liberty should not depend on the presence of domination. *Freedom with* is based on an ethic of love and does not require violence to sustain itself. It is a choice, one that is perhaps the ultimate exercise of *freedom to* and the continual re-examination of who is represented by *freedom from*. Central to *freedom with* are critical consciousness, learning to look inward and outward, awareness and acknowledgment of the truths of our shared realities, and community. *Freedom with* extends beyond resistance to transformation. It is to struggle with, to move through difficulty toward mutuality and interdependence. It can be viewed as inherently feminine, deeply relational, unitive, and wise. King prophesied that "the end is reconciliation, the end is redemption, the end is the creation of the Beloved Community."[468] Before

---

[467] hooks, "Love as the Practice of Freedom," 244.

[468] King, *Essential Martin Luther King, Jr.*, 38.

substantiating liberatory theories with an ethic of love, it is crucial to consider the limitations.

Problems with Liberation Movements

The struggle for liberation is just that: a struggle. It is often synonymous with persistent fight energy, which can lead to recreating forms of domination. Fight energy is not sustainable over time. Liberation movements can keep oppressed groups in competition with one another rather than seek to destroy the roots of oppression. They can also keep oppressor–oppressed locked into dependent cycles of resistance. While struggle and protest are necessary for liberation, when they become the primary energy people become disabled from connecting to other possibilities.[469] Furthermore, it does not challenge how centers of power imprison the minds of those who hold it, and as noted above, genuine freedom implies challenging even that which controls our thinking.

Many feel motivated to subvert domination only when it directly threatens their self-interests. Those content to remain in power rarely sustain allyship in liberation movements.[470] If liberation is to be taken seriously by White people to deconstruct a culture of whiteness, then we need a new language that moves beyond resistance and overcoming, beyond oppressor and oppressed binaries.

While freedom from is important, it is not an end, as it does not dismantle racist systems of power. That which one seeks freedom from demands our critical analysis rather than the movement itself. Historically, those who protest and engage

---

[469] Holmes, *Race and the Cosmos*, 31.

[470] hooks, "Love as the Practice of Freedom," 246.

in the work of liberation are more readily criticized than those who upheld systems of domination. Consider how media quickly pounced on BLM protests in the summer of 2020, calling them "rioters," "Antifa," and even "domestic terrorists"[471] instead of focusing on the systems being protested. This approach diverts attention away from real issues that require thoughtful, collective solutions. Furthermore, researchers found that the protests were overwhelmingly peaceful compared to inflammatory reports criticizing them.[472] The wisdom of Martin Luther King, Jr., still applies as he criticized the powerful for setting the timetable for another's liberation, paternalistically proclaiming support of the goals while criticizing the method. They hijacked the process and prevented meaningful engagement.[473] If we are serious about it, liberation needs to focus on the ways collective liberation is bound together.

The challenge of operationalizing freedom in a liberal democracy is agreeing upon methods to preserve it. There is potential for greater empathy toward those we perceive as our enemies if we can connect at the level of needs and values. When we can see one another's humanity and appreciate how we are similar and different, possibilities for peace and restoration increase.

For Whites in the United States to participate in liberation, we cannot remain satisfied protesting alongside as allies then returning to the arms of whiteness. We

---

[471] See, for example, Byman, "Who Is a Terrorist, Actually?"; Dewan, "Trump Is Calling Protesters Who Disagree with Him Terrorists;" Gonzalez, "Congress Should Investigate the Black Lives Matter Riots;" Steinmetz, "'A War of Words.' Why Describing the George Floyd Protests as 'Riots' Is So Loaded."

[472] Chenoweth and Pressman, "Black Lives Matter Protestors."

[473] King, "Letter from a Birmingham Jail," 73.

must also engage in the difficult work of disentangling from a culture of whiteness. Efforts toward liberation are not just about freeing the historically oppressed or marginalized but freeing ourselves, too. If I accept that a culture of whiteness has socialized every person in our country to some degree, then I also accept that we can choose to resist that socialization.[474] One cannot claim to be an abolitionist without making that choice and addressing the wounds racism has inflicted, be they hidden or apparent.

Liberation from whiteness cannot occur by maintaining our complicity with structural racism but by embracing a "culture of conversion" and employing public behaviors of love.[475] To borrow from Blackfoot philosophy, we must see ourselves as stewards of the breath of life,[476] not hoarders. We can exhale our energies into imagining a world that does not maintain systems of domination. One who uses power responsibly constantly asks, "Whose voice is missing here? What have I forgotten to consider?" If we have any inkling that love matters, then we must be willing to surrender to what we do not know to imagine a world governed by it. Here again, love and liberation cannot be mandated; they must be internalized as values.

Another problem with liberation movements is their alignment with God and theology. While liberation theologians argue against the typical White male God of Protestant Christianity, I assert that it is necessary to move beyond images of God altogether, especially idolatrous images of a God who colluded with white supremacy

---

[474] hooks, *Teaching Community*, 56.

[475] hooks, "Love as the Practice of Freedom," 243.

[476] Michel, "Maslow's Hierarchy Connected to Blackfoot Beliefs."

and enslavement. To get beyond the "religion of whiteness" that values individualism, domination, and favoritism, notions of God cannot be perceived as a separate, "out there" God on whom we depend for agency or intervention. If we want to achieve freedom, we must see ourselves as agents of it and experience the divine as an expression of the true self. It is as Frederick Douglass wrote: "I prayed for freedom for twenty years but received no answer until I prayed with my legs."[477]

I acknowledge the inherent conflict in removing conversations about liberation from the realm of religion or God. It might be more accurate to say that we need to deconstruct our understandings of both, especially Christianity as it has been abused by colonizers as a weapon of domination. Consider that African enslavement was justified by Christians as a way to "tame the savages."[478] Prior to the height of the trans-Atlantic slave trade, a pan-European, Christian crusade ensued against the predominately Islamic Ottoman Empire for nearly 400 years, blurring the lines between the emergence of White/Euro supremacy, Christianity, and Islamophobic conquest that would sharpen the divide between empires in the East and West.[479] Keller refers to a "thousand-year crusade" during which "humanist" Pope Nicholas V—the very same who permitted the exclusive plunder and enslavement of West Africans to the Portuguese—called for the Christian

---

[477] Holland, *Frederick Douglass: The Colored Orator*, 67.

[478] Reynolds and Kendi, *Stamped*, 6.

[479] Horne, *Dawning of the Apocalypse*, chap. 1.

unification of European nations to resist Muslim conquest.[480] Instead of the multireligious pluriversality proposed by some Christians, like the fifteenth-century cardinal Nicholas of Cusa, a pan-European supremacism arose.[481]

Imperial values influenced religious and racial formation because pluralism proved challenging both ideologically and practically. European supremacism ultimately translated into racial and Christian supremacism in the colonization of the Americas. Instead of religious freedom, the Western world exploded via religious violence.[482] Modern concepts of freedom are therefore intertwined with conquest and capitalism, what Keller refers to as a "crusade complex," that included Islamophobia and anti-blackness fueled by the enslavement of Africans.[483] Even though the Islamic Ottomans also enslaved people, including Christians, the European-driven trans-Atlantic slave trade ultimately dwarfed the Ottoman practice in scope and brutality. The colonial maneuvers Christianity brought to the "New World" were antithetical to freedom and love.

Keller asserts that longstanding habits of Christianity as a colonizing religion got naturalized as engrained as truth.[484] Therefore, spiritual liberation requires rejecting the use of religions as tools for domination and retrieving the transpersonal

---

[480] C. Keller, "Crusade, Capital, and Cosmopolis," 242.

[481] C. Keller, "Crusade, Capital, and Cosmopolis," 241.

[482] C. Keller, "Crusade, Capital, and Cosmopolis," 244.

[483] C. Keller, "Crusade, Capital, and Cosmopolis," 240.

[484] C. Keller, "Crusade, Capital, and Cosmopolis," 249.

love innate to their mystical cores. Keller quotes Cusa's call for peace between Islam and Christianity that invites not mere tolerance but inclusive multiplicity: "All the names are unfoldings of the enfolding of the one, ineffable name.... Although there could be many such unfoldings, they are never so many or so great that there could not be more."[485] His plea was overshadowed by imperialism corroborated by the Christian church even though, as Keller writes, "None of us (not even a cardinal) can . . . 'know' God, no religion can rule out the truth of other religions. For in all their difficult differences of name and way, each seeks the life that is beyond names."[486] To echo both points, liberation does not only belong to Christianity.

The liberatory roots of Christianity are evident in the teachings of Jesus and the early church, who sought an experience of the beloved and empowered community outside the walls of institutional religion.[487] Part of liberating Christianity from empires is to recognize that the symbol of the cross can both heal and hurt; it can empower and liberate as well as enslave and oppress.[488] It is a symbol of persecution and redemption. It is imperative to wrestle with these tensions and ask whether the worst abuses of Christianity will determine its final meaning or whether the underlying message of interrelatedness will prevail. Religious devotees ultimately determine its direction and expression.

---

[485] C. Keller, "Crusade, Capital, and Cosmopolis," 251.

[486] C. Keller, "Crusade, Capital, and Cosmopolis," 250.

[487] Sanford, *Mystical Christianity*, and John Shelby Spong, *The Fourth Gospel: Tales of a Jewish Mystic*, interpret Jesus's ministry as one of radical inclusion and liberation.

[488] Cone, *The Cross and the Lynching Tree*, 20.

Aligning liberation with a religion of individualism and personal salvation, as White Protestant Christianity is so often expressed in the United States, is a theological misinterpretation. Instead, theology ought to concern itself with the community who seeks to define, in every generation, its purpose for being in the world.[489] Liberation theology advocates for both social and spiritual justice. It takes very seriously the role of human activity in creating a liberated society by responding to the urgency of injustice and the need to restore Christianity to its anti-colonial origins.

As ineffable and impossible it is to define God, human concepts of the divine mirror our concepts of self and relationships. If we limit our capacities for justice, freedom, and love, we limit wise theology's relationships to human agency. The creative possibilities—and tensions—between a cosmic God who acts on our behalf and one who does not are limitless. As much as our images of the divine can invoke fear and trembling, I also believe they can draw forth tremendous possibilities for fulfilling our roles in the cosmic order of interconnectedness. Ultimately, however, liberation is not restricted only to believers. Liberation, like love, operates in between. It is both of us and wholly other than us. Both require our participation and engagement with the sacred other and with quite a bit of surrender to mystery to be fully realized.

Barbara Holmes and Vaclav Havel offer that liberation is seeded in self-transcendence and a preeminent belief in the transcendent other. As we enact justice and liberation in concrete ways without attachment to egoic goals or outcomes we

---

[489] Cone, *Black Theology of Liberation*, 9.

immerse ourselves in the process itself. We need pedagogies, philosophies, theologies, and psychologies of liberation that address the oppressed and oppressors so that it becomes a communal endeavor. Havel suggests that liberation is "an awareness of connections to a reality beyond our everything, a higher intention that is the source of all things, a higher memory recording everything, a higher authority to which we are all accountable in one way or another."[490] The ideal pursuit of freedom is active relation; inclusive, not exclusive; and cooperative, not competitive. It requires an engaged citizenry committed to a shared ethics of love.

Perhaps there is no beast to slay, only beasts to face, invite in, and ask what they can teach us. The solution for achieving a just, loving, liberated society is in the overlapping and infinite space between individual choice and shared commitments and values.[491] The right to choose is a significant component of a society that values freedom, but freedom with does not restrict the safety and belonging of others. It protects without force and challenges without coercion. I acknowledge that this feels infinitely more difficult to manage than our current system and requires ethical leadership at all levels. This fact alone feels like a barrier to imagining something different.

We cannot become anti-racists or abolitionists if we remain unwilling to interrogate the systems of thought, behavior, and belief that explain human behavior, especially those rooted in a Western, colonial, White patriarchal tradition. We cannot

---

[490] Holmes, *Race and the Cosmos*, 48. Holmes quotes Vaclav Havel's talk "A Sense of the Transcendent," given March 29, 1995.

[491] Holmes, 49.

throw the proverbial baby out with the bathwater, but we must remain open to deconstructing accepted knowledge. Achieving genuine freedom is not mere tolerance of differences but a total embrace. According to poet Audre Lorde, differences provide a "fund of necessary polarities between which our creativity can spark like a dialectic. Only then does the necessity for interdependency become unthreatening."[492] In a dialectic space that hovers between the margins and the center, and perhaps ever nearer to the margins, we can seek new ways to *be* and garner the courage "to act where there are no charters."[493]

Love as the Practice of Freedom

I know my mother loves me. I know she would say she wants the best for me, a good life. Yet her love often feels gripping, even in the way she claws the soft space between my shoulder and neck when she comes in for a hug. It feels like she loves me through the veil of her own grief and shame. It could be that she felt different, too; that she poked at the edges of acceptability in her family of origin. As Thandeka proposes, perhaps she suffered the loss of her mother's love because she did not play by the unspoken rules set for her by generations of adherents to whiteness who erroneously perceived that belonging equated with sameness.[494] *I don't know for sure. It seems, though, that some part of her is always missing, hiding in the shadowy hinterlands. She once offered backhanded solidarity to me, saying that she dated a Black man, but knew when it came to marriage, it could never work. It's strange how she both broke the rules and upheld them. Perhaps*

---

[492] Lorde, *Selected Works*, 39.

[493] Lorde, 111.

[494] Thandeka, *Learning to Be White*, 2.

she exists more in the margin than I can recognize. And perhaps it is the work of each generation to expand the edges.

If it is true that whiteness loves in this way, with parts of us missing, then it is not free. If love is the practice of freedom with both transpersonal and maternal qualities, then it entails recovering the cast-off parts of ourselves and others. "Love as the Practice of Freedom," as bell hooks's title suggests, is to show up in the margin as our full, embodied selves without clinging to identities and fixed expectations that do not serve wholeness. As White people, we must be willing to loosen the grip on misguided ideas of belonging and address the deep and inherited shame that perpetuates division.

…

At the heart of liberation is metanoia. At a minimum, it is to rethink a position and, at most, a transformative change of heart and behavior. It is critical to transform our philosophies, psychologies, and spiritualities so that how we think, talk, behave, and believe reflects the world I propose we create rather than reinforce binaries and divisions. Thoughts ultimately shape our destinies. Indeed, philosophy, psychology, and spirituality are often misconstrued as entirely theoretical, but a liberatory approach to these disciplines emphasizes the importance of embodied praxis. Any genuine change requires something beyond mere belief. Metanoia unites contemplation and action, both of which are necessary for liberation and serve as a dialectic that leads to greater possibilities for human becoming.

A rhetorical metanoia is a kind of self-correction that occurs in the moment. It is developing the awareness that when defenses arise, and we want to say, "But I am not racist! This does not apply to me!" We can soften and say, "Actually, having grown up in the context of the United States, I have likely absorbed racist thoughts or tendencies." As a part of speech, it can amplify, soften, or add precision to a statement. As a device, it can contribute to strengthening our self-awareness. It is a small transformation that creates openings for profound behavioral changes, perhaps resulting in psychological metanoia, the healing that follows a total breakdown in personality.

In the context of my dissertation, the necessary "breakdown" is unbelonging from a culture of whiteness so that we may discover the deeper self, which is the aim of both psychological and spiritual metanoia. A genuinely liberatory spiritual conversion requires some act of repentance and repair. Metanoia is incomplete without changes in thought and action. Such a transformation is rooted in transpersonal love that threads together ways of thinking, believing, and being. Guided by Baldwin's principles of "quest and daring and growth,"[495] I define transpersonal love as disruptive to the status quo that masquerades as peace aligned with actions taken on behalf of our own and others' growth and liberation.[496] Dussel suggests that an ethos of liberation is structured around *commiseration*, or being with another's suffering such that one feels the interdependent nature of authentic liberation. In this way, liberation is an other-directed, empathic, metaphysical justice that is oriented toward love of the other as sacred other. He also says that the interior experience of contradiction of loving the oppressed other forces one to grapple with the tenuous relationship between freedom and enslavement and to hurt

---

[495] Baldwin, *Fire Next Time*, 44.

[496] hooks, *All About Love*. Adapted and extended definition of love.

from the pain of it.[497] In this vein, love as freedom builds trust across difference because of deeper knowing.

Without overlaying liberation with love, we deny the needs of the soul in movement building. As a result, our efforts to liberate ourselves and others from internalized domination and oppression patterns suffer. If we cannot allow love to shape the direction of our radical aspirations, we are often drawn back toward allegiance or benign participation in systems of domination.[498] Part of holding freedom and transpersonal love in tandem with one another keeps us alert to present injustices while realizing that each of us is more than our political and social identities. The moment we choose freedom with is also the moment we choose love because *with* always implies relatedness. Both are moves against domination and toward communion.

A dominator culture is anti-love because it requires violence to sustain itself. Choosing love, therefore, is counter cultural. Love requires intention and action. It is an act of will, and will implies choice.[499] We choose to love. As children we need love to thrive, and the quality of love received informs behaviors. As we individuate, an ability to enlarge concepts of love informs social change.

I recognize that I have braided the fierce and slightly unruly love I experience as a mother with a public, transpersonal, justice-oriented love. What I hope to inspire is an archetypal maternal love that is protective, nurturing, and responsive. I do not

---

[497] Dussel, *Philosophy of Liberation*, 64–65.

[498] hooks, "Love as the Practice of Freedom," 243.

[499] hooks, "Love as the Practice of Freedom," 246.

always like my children's behaviors, but I go to great lengths to protect and nurture their rights to become their true selves. Maternal love is fraught with pain and openness to change as it requires letting go coupled with the faith that we may not know the outcome of our commitment for years to come. In a microcosmic, intimate way, motherhood requires that we cast a ladder in the sky from the very beginning. I hold great hopes for my children and lay the groundwork necessary to get them there, knowing that I will falter and that much of their becoming will hopefully continue after I am gone.

Dr. King's description of agape love almost hits the mark in that he describes it as more than a mono-directional outpouring from God to human. It includes more than friendship and affection as it is understanding, creative, redemptive, and charitable.[500] We love because we are cosmically loved, because we are fundamentally rooted in connection. In King's view, we love because God loves us, and as a result that love works through us. What King does not name outright is the feminine and maternal aspect of agapic love.

Public or transpersonal love has some of the same energy in that we are not required to like another person to envision the best for them and work to construct a society that upholds equity, freedom, and justice as its highest values so that each person has a fighting chance to become whole. As with a maternal love, public, transpersonal love embraces love for the sake of love. On a communal level, this is not unlike the Blackfoot community built on the foundations of reciprocity and intergenerational thinking. Nor is dissimilar from mystical Womanism that upholds a

---

[500] King, *Essential Martin Luther King, Jr.*, 26–27, 35.

sense of connectedness to everything and everyone in the universe, beginning with Black women who are so often cast as "the least of these."[501] Womanism also embraces the sacred indwelling of all beings, seeks integration of the earthly body and the soul's expression, and ensures continual striving toward liberation from all manner of oppression. My husband often gives the Black women he grew up with credit for carrying entire communities on their shoulders into every space they entered. As White accomplices to freedom movements, we, too, must imagine that we never enter a space alone. We carry not only the idea of liberation as an act of love, but the images of all those—including ourselves—we wish to see liberated from systems of oppression.

The types of love I describe—maternal, transpersonal, agapic, Womanist—extend beyond the self and intimate other, toward a higher calling. As love infused with these qualities passes through and between us, we are better able to see and tend to our blind spots and see beyond myopic tendencies. Love emerges as we notice, question, and disrupt dominator patterns and their tendency to thrive on exploitation.[502] For White people, the first noticing is whiteness itself: that we have a race and a racialized experience that is molded by domination and ontological expansiveness. Adopting transpersonal love as a public norm has the possibility to free us from these patterns.

---

[501] Wade-Gayles, introduction to *My Soul Is a Witness*, 1–8. Biblical reference to Peterson, *The Message*, Matthew 20:45.

[502] hooks, "Love as the Practice of Freedom," 244.

CHAPTER 5 | PRACTICING LIBERATION

This chapter intends to offer an antidote to the problems outlined in Chapter 3. By doing philosophy, psychology, and spirituality differently, with the whole as much in mind as the individual self, we might approach what I am calling the *via totalis* or *freedom with*. Our collective liberation is intertwined, and unbelonging from a culture of whiteness requires that we divest from systems and structures that seek to divide and dominate. We need to adopt and pass on new ways of thinking and being to foster intergenerational change. Inasmuch as our thoughts can be reoriented, they must ultimately inspire equivalent actions that seek to restore us to one another and liberate all people from systems that oppress. Our philosophies and what we believe to be true about the world inform our psychologies and spiritualities. Together these change our beliefs, behaviors, and systems.

A Philosophy of Liberation

A philosophy of liberation seeks justice, beauty, and equity. Achieving these entails harmonizing the conflicting interests of a diversified society without sacrificing the well-being of any one part. It involves freeing the mind from limiting beliefs and acting justly. The just and equitable person is free, and the just and equitable society supports each person's freedom. If dominator societies adopt and practice philosophies of liberation, it will shift economies driven by scarcity and competition. Dussel offers that the praxis of liberation facilitates a new political and economic order that is creative, inventive, and innovative that does not necessitate oppression.[503] Praxis enables conceiving of situated solutions that are specific to

---

[503] Dussel, *Philosophy of Liberation*, 64.

communities and corrects zero-sum thinking and uninspired universal programming. Practicing liberation includes and centers historically marginalized populations in creating new solutions and systems while the role of the center is to listen, facilitate where necessary, and empower.

Racism and racist policy are barriers to practicing liberation. Societies that deny justice and equity to some are not ultimately free. Liberation from racism requires a dramatic shift in consciousness from those who historically hold power to upend the accepted social order. In many ways, a philosophy of liberation is past, present, and future oriented as it requires repairing past harms to realize a just future. The past and future are forever synchronized by how they inform proximity to present problems and systems of power.[504]

Many theories of freedom are at odds with liberatory praxis. One could say that, as a praxis, the idea of freedom guiding the United States has been one of violence and domination that prioritizes the individual over the community. One could also say that American philosophy encourages a quest for freedom whose praxis lags. In either case, if we are interested in philosophy as activism, we are obliged to respond to the freedom-negating impact of a culture of domination and individualism. The expressed aim of liberation philosophy is to critique colonialism, imperialism, globalization, racism, and sexism articulated from experiences of exploitation—arguably all principles upheld by American policy and a culture of whiteness.[505] I propose White Americans seek liberation by deconstructing whiteness

---

[504] Dussel, 19.

[505] Mendieta, "Philosophy of Liberation," par. 3.

without co-opting the intent of liberation philosophy that specifically empowers the historically oppressed and marginalized. It requires a shift in position in which we align ourselves with the most marginalized and a shift in perspective in which we practice self-reflection and societal critique. White people in this country are not racially oppressed, but we are morally and spiritually repressed in so far as we remain loyal to a culture of whiteness. Liberation philosophy affirms cultural diversity, gender and racial equity, political sovereignty, and the language of "pluriversality."[506] It can provide a lens to help decolonize the impact of the founding ideas of the United States on our minds and behaviors.

"That all men are created equal, that they are endowed by their Creator with certain unalienable Rights, that among these are Life, Liberty and the pursuit of Happiness"[507] is a liberatory principle. We need to examine, revise, and expand interpretations of our constitutional philosophy and evaluate its implementation. What do we mean by "all," for example, and should "men" be changed to persons? Does "all" imply just a community of persons or all beings, including the land? What do we mean by Liberty and Happiness, and what is their relationship with Justice? A sound moral compass is among the highest human virtues, and a just society supposedly produces happier citizens. Often, the powerful abuse the idea of justice to achieve their interests and enact retribution. Our system teaches that if someone murders my family member, justice is served if the murderer is executed or suffers in return. Justice is transactional, and happiness is personal, usually attained by

---

[506] Mendieta, par. 3.

[507] United States Declaration of Independence.

consumption, exhibition, or production of goods or power. Justice and freedom must move beyond the individual level to be absorbed as cultural values. They cannot remain tied to race-based power and competition for resources.

White Americans need to engage in a period of de-centering, to realize that the virtues previously mentioned are not limited. Whiteness is so accustomed to zero-sum thinking that it hoards both resources and virtues. Enrique Dussel's diagrams of the center and the periphery are beneficial to further understand this concept.[508] The periphery represents historically marginalized classes, whether identified as a group or groups of people within a society (Blacks and Native Americans, for example) or one country or region's political and economic subjugation by another (Latin America by the United States). They are often deemed incapable of managing their freedom and, therefore, their rights to happiness. Conversely, those in the center are usually well-resourced and seen as more deserving of their wealth and position, especially in supposed-meritocracies like the United States.

Though there are many ways to diagram centers and peripheries within the United States, I will broadly say that whiteness is the center and non-whiteness, in rippling degrees, is the periphery. The trappings of the center, including wealth, power, representation, and so on, protect a culture of whiteness. When White people fall into the trap of believing we deserve our social and economic status, we perpetuate the myth of whiteness as standard-bearer.[509] Such thinking expects

---

[508] Dussel, *Philosophy of Liberation*, 2.

[509] Baldwin, "White Man's Guilt."

assimilation and supports actions like reducing welfare funding that impacts primarily generationally poor, non-white communities. If our philosophies and ensuing practices support the interests of the center who continue to believe that another's gain is their loss, the outcomes remain unchanged and even poor Whites suffer.

A limitation of Dussel's philosophy is that societies seem fated to recreate a dualistic or binary system and uphold a dominator–marginalized paradigm. Liberation from the center shifts power to the periphery, and the two engage in continual struggle. It focuses primarily on *freedom from* oppressive structures without offering a collective, albeit challenging, movement toward a more holistic *freedom with*. The latter depends on individual and group transformation, which is much more difficult to enforce and measure. It also depends on creating robust systems of belonging that do not dehumanize. There seems to be a rapidly disintegrating sense of belonging, evidenced by an obsession with keeping the "foreign other" out.[510] Communities entrenched in a culture of whiteness that perpetuate fears of replacement feel devoid of intellectual, emotional, and spiritual openness. The people in them remain atomized with their self-interests pitted against collective interests, as it feels like all citizens are vying for one thing: attaining and maintaining power. Individual emancipation cannot rely upon disengaging from society, but the redemption of society from atomization.[511]

Liberation, as postulated by philosophers, prioritizes the needs of those who have been historically oppressed or marginalized and affirms global cultural diversity. It is

---

[510] Morrison, *Origin of Others*, 95.

[511] Birt, "Quest for Freedom as Community," 98.

unsustainable to recreate cycles of domination and separation. Integration is not necessarily the goal of a liberated society as it often implies assimilation. Instead, it seeks to evolve from diversity to inclusion. Liberation is a metaphilosophy that critiques all forms of dependency and inauthenticity and rejects us/them thinking.[512] It begs us to critique philosophy itself, what beliefs we absorb and adopt through culture, and whether they endorse maximal human freedom and becoming. It is a philosophy of resistance and nonduality that requires a multilayered approach through pedagogy, psychology, and spirituality. It is a framework that can help us critique a culture of whiteness and move toward more inclusive, comprehensive approaches to freedom that do not uphold harmful binaries.

In Plato's Symposium, the wise oracle Diotima spoke of love as the space "in-between" gods and humans. To pursue universal love, beyond that which one has for an offspring, is to discover union and immortality.[513] Love is a tamer of opposites, a site that can withstand tension, a container wide enough to hold justice, liberty, and happiness, deep enough to transform injustice into justice. Love is a space of nonduality, a place of learning and growth that can also be deeply unsettling. It is a space of generativity and connection that is metaphysical and physical. With

---

[512] Mendieta, "Philosophy of Liberation," par. 16.

[513] Plato, *Symposium*, 73.

love, "all men are bringing to the birth in their bodies and in their souls"[514] the greater mysteries of wisdom, temperance, and justice.[515]

The discovery of love is not a singular move from A to B, but a continual process without origin or destination. It is a way of being, thinking, and moving through the world that leads to greater freedom. It is a dance, intimate and responsive, able to hold tension and difficulty. Can we imagine ourselves as mediators and choreographers, so that we are neither designated "peripheral" nor "central" in society but a multitude of differentiated centers seeking a fundamental connection with transcendent others? The wise feminine Diotima knew love to be beyond individual sentiment, wholly committed to the beauty of all other things. It is not coincidental that she compares such knowing to birthing.[516] Dussel suggests that we will recover the loving and intimate aspects of liberation once the denigration of the feminine is no longer acceptable. Further, "the pulsion toward the mother is at the same time toward the ancestral."[517] Dussel and Diotima amplify my sense that liberation from racism at its core is feminine, maternal, intergenerational, and transpersonal.

In the margins we can grapple with and expand concepts of liberty for a pluralistic society and create places of profound change and belonging. In such

---

[514] Plato, 71.

[515] Plato, 74.

[516] Plato, *Symposium*, 77.

[517] Dussel, *Philosophy of Liberation*, 85–87.

spaces, the roles of oppressed and oppressor dissolve and a willingness to see ourselves and one another from both outside and inside perspectives grows. Though a philosophy of liberation was conceived for marginalized populations, the work of genuine liberation needs to happen in between the periphery and the centers of power. It is a chosen space where we deconstruct rigid boundaries set by race, class, and sex domination and reconstruct spaces of radical openness and possibility.[518] I am suggesting liberation from the isolated selves to become whole selves in proximity to different others. Embracing the other is an act of transpersonal love that is simultaneously intimate and universal. Like Dussel, I assert that liberation philosophy is simultaneously other focused and embraces our own otherness. It possesses an interiority and exteriority in that a liberator is responsible and faithful to someone else's concrete uniqueness because they also possess their own.[519]

Philosophy aims to transform our way of thinking, being, and living. It is a quest for wisdom that incorporates praxis and seeks the unification of mind and body, thought and action, head and heart. We cannot just think our way toward freedom but, as hooks says, "create a culture of conversion where there is a mass turning away from an ethic of domination."[520] Love is consonant with change and requires a willingness to move away from fixed positions and toward fluidity and acceptance.

---

[518] hooks, "Choosing the Margin," 18.

[519] Dussel, *Philosophy of Liberation*, 64.

[520] hooks, "Love as the Practice of Freedom," 243.

If we are bound by "center" or white supremacist thinking, White people cannot operate in accordance with love and existential freedom. Using Robert E. Birt's distinction between philosophies of situated and existential freedom,[521] I suggest reordering our thinking about freedom, shifting from individualist notions of liberty deeply rooted in a culture of whiteness toward communal freedom that practices commiseration.[522] "Our freedom," Birt writes, "hence our very *being*—is an active relation of self to others and the world."[523] Genuine freedom implies empathy. When a community has the capacity to love individuals into becoming who they are meant to be—because of differences, not despite them—members are more likely to experience existential freedom. Whites in the United States assume situated freedom in many spaces. We often insist on individual rights rather than communal rights, exposing our limitations in understanding existential freedom. If we prioritize the isolated self over communal belonging, we cannot experience existential freedom.

Birt's notion of freedom is cyclical, reciprocal, and expansive as it is both individual and communal, autonomous and mutually enhancing. It incorporates both positive and negative freedom: freedom from dehumanizing systems and freedom to become oneself in the context of community. "*Being* human is an activity of becoming,"[524] and *becoming* is an act of transcendence. Instead of a binary

---

[521] Birt, "Quest for Freedom as Community," 88.

[522] Dussel, *Philosophy of Liberation*, 64–65. See also the section above, "Love as the Practice of Freedom."

[523] Birt, 88.

[524] Birt, "Quest for Freedom as Community," 87.

center/periphery approach, I imagine multiple centers of mutually supportive communities that do not succumb to zero-sum thinking. However, multiple centers are the antithesis of freedom if they do not honor intersectionality. Insofar as whiteness is a center that values assimilation, grieves the perceived losses of personal freedom, and maintains misperceptions of replacement, it is not liberatory but a guardian of center thinking.

Degrees of freedom, first and foremost, constitute the being of the human, and our humanness is only ever in conviviality with other humans. We are all situated beings, and our social contracts erode when we concern ourselves more with individualism than with community. Existential freedom is thus nearly impossible to fully realize on an individual level without also embracing communal freedom. If someone else's domination necessitates our freedom, then we are not truly free. I assert that genuine community preserves and actualizes the creative expression and uniqueness of the individuals within it. A community that affirms individuality and interdependence can engage in psychological reflection, philosophical discourse, and social praxis. It asks questions like, "Who or what is left out here? Are there voices in the community we have not considered?"

Birt invites us to reimagine community, solidarity, and liberty. To do so requires transcending the limitations of how we have previously defined all three. He writes, "We have no blueprints awaiting us. And perhaps it is just as well. This is a time for inventions, for making discoveries,"[525] for recreating a democratic society

---

[525] Birt, "Quest for Freedom as Community," 99.

that values interdependence. For White people to embrace a philosophy of liberation to emancipate ourselves from a culture of whiteness, we must consider the following:

- Colonization and oppression are historical characteristics of whiteness. We are responsible for knowing and understanding how our systems, history, and a persistent culture of whiteness play a part in fostering and continuing injustice.
- We can work to dis-integrate ourselves from a culture of whiteness through raising consciousness, listening, and engaging.
- We will not obtain all the answers and do not have to direct the process. The goal is to remain humble and curious.
- Liberation is a continual, dynamic process. In a sense, we are always in-between and deepening into the actualization of freedom.
- We are the subjects and agents of our liberation. A philosophy of liberation is entangled with the project of imagining a utopia (defined as a differentiated unity) where all beings have the right to thrive.[526]
- A move beyond dualism and binary thinking.

Liberation extends beyond a relationship between things, beyond facts and ideas, beyond perpetual flight-or-fight energy, beyond transaction. We are not things. Deconstructing America's racial caste system requires our relationships with one another to move beyond Martin Buber's concept of "I–It" toward "I–Thou," which entails the realization of freedom with. We can only become an I through a You; I

---

[526] Mendieta, "Philosophy of Liberation," par. 16.

form in active relation to the community.[527] When I address You as *Thou*, I speak with my whole authentic being. I speak to the separate You and the You within Me. I am simultaneously surrendering the self and inhabiting shared presence, no longer seeing You as a means to an end but as a holy extension of self who is also wholly other than me. An I–Thou philosophy disrupts us/them, center/periphery thinking. It is characterized by mutuality, presence, transparency, and ineffability. It reaches a heightened form of fully inclusive and wholly relational empathy.[528] The end goal is not a perfect, uniform utopia but a vision of cooperative self-creation. The transcendent other is affirmed rather than denied, the community preserves each person's unique otherness, and individuality affirms plurality.[529]

Exemplified by Diotima's wisdom that love and therefore freedom is not specifically located but experienced in between, the feminine voice is echoed throughout philosophy. More than a millennium after Plato's *Symposium*, Lady Anne Conway was one voice that critiqued Cartesian dualism in favor of a philosophy of transpersonal love. In a direct response to Rene Descartes, she boldly declared that humans are truly alienated in a Cartesian universe and that dualism of any kind fails as a philosophy because it is incapable of explaining interrelatedness.[530] She draws upon nonviolent Quakerism and the Lurianic Kabbalah, predicated on a restored

---

[527] I am drawing from interpretations of Buber's *I and Thou*.

[528] Buber, *I and Thou*.

[529] Birt, "Quest for Freedom as Community," 92.

[530] Conway, *Principles*, xv–xvi.

universe based on mutuality. She had the courage in the late 1600s to advocate for ideals of tolerance, liberty, and equality despite opposition. Her ideas about human freedom did not distinguish between spiritual and physical realms, emphasizing the role of acquiring knowledge, developing sensitivity, and consciously choosing improvement.[531]

I amplify her voice here because we need a resurgence of such philosophical ideals, an adherence to the ensoulment of all things as capable of change and worthy of love, dignity, and liberty. Hers is a philosophy of love as a means of liberation while never wavering from the position that humans ultimately have the power to choose and "reconstitute the world."[532] She is ultimately hopeful about the ability to evolve into our highest selves, "for nothing is so dark that it cannot become bright. Indeed, darkness itself can become light."[533] Furthermore, she claims that while we are programmed to love similarity, "there is also a certain universal love in all creatures for each other" by virtue of being "like parts or members of the same body."[534] When one part of the body suffers, the whole body is compromised. Conway's philosophy supports a differentiated unity that is imperative to any movement toward genuine freedom. In adhering to liberatory philosophies based in transpersonal love, we facilitate self and societal transformation. As I see it, the goal

---

[531] Conway, xviii–xix.

[532] Rich, "Natural Resources," 67.

[533] Conway, *Principles*, 38.

[534] Conway, 47.

of philosophy is not to eradicate the darkness; only our fear of it so that we might relate to it as a source of infinite wisdom.

Prevailing notions of individual liberty are inadequate for imagining the kind of freedom I am proposing. We are not required to lose ourselves but to discover our true selves within community. Liberation philosophy can help deconstruct a culture of whiteness and shift policies and practices toward an empowered and empowering community. If allowed to inform psychologies and spiritualities, we can learn to think, dream, and act beyond "Me." We will not repair systems of white supremacy if we distance ourselves from the sacred other and deny interconnectedness. We can adapt our languages and practices so that they can explain, bear, and transform the weight of our fragmented reality. Again, I highlight my insistence on using "we," as uncomfortable and unspecified as it is, so that we can find ourselves somewhere in it and from that we-ness, clasp hands and hearts with others who long to reconstitute the world.

Love is strengthened or distorted by the ways we practice philosophy, psychology, and spirituality. There is wide overlap between the three in that their liberatory forms start from a place of we-ness, not me-ness. A focus on me separates whereas we unifies and honors difference. The praxis of liberation philosophy facilitates embodied transcendence, ultimate belonging, restorative justice, and psycho-spiritual transformation as it seeks to know the other and the self in community with others more deeply.[535] Love is the practice of freedom; liberation is also the practice of love.

---

[535] Dussel, *Philosophy of Liberation*, 104.

A Psychology of Liberation

Psychology has long been clear about the necessity for personal liberation, for people's need to gain clarity and insight about their existence. While a necessary aim, it has not been clear about the relationship between the liberation of a single person and the liberation of a whole people. Instead, it often pathologizes individual behaviors as if they are separate from one's sociopolitical history.[536] None of us forms in isolation, and circumstances impact our development. I have made the case that whiteness has had a collective psychological impact on the formation of United States. In an increasingly diverse and pluralistic society, however, multiple narratives are needed. Psychological unbelonging is an intentional divestment from the kind of primitive narcissism that assumes whiteness is a ubiquitous narrative.

Liberation psychology aligns with Martin Buber's I–Thou philosophy, which follows the natural order of autonomy and embeddedness. I–Thou is an encounter with the sacred other in which a new relational dimension manifests in-between the self and other.[537] Liberation psychology is the mental formation and praxis of liberation philosophy in that it is relational, rooted in an ethic of care, and deeply concerned with the overall project of human liberation. The qualities of care, relationality, and interconnectedness are aspects of the archetypal feminine. Through relationships, we become our authentic selves, the revelation of which is the aim of psychology. Though primarily inspired by the work of psychologist-philosopher-

---

[536] Martín-Baró, *Writings for a Liberation Psychology*.

[537] Buber, *I and Thou*.

theologian Ignacio Martín-Baró,[538] it also aligns with Fritz Künkel's psychology of "we."[539] It incorporates individual depth psychology that affirms one's embeddedness in the collective unconscious, and it is also a psychology of mutual empowerment that aims to understand and transform oppressive sociopolitical dynamics.

Liberatory psychology extends beyond the individual operating within a single-family system. It seeks to understand the individual in a broader setting of communities, nations, and time periods. Furthermore, it asks questions about the meaning of the human in the context of evolutionary time and the purpose of the individual within a specific time.

As with liberation philosophy, for genuine, lasting change to occur, liberatory psychology should not rely solely upon the historically marginalized to lead the way. It is imperative to recognize that all people in a society are traumatized by dominator systems that perpetuate racism.[540] As Dr. King reminds us, "we are caught in an inescapable network of mutuality, tied in a single garment of destiny. Whatever affects one directly affects all indirectly."[541] I remind us, here, of my earlier proposal that oppressors suffer from a myopic sense of self and reality. By King's logic, the oppressor who aligns with a culture of whiteness is also indirectly oppressed by it.

---

[538] Martín-Baró, *Writings for a Liberation Psychology*.

[539] Sanford, *Fritz Künkel*.

[540] This sentiment is echoed by Tochluk, *Living in the Tension* and Menakem, *My Grandmother's Hands*.

[541] King, "Letter from a Birmingham Jail," 65.

We must unsee whiteness as the ultimate social destination and metaphorically die, or unbelong, to the ways we have believed it to be superior or "normal." We must step outside of inherited scripts and seek to understand how hyper-individualism furthers fragmentation in the self and society. A culture of whiteness unambiguously centers on me. The psychology of we unambiguously centers on creative, restorative, empowering relationships with the understanding that selfhood emerges in the context of community. Künkel writes, "The Web is alive within the individual, and the individual within the We."[542] The radical aspect of Künkel's psychology provided Western models the revelatory notion that the self is a contextualized being. It is one thing to say that I am immersed within the collective unconscious, but it is quite another to say that I am in direct relation with You. I *or* we is reductive; I *and* we is nondual.

If depth psychology aims to explore and uncover what keeps us from inhabiting an intrinsic wholeness, it must extend beyond the individual and toward the relationship to one's community and history. Our pathologies and defenses do not form in isolation or separate from our lived realities. When one's identity is shaped within an oppressor–oppressed dynamic, efforts toward restoring selfhood must include strengthening the individual's relationship with the community and the community's capacity to imagine collective healing and action. Our liberation depends on abiding by relatedness, interdependence, and understanding the self within the matrix of the social structures in which we are embedded.[543] For White

---

[542] Sanford, *Fritz Künkel*, 70.

[543] Martín-Baró, *Writings for a Liberation Psychology*, 3.

Americans, this entails understanding ourselves in the context of our ancestry and how we are products of a sociopolitical culture that favors whiteness. Co-creating ways to repair harm and conceiving of new policies and systems that usher forth dynamic pluralism can contribute to collective healing.

Principles of Liberation Psychology

The inherent tension in applying liberation practices to White Americans is that we cannot co-opt or appropriate identity based on racial oppression. While we may experience trauma and exploitation, our race is not the reason for our sociopolitical suffering. The injury White people suffer is to our humanity, owing to the lack of love shown to historically oppressed people via our complicity or silence. A culture of whiteness creates and perpetuates the conditions from which we need liberating. I imagine a post-racist world that does not negate ethnic and cultural diversity but ceases to assign or deny privilege on this basis. A culture created by white supremacy keeps us from forming sustainable, emancipatory alliances across race and class. It also keeps us from unlearning shame and denial as discussed in Chapter 3. Following are the basic principles of liberation psychology that can help articulate the impacts of a culture of whiteness on our autonomous and embedded selves.

1. The role of psychology is to assist people in understanding their realities by reflecting on their social and historical experiences, both the positive and negative, the light and shadow aspects.

While individual work is crucial to co-creating effective social change, it is not an end. We are situated beings, located not just in a specific time, but in entire ancestral and cultural histories. These histories, including traumas experienced, inflicted, and observed, are passed down like an imprint or a breath from generation to generation. Each one of us has a personal and historical memory. The field of epigenetics continues to study the impact of inherited behaviors, histories, and environments on the expression of our genes. The Haudenosaunee Nation believes that definitions of community transcend time and space such that every action impacts seven generations backward and forward.[544]

Every age bridges the gap between the no longer and the not yet, between past and future. Viewed through this lens, I clearly see how my family ancestry informs my inherited assumptions, how it braids with my husband's history, and how together we reconcile them. My mother-in-law once said, "[The boys] are her great-great grandmother's wildest dream." Cecelia Charles never met my sons, but I am certain she dreamed them into being. What wild dreams are available as we seek to change systems that keep racial oppression and division in place?

Unequal and dehumanizing social conditions thwart individual development, whether we suffer from, maintain, or inflict them.[545] We cannot afford to assume whiteness or Americanness as the standard for freedom and humanity. Instead, we need to learn from the situated knowledge of the generationally marginalized while we conduct an inventory of our own to imagine undoing a culture of whiteness. The focus on me needs to be decentered and we redefined beyond those who share our race, ethnicity, or family history. We will not achieve psychological freedom if we disregard our relationship with and responsibility for the welfare of others. Each of

---

[544] Wall Kimmerer, *Braiding Sweetgrass*.

[545] Martín-Baró, *Writings for a Liberation Psychology*, 114.

us is embedded in a historically grounded social location. Seeking to understand it as a facet of identity is both liberation and reclamation of the situated self.

…

I wanted my history to be all rabble-rousers and disrupters, people who stood for freedom and justice. Mostly they put their heads down and got to work. Nothing is so simple, but complex and multilayered and, therefore, inevitably more beautiful and heartbreaking than I could have imagined. My family members have waved away so much with the excuse of "not knowing better." Don't we always have access to knowing better, some higher reality that is a deep hunger for wholeness? I need to believe we do, so that we can lean far beyond our present fears and toward unseeable ladders in the sky. My son once penned a letter to John Chandler that said, "You need to know that we are not 3/5ths of a human being. You need to know that I am human. You need to know that I am here." If only we could bend time and retroactively change the course of history.

Baró wrote that "all human knowledge is subject to limitations imposed by reality itself. In many respects that reality is opaque, and only by acting upon it, by transforming it, can a human being get information about it."[546] *Often, we choose to keep reality hidden so that we do not have to face the harsh or unkind truths about ourselves, our families, and our communities. This hiddenness protects us from feeling deep grief about the way things are and limits our understanding about how beautiful the world could be. The potential for rupture is enormous when we learn the truth after withholding it for so long. For some, it is safer to stay in denial, maintain myopia, and believe that the cave's dancing shadows are the only reality. Secrets so often conceal shame on the personal and collective plane.*

---

[546] Martín-Baró, 28.

When the James Webb Space Telescope published its first celestial images of ancient star systems, I experienced a strong temptation to minimize and say, "That can't be." Newness does that; it makes us feel simultaneously thrilled and terrified. Both the numinous beauty and the rich vastness of deep space feel mythic, but they have, in fact, always been. Perhaps it even longs to be known if the universe can experience such a thing as longing. The point here is that mystery awaits, and discovery requires imagining beyond what is currently known and trusting it can be made real. It is true for our relationships with one another just as it is for the physical universe.

I read about ancestors who enslaved people just as I read about others lauded for their community leadership and innovation. I am aware that my father ran up against some uncomfortable edges when researching my mother's genealogy. I am aware that I am related to inventors and innovators and heroes. Simultaneously, I am aware that my family's gradual wealth originated from stolen land, free labor, and inclusion in a culture of whiteness.

Alternatively, I read about Elizabeth Margaret Chandler, an abolitionist, writer, and activist who bought only free cotton, sugar, produce, thread, and other cased goods.[547] *I felt fascinated reading about William Edward Chandler, and it did not occur to me until later to wonder about his mother, the daughter of a former enslaved woman. She, too, is my ancestor, but again, a no-named dead end who was not counted on the basis that she was not married to William's father. I share this to illustrate that families and individuals contain multitudes. There is no single narrative, and we need ways of unearthing them so that we may begin to hold the complexities of our collective lives.*

The parallels between my family and society at large are stunning and, yet, disarmingly obvious. From hiding mass graves of Black prison laborers in Sugar Land, Texas, to uncovering the remains of 7,000 Native Americans at Harvard University that helped further bogus race

---

[547] *History of American Women*, "Elizabeth Margaret Chandler."

theories,[548] *this country has buried its shame in the same way that families come to believe that not speaking of a thing wills it away. I met a woman in Charleston, South Carolina, who learned that her inherited wealth came from the underground slave trade. She sought amends by creating official placards of all the sites—now boutique hotels, stores, and restaurants—where enslaved people were held, chained, and sold. If nothing else, she brings souls into awareness as tourists gorge on She Crab Soup and coo over the mastery of sweetgrass baskets. She integrates past with present for a more honest future. When brought to light and woven into our lives, stories help solidify our identities, increase our stamina for difficulty, and create possibilities for meaningful repair. They integrate unknown or unfaced aspects into our collective psyche.*

…

2. Psychology needs to develop a critical consciousness that moves toward an ethical praxis to which the issues of human liberation are central.[549]

In individual work, this principle begins with reorienting our attitude toward life, to consider not "what we [expect] from life, but rather what life expect[s] from us."[550] It entails being in right action with the world and working toward fulfilling one's tasks that point ever closer to meaningful participation. It is grounded in what is and what is not and can therefore orient toward what can be. Indeed, this principle presumes a shared priority of human liberation.

---

[548] See, for example, Binkovitz, "Sugar Land prison cemetery recalls era of forced labor" and Mitchell, "Harvard University is still holding on to the remains of 7,000 Native Americans."

[549] Martín-Baró, *Writings for a Liberation Psychology*, 6.

[550] Frankl, *Man's Search for Meaning*, 79.

When we operate from the critically conscious self who is ethically grounded, we can make choices consonant with those ethics. The aware self does not abdicate taking a stand in service of remaining unbiased and neutral, especially when bias results from an ethical choice.[551] For example, a liberation psychologist can seek to objectively understand the racist act or actor and still take a position of anti-racism. Liberation includes accountability and personal responsibility.

Baró challenges the field of psychology to veer away from scientific purity often aligned with institutional power. If psychology is to advance his challenge, it must come alongside the dominated rather than the dominator and facilitate a departure from predominant, patriarchal forms of research and analysis. It must also push the dominator to examine the limitations of power. The point is to use psychological tools to understand the world, find one's place in it, and then to change it. To do so entails tending to three urgent tasks: recovering historical memory, de-ideologizing everyday experience by empowering groups and individuals to articulate their realities and utilizing community strengths to disengage perpetual struggle.[552] For White-identified people, this process looks first like recovering and revealing even the most difficult truths about our histories. Secondly, we must recognize rather than idealize the limitations of a culture of whiteness.

Thirdly, psychology cannot ubiquitously bend to the rules of whiteness so often protected by the institution. It must liberate itself through transformative praxis. We must allow it to form more participatory, dialogic, and action-oriented

---

[551] Martín-Baró, *Writings for a Liberation Psychology*, 29.

[552] Martín-Baró, 31.

clinical research and analysis that is directed by participants and links individual change to societal change. A transformative, liberative process involves changing the self and changing relationships, including our relationships with institutions. The goal is to erode the invisible but felt borders that separate us from others and hidden aspects of the self. We need to be questioners, listeners, and providers of answers as well as receivers. Finally, we can discover the virtues of being White without assuming a mantle of superiority. Individualism is a virtue of a robust sense of self embedded in a larger whole that furthers the cause of liberation. In this sense, individualism is supplanted by individuality, and we approach a diversified unity.

When perceived or real threats to identity occur, the instinct is self-protection and preservation. The tendency is to pull inward, to retract. In such a state, others who are similarly constricted validate us, and we form anemic communities bonded by feelings of isolation, fear, and victimization. We see this in the rise of white nationalism and Trumpism, whose followers fall prey to replacement theories and zero-sum thinking. Psychology, then, must develop the tools and the stamina for pushing past self-protection toward a more inclusive ethic of group protection that defies exclusion.

It would be unwise to mandate participation in individual psychotherapy, but we can infuse liberatory practices in schools, community centers, and public institutions. My work is neither a curriculum nor a manual, but it invites consideration of the power of asking children to imagine and map their social and familial solar system, to conceive of themselves as embedded members of communities. Despite differences in family systems, a well-facilitated group would experience connection across difference. Similarly, consider the power of Thich

Nhat Hanh's prayer before eating: In this food, I see clearly the presence of the entire universe supporting my existence.[553] It gives just enough pause to consider every hand, element, and process that went into our nourishment. Even further, imagine what it could mean to have public, digital story-collecting booths in every county or public art practices that honor healing. These practices alone could do wonders to reinforce belonging, awareness, and interconnectedness. The praxis of liberation psychology happens in and among the world, not in protected institutions or private offices.

3. Liberation psychology bleeds into depth psychology and spirituality with the goal of individuation, or the ability to embrace the tension of opposites.

This principle recalls Diotima's principle of love as "in between."[554] Individuation is an ongoing process of coming into oneself and embracing one's innermost uniqueness. In that process, we become authentic members of a community. It is not necessarily begun consciously but thrust upon us by an instinct for wholeness.[555] This instinct for wholeness is individual, collective, and cosmic. It is the goal of depth psychology and the direction of the principle of unity in diversity. Wholeness is unattainable without struggle and wrestling with discomfort and change. Liberation psychology provides tools for adapting to change.

I place individuation between sections on psychology and spirituality because it is entangled with both. It recognizes the "Christ within," the Godself, or capacities

---

[553] Hanh and DeAtonis, *How to Eat*, 97.

[554] Plato, *Symposium*.

[555] Sanford, *Fritz Künkel*, 24.

for self-transcendence. It is a mystical concept. In the Jesus story, it is the moment Jesus receives a kiss from his betrayer, Judas, and calls him "Friend."[556] Judas symbolizes the shadow aspect, which Jesus integrates in a final act of mercy. He sees himself in the face of the betrayer and realizes that loyalty to a radically different, liberated future requires the betrayal of old ideas. Symbolically, individuation may oblige individuals to reject collective loyalties to the status quo but accept it as part of them.[557] Instead of denial, rage, or fear, Jesus extends Judas grace and draws the shadow aspect into the Self. It is a radical moment of poiesis, a seed of transformation.

"Friend. Why have you come?"[558]

Having referred to his betrayer—or the betrayed aspects of himself—as "friend," Jesus goes to his death.

It is a moment of wholeness, of death to the ego, and the release of the false self who rejects and divides. It is an encounter with genuine freedom. Death is inevitable where radical love is present. The Greek translation of resurrection is something akin to "standing back up into life."[559] We live an enlarged life when we stand up for virtues like justice, freedom, and love. My concept of conversion as

---

[556] Peterson, *The Message*, Matthew 26:50. See also Edinger, *Christian Archetype*, 82–83.

[557] Edinger, *Christian Archetype*, 83.

[558] Peterson, *The Message*, Matthew 26:50.

[559] Presented by my mentor and friend, Dr. Bill Kerley in a 2022 lecture titled "Shift Happens."

explicitly feminine is illustrated by the telling that Jesus's life, death, and resurrection are witnessed by an annunciation, visitation, and appearance to the feminine. Transforming a culture of whiteness awakens us to the feminine energy of birth, death, and rebirth.

Our Judas is a culture of whiteness, not the physical characteristic of being White. To "convert," we must realize that it is part of us while betraying its toxic hold on us. A culture of whiteness betrays our interconnected nature and seduces us into believing in the separate self, and zero-sum thinking while denying the other. Judas may confront us in the form of the single Black mother caring for many children, a migrant worker who tends to our space but whose name we don't bother to know, or even the poor White person so deploringly called "trash." These are the "strange others" whose personhood a culture of whiteness rejects and betrays because it cannot bear to imagine connectedness. Our disdain for them fuels superiority and furthers denial and disunion. They are the ones we must draw near and call friend.

Judas may reveal himself to us through our denial and defensiveness when confronted with brutal truths and buried narratives. Will we cling to the old stories, or will we face truths about racism, exclusion, and a culture of whiteness? If we choose to listen and speak truths, we journey toward the proper destiny of wholeness. Integrating the various Judases shapes us into becoming the best versions of our autonomous and embedded selves. When we do not cling to defenses and old ways of knowing but stand back up into life with expanded consciousness, we develop new awarenesses about how a culture of whiteness imprisons our true natures.

There has always been division, at times felt more acutely than others. Individuation seeks wholeness and freedom from division, allowing us to sit with the wounds differently. Freedom from hyper-individualism requires compassion for the part of us that once worshipped Mme as the ultimately center and ostracized the other as "it." As we deconstruct the seduction of whiteness as just human or just American, we gain humility for how our humanity is privileged and commiseration for those whose are not. Letting go of zero-sum thinking allows us to live in a place of abundance and generosity, to imagine equitable redistribution of wealth and resources. Finally, facing what we have denied in ourselves and our histories, not necessarily intentionally but to avoid confusing shame and pain, allows us to live with integrity. Compassion, humility, generosity, and honesty are all qualities of the kind of transpersonal love that can govern a genuinely liberated society.

It is disingenuous for me to lead anyone to believe that individuation does not come at significant risk to the comforts of belonging. It may feel like an internal war as something old dies and something new is born. If we can see it as symbolic of human potential, we might find comfort knowing that Jesus was unrecognized in his transformed, resurrected state and perceived as a stranger. He was not in perfect condition. His body bore evidence of his wounds, but he was also somehow lighter and brighter.

Sadly, Judas could not integrate his shame or grief and committed suicide. Individuation is difficult. Many choose silence or neutrality because the loss of familiarity produces anxiety. Making the ethical choice requires great ego strength, a strong sense of I rooted in a larger sense of we that transcends tribal or ego-motivated affiliations. Transpersonal belonging extends beyond a single generation, beyond a single community. When we belong wholly to love, we stand at the same time wholly in the world.[560]

Through the process of individuation, we discover the Self, our inner unity. As Fritz Künkel wrote, "This Self is our Center, our wholeness, our totality, our uniqueness. . . . [It] is the circumference of our personality, that which bounds everything and contains everything within it. . . . The Self is not only the center of our personality but exists between us and others."[561] There is an authentic Self in each of us which overflows with creative potential that is enlivened in community. The great paradox is that the revelation of the authentic Self is possible only because of self-transcendence.[562] Self-transcendence is fundamental to unbelonging from whiteness and discovering greater belonging.

From Me to (Mature) We

As we individuate from a culture of whiteness personally and collectively and become more wholly ourselves, the paradox is that we also become more wholly embedded in a culture of "We." There is a difference between a nascent, almost-instinctual We and a "Mature We." The former is a natural inclination for connection with caregivers. The family structure provides the first experience of We-ness and our first experience of I. A sense of I forms because of the positive and negative interactions with those around us. Ideally, the family structure respects, nurtures, and challenges all members to become their authentic selves. Still, even in the healthiest

---

[560] Bonhoeffer, *Ethics*, 185.

[561] Sanford, *Fritz Künkel*, 25.

[562] Frankl, *Man's Search for Meaning*, 107.

circumstances, there is a rupture of we in which I must come to know myself apart from it or else I can become enmeshed and codependent. Socially speaking, a culture of whiteness reinforces the White child well into their adulthood, social belonging is unchallenged, and an incomplete or primitive sense of we and a fragile sense of I results. There is no struggle, no process of individuation, no death to the egocentric me at the level of society. Künkel names this expectation to conform and defer to unchallenged standards of public opinion "We-sickness."[563]

White people suffer from We-sickness when we refuse to see structural racism and inequity operating, discount the experiences of our non-white brethren, or do nothing at all once we do see. Submission to a culture of whiteness does not foster individuation. Some lament a loss of "the good ol' days" and remain part of the powerful but "innocent" milieu. Such positivism remains blind to the most complex and vital aspects of human existence. As Baró points out, the "problem of positivism is rooted precisely in its essence; that is, in its blindness toward the negative."[564] It is how we convince ourselves that racism is a thing of the past, or on the flip side, continue believing, for example, that IQ tests are an objective, culturally universal measure of genuine intelligence that rationalize White superiority. Evidence is applied indiscriminately to suit biased views as positivism subverts facts and disables holding the good and bad of our social circumstances in tension, therefore denying reality.

---

[563] Adapted and paraphrased from Sanford, *Fritz Künkel*.

[564] Martín-Baró, *Writings for a Liberation Psychology*, 21.

The Maturing-We, on the contrary, is in Künkel's words, "characterized by the responsibility of every member for the whole group."[565] In contrast to primitive narcissism, it echoes the Blackfoot concept of community actualization and holistic womanist theologies. Successful individuation or actualization is measured by how well we integrate all aspects of experience to foster community well-being. The Maturing-We creates and upholds the space for individuation without endangering unity. It does not tolerate enmeshment where difference threatens to topple the expected order. It follows the principle of cooperation and dialectical ideal of unity in diversity. At the collective level, a Maturing-We does not rely upon personal friendships or relationships but a fundamental reverence for individual personhood. It seems obvious, but I am suggesting something quite radical, not unlike Martin Buber's *I and Thou* nor the gospel teaching to "Love your neighbor." Transpersonal love becomes the starting point for establishing policy, process, and diplomacy. It is radical because it is yet to be achieved.

It is essential to develop personal consciousness and awaken to one's participation in advancing a world consciousness that is foundational to the creation of Beloved Community. Balancing the tension of differentiation with integration is fundamental to the Maturing-We. The concept aligns with feminine, maternal values because it is rooted in transpersonal relationality and an ethic of care. It prioritizes a just process over a particular outcome. Perhaps achieving a balance between masculine and feminine principles can provide the necessary agency to operationalize an ethic of care.

---

[565] Sanford, *Fritz Künkel*, 98.

I align We-psychology with liberation because it is grounded in cooperation, not competition. It does not supersede other psychological pathways, nor does it pretend to be nearer to the truth than they.[566] It is not a complete system at all. Still, it calls attention to the often-neglected relationship between I and we and incorporates a sense of we into any praxis of liberation. A Mature-We psychology helps us to embrace a responsible love toward our intimate others and the broader community. It advocates for accountability over complicity. Here I invoke "quest and daring and growth"[567] and ask us to embrace a "love that is not the emotional attachment so often meant by the word, but rather a sincere, intelligent, courageous concern for the common welfare."[568] In some sense I am proposing that White people in the United States individuate from individualism, that we continue self-improvement and acceptance while embedding the improving self in a social context dedicated to justice and liberation.

I arrive at a pivotal point in my dissertation. Excavating aspects of the United States's racialized history alongside my ancestry illustrates the impact of racism on personal and collective economic, psychological, and spiritual outcomes and leads me to conclude the following: (1) We live in a culture of I and Me, not We and Thou. (2) A public understanding and practice of love is necessary if we are to imagine and create something different and altogether *more* than our current reality.

---

[566] Sanford, *Fritz Künkel*, 21.

[567] Baldwin, *Fire Next Time*, 44.

[568] Sanford, *Fritz Künkel*, 98.

Love is the ultimate destination of my ladder in the sky, and the only possibility for extending beyond it. It is a container for the "all of it" and the only sensible definition of the divine that I have. Love is where I intended to land, and I cannot disaggregate it from my understanding of liberation psychology or spirituality. Love is the ineffable energy that tames the opposites and keeps us pursuing what William James called "the more."[569] Only by inhabiting it with everything we've got can we cultivate at I–Thou relationships or the Maturing-We. Perhaps we have three fundamental choices in life: to face it with fear, indifference, or love. Choosing love does not erase the other two. It fortifies us with the courage to move through them, whereas fear and indifference feed on more of the same. Love is disruptive, subversive, and rebellious. Paradoxically it is also restorative, loyal, and conciliatory. I operationalize Love as public discourse and praxis in a later section. Still, it is crucial to recognize that it belongs here, in the space between—or perhaps more apt—as the thread that unites philosophies, psychologies, and spiritualities of liberation.

A Spirituality of Liberation

Concepts of liberatory spiritualities emerge from the field of liberation theology. My rationale for broadening the conversation beyond Christian theology and toward an interfaith dialogue is first because liberation theology is a phenomenon of global Catholicism that was almost entirely embedded in a Latin American context.[570] Secondly, liberation should not limit itself to a specific religion or deity. Aligning liberation strictly with Catholicism has all sorts of implications

---

[569] James, *Varieties of Religious Experience*, 346.

[570] Mendieta, "Philosophy of Liberation," par. 23.

around who is or is not included in religious paradigms. We cannot overlook the Catholic and Protestant church's roles in enabling and upholding a race-based slavery system, extreme wealth disparities between the church and its people, sexual abuse, and cultural annihilation because of inquisition and evangelism. Nor can we overlook the treatment or exclusion of women, LGBTQIA+ individuals, Native Americans, and countless others.

I am interested in thinking about liberation beyond a specific religious paradigm in solidarity with all beings precisely because religion aligned with imperialism and a culture of whiteness is a tool that perpetuates domination and the "light supremacism" of Euro-American religious ideals.[571] We must come to a complete understanding that the world in its entirety is the "church" and needs to disentangle from tools of oppression, both religious and secular. A liberatory spirituality is an integral, pluralistic spirituality inseparable from social and political action. Engagement with the world—with other bodies—is transcendent action in that our relationships with one another constitute our relationships with the Sacred.[572] My notion of divine immanence has everything to do with embodied relatedness.

While I aim to highlight the need for anti-racist dialogue in an interfaith context, I am admittedly rooted in an Abrahamic religious tradition. Thus, my experience, examples, and perspective emerge primarily from a Christian upbringing. However, I share the view that mystical expressions of the various faith traditions are

---

[571] C. Keller, *Face of the Deep*, xvii.

[572] Haight, "Theological Trends," 50.

the common and wise root of all religions that pursues union with reality. From an interfaith point of view, Howard Thurman declared that mysticism should be the basis for involvement in social transformation. His view was that the personal is social, that unity results from the insight that "love binds all things into a single whole. . . . To live and to love are to do one thing."[573] Further, mysticism entwined with social action is intended "to deepen one's sense of self, meaning, and relatedness to others."[574] Because I advocate for a psycho-spiritual transformation as fundamental to unbelonging from a culture of whiteness, I support that anti-racism is ultimately the work of ordinary mystics who seek to deepen relatedness with transcendent others. The ordinary mystic's social agenda, therefore, is to resist whatever separates—human from human, human from divine, and human from creation.[575] The psycho-spiritual transformation of the self, relationships, and ultimately societies is our covenant with the great mystery that governs existence and our path to liberation. I am mostly informed by the Christian tradition, but my perspective is influenced by mystics of many faiths.

The complex paradox of Christianity is in the ways it manifests as both an exclusionary and liberatory religion. There have always been discordant strains of Christianity, one that arose from under the thumb of the other. One is a religion of the colonizer and the other of resistance. Particularly the White, patriarchal, Christian church is consumed by individualism, consumerism, and competition for "right

---

[573] Thurman, *Mysticism and Social Action*, 31.

[574] Smith, foreword to *Mysticism and Social Action*, 8.

[575] Thurman, *Mysticism and Social Action*, 25.

doctrine." It has been complicit with land acquisition, enslavement, and segregation as part of the divine order. In direct contrast, James Cone suggests that the Black Prophetic Christian tradition speaks the truth, exposes lies, and bears witness to the public at great personal and communal risk; it is future-focused and refuses tolerance of present inequities; and it insists that God's identity is revealed in the struggle for freedom.[576]

Womanist theology goes further and challenges the patriarchy within the Black church. God was not just the liberator of the poor and the oppressed in general, but of the Black woman. Many Black Christian women testify that a liberatory God helped them make a way out of no way in response to pain and bondage.[577] It is difficult to make sense of a single religion with many competing agendas. How, as Willie James Jennings implores, might we get these discordant threads to *know* one another? Not in the familiar sense, but in a deeper order of knowing, sensing, and imagining.[578] Here again our knowledge of intimate, maternal, familial love may guide us in creating social systems undergirded by an ethic of care.

It behooves the White church to take the liberatory teachings of Jesus seriously, as indicators of how we ought to live with and love one another to foster the kingdom of heaven here on earth. Christianity possesses a "breathtakingly powerful way to imagine and enact the social, to imagine and enact connection and

---

[576] Cone, *Black Theology of Liberation*, 4, 15.

[577] D. S. Williams, *Sisters in the Wilderness*, 5.

[578] Jennings, *Christian Imagination*, 14.

belonging."[579] Any notion of God remains absent from the world insofar as we neglect the imperative to love one another as embodied beings. Our distorted racialized history exposes the limitations of our relational imagination. As Bonhoeffer suggests, the transcendence of God is not discovered by escaping this world, but precisely within and between humans.[580] Seen this way, transcendence is immanence, encountered in the activity of ordinary life.

Inspired by the South and Central American Jesuits, a legacy of Black, feminist, queer, Asian, Latinx and other liberation theologians added their voices to a religious conversation that challenged colonial, patriarchal, White religious norms. Liberation from oppression and practicing transpersonal love is the core of Jesus's teachings and the basis of the Beloved Community. Howard Thurman describes it as a vision of a "harmony that transcends all diversities and in which diversity finds its richness and significance."[581] Further, the devotion to the individual self is derivative of the ties that unite oneself to every other self, not the other way around. While individual congregations may strive for intentional connectedness and collective liberation, the White Church overall has missed the power of salvation within community because of its obsession with individual salvation.

Conceiving of a theology of liberation from whiteness needs freeing from myths of dualism and individualism. The White church needs to reckon with and repair the ways in which it has acted discordantly with the greatest commandment to

---

[579] Jennings, 15.

[580] Bonhoeffer, *Ethics*, 25.

[581] Thurman, *Search of Common Ground*, 6.

love the transcendent other. The mainline White Christian church seems to avoid plumbing its depths and reconciling with its ancestral and national aggressions that actively undermine love. Yet, as Keller suggests, "such preconditions have shaped, privileged, and deformed 'me'—like a contagious disease."[582] Liberatory theologies and spiritualities can heal the disease of whiteness and a distorted relational imagination that prohibits connection and belonging.[583]

Liberation theology informs liberation spiritualities with a preferential option for the poor and historically marginalized, an imperative that critical reflection emerges out of a committed praxis, a focus on changing society, and a widening of who is meant by "community."[584] Theology provides language around transcendence, mysticism, and meaning. I am not suggesting we remove God or theology from discussions of spirituality, just that we do not bind liberation to a specific religious denomination or conception of God. Liberation is ultimately seeded in transcendence in the world because it transgresses boundaries that divide and dominate. It requires more than socially or legally engineered structures and abides by a fundamental agreement that unity is possible only by embracing the diverse, sacred other.

William James defines religion as a person's total attitude toward life and morality as one's acceptance of the universe, which is to say reality, that is characterized by "the feelings, acts, and experiences of *individual* [persons] in their

---

[582] C. Keller, *Face of the Deep*, 80.

[583] Jennings, *Christian Imagination*, 16.

[584] Mendieta, "Philosophy of Liberation," par. 24.

solitude, so far as they apprehend themselves to stand in relation to whatever they may consider the divine.'[585] There are two concepts to consider here as I work toward a definition of an interfaith liberation spirituality.

First, we must challenge the insistence on individualism. Indeed, spiritual experiences are often individually experienced, whereas religious ritual is often in community. However, as James suggests, we must allow that spiritual experiences are always in relation to others—seen or unseen, like or unlike, living or nonliving—and how well we love them.[586] As with deconstructing a culture of whiteness, we must push past notions of the separate individual and allow our most private moments of contemplation or prayer to impact our ability to lead, listen, and love within a community. The most profound spiritual experiences inspire us to change in some way, thus they can be understood more through subsequent action than description. This amplifies what Shelly Tochluk means by encouraging White allies to contemplate social justice and action in a personal spiritual practice. A question she suggests pondering is, "How do I have to be in order for others to be free?"[587] In working for another's freedom, we simultaneously free ourselves. It transcends self-interest, and in this way, meditation becomes a political act.

Second, whatever images or concepts of the divine we have must be inclusive of, if not preferential to, real beings, real people, and real experiences rather than imagined. As with repudiation of the separate self, we must also reject a separate,

---

[585] James, *Varieties of Religious Experience*, 32.

[586] James, *Varieties of Religious Experience*, conclusion.

[587] Tochluk, *Living in the Tension*, 21.

unseen God who intervenes on behalf of some but not others. We must disavow a God who is anything other than whole-making, the sum of all our complex parts. We might even consider letting go of God as *a* being, especially the idolatrous image of a bearded White male entity in the sky, and consider it instead as *being and becoming*.

Liberation spiritualities tie our rituals, images, and myths to conscientious actions relevant to the time, space, and circumstance in which inequities exist. They embrace the interconnectedness of all things and honor a plurality of spiritualities. They relax the focus on me and fortify concepts of we and Thou without diluting the importance of a personal spiritual practice. Liberatory spiritualities transcend and include parochial notions of God and allow that we are co-evolving with the divine. As much as our ideas about God limit ideas about who belongs and who does not, we must challenge our limiting beliefs. Interfaith liberatory practices must break out of their enslavement to orthodoxy over orthopraxis, or a commitment to right action over right doctrine.[588] Thurman further challenges us to consider religious categories constructions of the mind that reflect cultural and social patterns of individuals within them, but that everyday mystics are not fundamentally concerned with such categories insofar as they are divisive.[589] Spiritual liberation, then, requires that we see beyond the limitations of our situated selves.

The wise religions I have learned from—primarily Judaism, Sufism, Buddhism, and Christianity—share a liberatory and mystical core. In a liberatory sense, they support the expression of the true self through a process of individuation

---

[588] Martín-Baró, *Writings for a Liberation Psychology*, 26.

[589] Thurman, *Mysticism and Social Action*, 25.

and freedom from worldly oppression. In a mystical sense, they uphold the inherent oneness of all things. Abiding in oneness serves the values of love, justice, mutuality, freedom, and truth without attachment to a specific doctrine. As we deepen our commitment to these values within our chosen tradition, the waters of all wise religions flow together. A nondual mystical path leads to spiritual metanoia and revelation of the deepest self, which is also in concert with the great mystery in which we live and move and have our being. There is no possibility for lasting justice and human solidarity without a change of heart and behavior.

Furthermore, it is impossible to authentically contribute to another's liberation without undergoing one's own process. If we are a person who experiences social and political freedom in the world, then our freedom is, as one Jesuit describes it, "in one way or another for the freedom and liberation of others."[590] Ultimately, when whiteness perpetuates dehumanization of the other, it also dehumanizes the self. Mystics have understood the reality of interconnectedness all along, and we can draw upon their wisdom to imagine a society in which I and Thou are sacred, in which *We* are healers and change agents. To echo the continuous thread of interconnection, I borrow from twentieth-century Hindu-Catholic nun Sara Grant, who borrows from the nineteenth-century ethereal poet Francis Thompson.

"All things by immortal power,

Near or far,

Hiddenly

To each other linkéd are,

---

[590] Haight, "Theological Trends," 51.

>That thou canst not stir a stone
>
>without troubling of a star."[591]

Our interconnectedness to all that is traces back to the beginning of time.

In the Christian tradition, a spirituality of liberation focuses on the historical Jesus, whose teaching about a transformed society that upends the status quo is central. His parables are grounded in the natural world and always entail transgressing social boundaries. A mystical reading of the teachings of Jesus reveals that he does not demand belief in him as much as participation in creating the kind of world he teaches us to imagine.[592] If we give ourselves over to what we are for, and if what we are for extends beyond essentialist claims of the small self, then we become co-creative agents of change and couriers of love.

Liberation is neither easy nor instantaneous, but rather a lifelong discipline that requires a willingness to encounter struggle and an openness to the unseen parts of the self. In a culture of domination established by racism and sexism, the feminine remains deeply hidden. As a teacher, Jesus valued the feminine. He addressed women directly in public with great respect and care. They are often recipients of his teachings and the fertile ground of transmission.[593] Jesus is part of a long line of

---

[591] Written by Thompson, "Mistress of Vision," 96–102.

[592] John Sanford's book, *Mystical Christianity: A Psychological Commentary on the Gospel of John*, is an excellent resource on this topic.

[593] Several biblical stories amplify this assertion. Examples include the following: the announcement and birth of Jesus came to and through a woman (Luke 1); transforming water into wine was done in front of a group of servant women (John 2); Jesus told a Samaritan woman at the well to go a spread wisdom (John 4); Mary Magdalene was one of the most important disciples, as evidenced by her presence at the crucifixion, burial, and resurrection.

liberators with whom we can choose to stand, regardless of our faith tradition. It is as Hindu-Catholic-mystic Sara Grant wrote: "It was not The Way because Jesus walked it. Jesus walked it because it was The Way."[594] In our own right, each of us is invited to walk in The Way.

Liberatory spiritualities rest on non-duality. The whole of existence is underpinned and permeated by a fundamental unity that is realized by making differences sacred.[595] The mystical path of radical love and genuine, relational freedom is not simply chosen but practiced and inhabited. In Bonhoeffer's view, mystical knowing "now means the establishment of the relationship to oneself; it means the recognition in all things of oneself and of oneself in all things."[596] Disunion with the self is disunion with the other and vice versa. Restoring union liberates both the oppressed and oppressor. Steeped in these roles, we remain in *against* energy, trapped by beliefs about the separate self. Practically speaking, then, how might a mystical, liberatory spirituality can help us implement practices to realize a post-racist society? I outline in this section the key ideas critical to developing a mature, liberatory spirituality.[597]

---

[594] Grant, *Toward an Alternative Theology*.

[595] Grant, 26.

[596] Bonhoeffer, *Ethics*, 26.

[597] These are principles taught by my mentor and spiritual teacher, Dr. Bill Kerley. They are informed by Jungian psychology, mystical teachings, and experience. I have expanded on what each one can mean in the context of individuation from a culture of whiteness.

Decolonizing Transcendence

In Chapter 3 I discuss how our misguided ideas about transcendence aimed at getting beyond embodied human existence led to increased shame and separation, thus undermining the kind of psycho-spiritual transformation I propose. I allude to the need to reframe transcendence as an aspect of immanence, or embodiment. Before introducing the steps toward spiritual liberation, it is important to decolonize our ideas about transcendence, which entails rejecting the idea of a wholly otherworldly, paternalistic God that enshrines whiteness as good. A decolonized vision of transcendence-through-immanence allows us to envision ethical relationships between human beings and between humans and other creatures.[598] If there is a divine force operating among us, then let us presume that it operates within each of us. If it is cosmic energy that formed us, then it, too, flows through each of us. Both are astounding considerations. Not even one of us is separate from this reality. In that sense, we are both the same and unique expressions of difference.

Engaging with the characteristics of spiritual liberation leads us to revise our perceptions about the "other." Catholic priest Romano Guardini once said, "I am not you; I am not other than you either."[599] This goes on and on, implicating the whole universe in being both distinct from and part of us. It is a mystical vision of nonduality. It recalls Meister Eckhart's thirteenth-century sermon in which he wrote, "The eye through which I see God is the same eye through which God sees me."[600]

---

[598] Rivera, *Touch of Transcendence*, 2.

[599] Guardini, *World and the Person*, 31.

[600] Eckhart, *Meister Eckhart's Sermons*, 25.

This is the invitation I extend, to consider the other as an aspect of self and wholly distinct from the self. It is an invitation to consider that difference is neither wrong nor bad, but necessary for a thriving planet, a just society, and transpersonal love.

Introducing her book *The Touch of Transcendence*, Mayra Rivera writes:

What would divine transcendence look like if we revised our conceptions of difference? What if we no longer assumed that difference entails separation? What if transcendence were not understood as that which radically distances God from creatures, but rather as a theological concept that makes difference significant, especially our differences from one another?[601]

She offers that transcendence is not beyond us, but within and between us, that each of us is wholly other in a way that also represents the face of something ineffable and unqualifiable yet fundamentally knowable through experience. Transcendence implies "beyond." Drawing on the root of trans as "across" or "change," let us consider transcendence a process of becoming, a lateral experience of connectedness in which we reach toward one another.

The direction of the cosmos is toward differentiation in communion.[602] Such a trajectory does not support hierarchy and dualism, but cooperation and interdependence. It rejects us–them paradigms and breaks down social, racial, and economic pyramids. A liberated spirituality primarily concerns itself with lived experience and only secondarily with metaphysical speculation. It assumes that our lived reality is both sacred and shared and worthy of social conditions that affirm it.

---

[601] Rivera, *Touch of Transcendence*, x.

[602] Swimme and Berry, *Universe Story*, 77.

From a spiritual perspective, each person is a unique representation of the cosmic imagination, an integral, sacred part of the whole. Suppose our spiritualities can develop a relational transcendence that affirms the complex difference and inter-relatedness between all beings. Suppose we experience transcendence because of our immanence, because of "God" as a force that operates within and between human lives. In that case we can no longer identify the "other" as wholly separate because love becomes knowable, perceivable, and graspable in the space between. In some sense, all of us are "transcendent others."[603] It is our shared otherness and our difference that creates and sustains unity.

I am asking that we embrace the possibility of "what if." What if we could love each other's difference so fully and so hard that we couldn't help but get beyond whiteness that insists on a sameness and exclusion? What if we lean into the following behaviors that aim to facilitate unbelonging to foster greater belonging?

Self-awareness

Self-awareness is critical to the type of spiritual liberation that fosters unbelonging from a culture of whiteness. While there are many guides and resources toward deepening self-awareness, the goal is to be in tension with self-acceptance and self-improvement.[604] With healthy ego formation, one is more likely to accept one's capacities and limitations. Consider a charge like, "All White people are racist." A person with enough self-acceptance can acknowledge the sting and hear it with

---

[603] Swimme and Berry, 4.

[604] Tochluk, *Living in the Tension*, chap. 2.

curiosity rather than defensiveness and manage a productive response.[605] Because our self-awareness and social awareness is formed in reciprocity with the communities with which we interact, they expand or constrict accordingly. It helps to accept that whiteness operates so deeply in the US social matrix that none of us are immune from it.

Part of cultivating self-awareness is asking how whiteness has shaped us specifically while still maintaining enough depersonalization to understand that none of us created the conditions that perpetuate it. However, because so many White people remain disconnected from collective racial wounds, attending to them in ourselves does not always resonate.[606] Self-acceptance balanced with improvement provides the necessary grace to be with current thresholds of consciousness while also acknowledging our limitations. A pitfall is that awareness of our shadows and the ways we have been conditioned in a culture that privileges whiteness can lead to shame and guilt. As discussed in Chapter 3, dwelling in shame leads to avoiding or denying the very issues that need our awareness to change society.[607] When we lack awareness around racial issues and our situated selves, or when we lack self-acceptance about where we are in the journey of anti-racism, we may attempt to gain validation from others, especially those who are non-white. Therefore, it is useful to establish awareness and remain open to feedback from trusted others about our habituated behaviors when uncomfortable or challenged.

---

[605] Tochluk, 54.

[606] Tochluk, 58.

[607] Tochluk, 68.

Committing to acceptance and improvement is a necessary tension that increases capacities for empathy and compassion for self and others. As a result, authenticity and vulnerability increase and reactivity decreases. We will take imperfect action, and we will not always get it right, but showing up with humility and a willingness to learn relaxes the field.

Curiosity

Curiosity is key to creativity, and creativity is central to the "human element." Because of curiosity, we continue to probe the mysteries at the heart of the universe. If we remain curious about one another, open to who we really are, and willing to see with our hearts, we might begin to soften our edges and deepen our listening. We hope to lessen the degree to which we act from our wounds and anxieties.

Curiosity is twofold for White people who want to imagine and enact an anti-racist society. First, we cannot assume that we know another's experience nor that we are the experts on how racism looks and feels. Curiosity is humble, an essential quality of wisdom, but it is not afraid to ask appropriate questions and discern whether the answers serve the values of love and liberation. The second aspect of curiosity is about our personal and familial histories and whether they have been complicit with white supremacy. I don't underestimate this difficulty because of what each generation withholds or denies. That said, curiosity is the ultimate opening for individuation and integration. It is necessary for nurturing the radical imagination. It is also our salvation, for "if you bring forth what is within you, what you bring forth will save you. If you do not bring forth what is within you, what you do not bring forth will destroy you."[608]

Curiosity allows softening to occur. Instead of insisting something like, "I don't have a racist bone in my body," curiosity invites us to consider that this is the water in which we swim, and in one way or another each of us has adapted to survive in it. A curious question might ask, "In what ways have I been complicit with white supremacy? How has it benefitted and limited me? What am I willing to let go of?" Curiosity is a long look in the face of the "transcendent other" as much as it is an inward gaze. In doing both, we increase our endurance for uncertainty.

Uncertainty

If a lack of creativity produces anxiety, then anxiety fosters the need for certainty. A need for certainty manifests as fundamentalism of all kinds. Certainty should not be confused with conviction about one's closely held values, like freedom, justice, truth, and love. Certainty triggers defensiveness and rigidity about one's beliefs and behaviors, causing inflexibility with process in complex situations. It is the opposite of faith and keeps one locked in the small self in service to the ego's gratification.

Uncertainty maintains an openness to process and mystery. When we engage with them seriously but not literally, myths help us make sense of universal questions and engage with uncertainty. In the same sense that concepts of the divine cannot be fully known or named, there is an aspect of mystery in each being that is ineffable and deserving of our wonder. Patriarchal interpretations of the sacred and the

---

[608] Bauman, *Gospel of Thomas*, 145.

human other connote separation, independence, and individualism. Mystery saturates the human project. We perpetually ask questions about our origins, purpose, and destiny. We address them privately and within our communities and cultures. Whether answerable or not, we ought not to disregard our responsibility to the mysterious, transcendent other in trying to ascertain answers.

When deconstructing a culture of whiteness, uncertainty furthers curiosity and flexibility. Comfort with uncertainty is necessary for unbelonging from a culture of whiteness because we do not yet know what a world without racial hierarchy looks like. We are creating it as we unlearn it. I have often sat in rooms where well-intended White people want to explain to non-white people why something is or is not racist. It is important to recognize such behavior as a need for certainty that protects from discomfort, vulnerability, and opening oneself up to "the radical mystery of the other."[609] An uncertain response might look like sacred silence or sound like, "Tell me more. I want to understand." Here there is vulnerability. Here there is the possibility of transgressing constructed boundaries. Here there is freedom, a removal of what Baldwin refers to as "the masks that we fear we cannot live without and know we cannot live within."[610]

Needs for certainty may also show up as control. I see this in philanthropy spaces where primarily White donors want to dictate who, where, and how they distribute their dollars. White donors often have access to generational wealth because of historically inequitable opportunities and resource allocation.

---

[609] Hollis, *Living an Examined Life*, 103.

[610] Baldwin, *Fire Next Time*, 44.

Furthermore, many families like my own obtained land and resource wealth first, by usurping Native American land and second, by participating in a slave economy. Wealth redistribution is a reparative act that can be difficult to govern, track, and manage. One democratic solution is for cities, counties, and organizations to establish community funds controlled and distributed by impacted community members. These could be funded by individuals or through a revised tax system. To imagine a more participatory and equitable economy, philanthropy needs to engage with the spiritual quality of uncertainty.

Marion Woodman states:

It takes a strong ego to hold the darkness, wait, hold the tension, waiting for we know not what. But if we can hold long enough, a tiny light is conceived in the dark unconscious, and if we can wait and hold, in its own time it will be born in its full radiance.[611]

Waiting in the dark, allowing uncertainty to birth new understandings, breeds spiritual liberation. As her title indicates, we—White people—must leave "the father's house" dominated by White male patriarchy. This is true for men and women alike.

Personal Responsibility

Defensiveness, reactivity, and an inability to take personal responsibility dominate when we operate in certainty. In this state, it is easy to believe that life happens to us rather than with us as co-creators and co-conspirators. To develop a mature spirituality, lingering beliefs about a separate divine entity that works for or

---

[611] Woodman, *Leaving My Father's House*, 115.

against us, to whom we can appeal to intervene in times of distress, must be challenged. We are in service to life when we take responsibility for it. Individuation, both spiritual and psychological, is a process of growing up, of being able to ask oneself, "What am I asking of another or God that I am not asking of myself?" We can shift our gaze from "out there" to within and enable a fundamental change in our center of gravity. Some part of us knows when we are avoiding, defending, or rationalizing to escape responsibility because the consequences begin to make themselves known through behaviors.[612] When we neglect personal responsibility, we pass it to the next generation, and neglected problems risk becoming family traits. Menakem argues that racism is embedded in White culture because the horrors of it were never openly addressed at the family, community, and political level.[613]

The belief in a personal God who is exclusively *for* us assuages anxieties about our smallness and connects us to ineffable mystery. Insofar as a personal God attends to the gratification of the ego or individual gain, our prayers and energies are misdirected. If a personal God stands on the side of the oppressed and marginalized, it nudges believers to plumb their depths in ways that lead to transformation and urges one to recognize the essential dignity and value of all persons, it is a God worthy of our pursuit. A God that favors a single nation over others, a single race or person over the whole, or even a particular religion is an exclusionary God. A God

---

[612] Hollis, *Living an Examined Life*, chap. 2.

[613] Menakem, *My Grandmother's Hands*. Menakem refers to racism in terms of inherited traumas, but it applies to any unresolved psychological or spiritual situation.

of love has many names and faces. We must examine inherited personal and cultural hermeneutics and how they inform our belief, non-belief, and needs for control.

Racism is embedded in American culture, and those who have inherited it through transmitted beliefs and behaviors bear responsibility for naming and undoing it. Personal accounting begins to shift the ethos of families and communities. Truth and reconciliation processes are inspired by curiosity and urge personal responsibility. However painful resurfacing wounds of the past can be, they remain unhealed until they are named. As of this writing, Pope Francis is embarking on a penance tour of Canada as part of the country's Truth and Reconciliation Commission to ask forgiveness of Indigenous Americans impacted by the physical, sexual, and psychological abuses inflicted by Catholic residential schools.[614] Admissions, apologies, and seeking forgiveness are not ends. Here personal responsibility meets curiosity and uncertainty. Once truths are shared, we can ask, "What can we imagine together? What can we build upon to ensure growth and change? What do you need from me?" It could be that for a very long time, we need to listen. Taking personal responsibility for our silences, complicity, actions, and ignorance is part of community action.

The path of personal responsibility should not drown us in shame. Quite the opposite: it liberates. It is a commitment to naming what is and grappling with it until it begins to make sense and calls us into a new way of being. Grace and tenderness belong on this path as much as strength and courage. Every one of us has a calling, a summons to show up and participate in life. Some of us are healers and

---

[614] Jacobs and Rascoe, "Pope Francis Visits Canada."

caregivers. Others are builders and creatives, and still, others are thinkers. Some are explorers who push the boundaries of what we believe to be possible, while others ask all the preparatory questions. For the "human element" to thrive, we must allow that everyone belongs, and each person has a part to play. We dip into the small self, protected and fearful, when we believe there is no room for failure or doubt. The integrated self does not discount fears and limiting beliefs but goes through them.[615] She knows that by going through, she will change and die to old fears and patterns so as not to repeat the fugitive past. The going through leads to transformation.

Change

As I see it, the more we rely on external entities or forces to tell us what to do and how to live, the more averse to change we become, and the less we can accept an evolutionary, constantly evolving reality. Wholeness is impossible without change. Jungian analyst James Hollis asserts that individuals are freer than ever to choose their life path, that presumably fixed identities like gender, sexuality, religious preferences, and even racial and ethnic expressions are more fluid. Even though the nature of our psyche is open to change, growth, curiosity, and creativity, there are primitive elements that retain a commitment to what is known and familiar, even when constrictive.[616] I interpret current backlash to progress toward greater equity as an emotional divide between those who are trapped by zero-sum thinking and those who are not. Tensions and conflicts arise from anxiety about change, the erosion of certainties, and subsequent challenge to essential identities. Predatory politics takes

---

[615] Hollis, *Living an Examined Life*, chap. 9.

[616] Hollis, chap. 3.

advantage of and further stokes these anxieties, creating a world ruled by fear rather than one ruled by hope.[617] Although it is ever-present in our all-encompassing reality, embracing change is difficult. It requires all the qualities of a liberated spirituality: curiosity, acceptance of uncertainty, and taking personal responsibility. The degree to which individuals and communities tolerate uncertainty and change and their openness to receiving the transcendent other defines the moral measure of a culture.[618] By that definition, our society overall is not doing well.

Attachment and loss, birth and death, love and fear are central to the human story. Whether we respond to situations by clinging or adapting, constricting, or expanding is related to our spiritual and psychological liberation. It is impossible to separate our personal responses to these dynamics from society. Our acceptance of change is almost entirely related to our ability to stay present to the self and the we that surrounds us. It is to move from rugged individualism to Beloved Community, to be what Martin Luther King, Jr., calls a "transformed nonconformist" who never yields to passive patience as an excuse to do nothing.[619] For White people, it is listing toward a willingness to be nonconformists in a culture of whiteness that excludes. In any manifestation of the Beloved Community, we are called to be loyal to something beyond the self as well as to a deep knowing within the self. Josiah Royce names it loyalty to loyalty that is beyond militarism. He invokes familial and romantic love, daring that one's neighbor and the stranger, too, is loved as "one of the lovers." Dr.

---

[617] MacKenzie, "The Predatory State by James Kennth Galbraith, 881.

[618] Hollis, chap. 3.

[619] King, *Strength to Love*, 27.

King calls it agapic love that both includes and extends beyond interpersonal relationships.[620] I refer to it as a deeper belonging beyond essentialism and tribalism that has specific maternal qualities and borrow from Thurman's concrete practice of love in an interfaith context. When we commit to unbelonging from whiteness and allowing that each person's essential personhood is fulfilled in the context of community, we participate in an abiding trust that the heartbeat of the cosmos is justice.[621]

Regardless of our religious affiliation or adherence to specific doctrine, we are called to devote ourselves to a unitive cause guided by the interests of the ideal community and respond to its changing needs from age to age.[622] Agapic love, loyalty, and deeper belonging are actively sought. Not only are we called to cultivate them, but to pursue change so that the Beloved Community continuously expands to achieve maximal inclusion. Through the experience of personal and transpersonal love, we gain the strength to stand against injustice and recognize that change is slow but remain passionately committed as though it is imminent.

A prosocial, restorative community of belonging is both a source of accountability and security in times of change. Moreover, a solid intergenerational presence provides perspective and wisdom when insecurity arises. Remaining open to change and aware of the present moment allows us to regularly sift through our histories and attitudes and discard what is no longer relevant to growth. Over time I

---

[620] Herstein, "Roycean Roots of the Beloved Community," 97–98.

[621] King, *Essential Martin Luther King, Jr.*, 27.

[622] Herstein, "Roycean Roots of the Beloved Community," 97.

have found that a regular spiritual practice deepens openness and awareness. According to Buddhist teachings, "We are what we think. All that we are arises with our thoughts. With our thoughts we make the world."[623]

It is evident that embracing change is relevant to liberation from a culture of whiteness. We need not look very far to notice how different social demographics and dynamics are today from 60 or 100 years ago. Less than a lifetime ago, I could not have married my husband. Less than ten years ago a woman could not legally marry another woman. The tension between active resistance and passionate acceptance of social change cause many to feel caught between polarities. There is no going back to "the way things were." Sixty years ago, Martin Luther King, Jr., lamented that "privileged groups seldom give up their privileges voluntarily."[624] Individuals might, but groups, he says, are seldom as moral as individuals. To do more than tolerate change, what would it look like for White people to actively participate in bringing it about without waiting for historically oppressed groups to demand it?

When we are willing, conscious participants in individuation and evolution, the true self emerges, and the true self embraces the emergence of the transcendent other. Emergence relies upon the various parts interacting with a broader whole while supporting the integrity of each piece. The emerging whole becomes something inclusive, different, and more wholly human than the sum of the parts. To me, the more human thing is to be in wild pursuit of transpersonal love.

---

[623] *The Dhammapada: The Sayings of the Buddha*, 3.

[624] King, "Letter from a Birmingham Jail," 68.

Institutional Responsibility and Change

An extension of personal responsibility and openness to change is how we choose to hold our religious and spiritual institutions accountable. In the wake of George Floyd's murder, many predominately White worship spaces hung Black Lives Matter flags or made a statement about a renewed commitment to diversity, equity, and inclusion on websites and social media. While the intent was good, changes were not very significant, mostly stopping with book groups, a training or two, or a fiery sermon. Public apologies are a start, but they are not enough to push the needle. Many White people and institutions seemed baffled about what to do next. In my personal experience as a co-teacher in a spiritual formation class, the more we talked about racism and spiritual reckoning, the more pushback we got, and some people ultimately asked us to stop addressing it altogether. Change is disruptive and often uncomfortable.

There is a desire among religious centrists and self-identified progressives to disassociate not just with the past but from those deemed "the bad White folk." In the process, they recuse themselves from responsibility, accountability, and acts of repair. The Methodist church, of which I am a part, has a contradictory history with enslavement. As support for abolition grew during the Second Great Awakening in the United States, many denominations were encouraged to take a stand.[625] Most denominations split into several branches for and against enslavement, sometimes

---

[625] Subsequent information is based on what I have learned over the years and supported by information from Lawrence, "Slavery and the Founders of Methodism," and The Faith Project, "Abolition and the Splintering of the Church."

along those same lines as the Confederate and Union states, while others split within the same state.

On the one hand, John Wesley, the father of Methodism, was adamantly against slavery and favored harsh judgment for those who enabled it. The first Book of Discipline in 1785 included legislation forbidding the buying, selling, or owning of persons unless bought to free them. Any person caught doing so was to be immediately expelled, and pastors were encouraged to act against the evil institution from the pulpit and public.[626] There were expectations and accountability measures in place should a Methodist violate Wesley's decree

On the other hand, the commitment to anti-slavery was short-lived and perhaps disingenuous. Rather than keep accountability measures in place, the Methodist church chose to split along North/South state lines when it became more common for appointed bishops to arrive at their posts with a cadre of enslaved persons as part of their belongings.[627] There was no longer a denomination-wide commitment to abolition. The self-appointed superiority of whiteness and the correlative rise of anti-blackness warranted a more substantial commitment than religious values that supposedly superseded racial division. James Baldwin accurately wrote, "I will flatly say that the bulk of this country's white population impresses me, and has so impressed me for a very long time, as being beyond any conceivable hope

---

[626] Lawrence, "Slavery and the Founders of Methodism," par. 8–12.

[627] Lawrence, par. 15–16 and Faith Project, par. 5–6.

of moral rehabilitation. They have been white, if I may so put it, too long."[628] He calls attention to the fact that whiteness equates with immunity or indifference to inequity and injustice, even in spaces that should actively work against it. Research, experience, and anecdotal evidence points to the fact that White Christianity is not only the creator of the racial caste system in the United States but also continues to promote and preserve it.[629] Here again, White Christians have much to learn from Jesus's message of radical inclusion as well as from liberation theologians, like Father Haight, who believe that "God acts in the world through human freedom."[630]

In his speech delivered July 5, 1852, marking the seventy-sixth year of freedom from British rule, Frederick Douglass called attention to the hypocrisies of the White Christian church, calling out its duplicitous complicity with the Fugitive Slave Act, even in supposedly free states. As worshippers bowed down in gratitude for their freedom from Imperial Rule, they were utterly silent in respect to the bondage of others. White men from the colonies went so far as to guard the coast of Africa to prohibit the international slave trade while breeding their own like domestic cattle.[631] In my view, if religion is to have any positive future significance in an increasingly pluralistic and spiritually open society, two things need to happen. First, it cannot preach freedom *from* this world, but rather *in* and *with* it. Bonhoeffer echoed

---

[628] Baldwin, *New York Times*, February 2, 1969, quoted in Jones, *White Too Long*, epitaph.

[629] This is one of the premises of Robert P. Jones' *White Too Long*.

[630] Haight, "Theological Trends," 49.

[631] Douglass, *What to the Slave Is the Fourth of July?*

this sentiment in his letters and writings before his execution by the Nazis in the closing days of World War II. He realized that the only option was to take on the mantle of *being love*. Religion needs to be something embodied and lived, not believed in or used as a source of power and coercion. It needs to be an experience of loving and being there for others.[632]

Second, pertinent to White Evangelical and mainline Christianity in the United States, religion must break with White racism. If affiliated with a predominately White church, one must recognize how it continues to uphold archaic rules about structure, legacy, patriarchy, and exclusion. Robert P. Jones asserts that the theological core of mainline White Christianity is "thoroughly structured by an interest in protecting white supremacy."[633] He also found that a person's racist attitudes correlated with their religious affiliation, specifically those who admit to racist thinking tended to also identify as Christian.[634] One wonders what is worth salvaging, as white nationalists have so crudely co-opted Jesus and the symbol of the cross. Is the reality of a thing defined by its intent or by what it becomes in the hands of culture? It resonates that Jesus needs liberation from Christianity, which too often aligns with nationalism.

---

[632] Bonhoeffer, *Ethics*, 90–101.

[633] Jones, *White Too Long*, 13.

[634] Jones, 181.

"I stop and stop again to hear the second music,"[635] which in the Christian narrative is liberatory and inclusive. I, too, must remember this quiet but steady drumbeat of love that coils through history and keeps her moving on and on.

Consider the radical grace extended to Dylann Roof, the twenty-one-year-old guilty of murdering nine people in a Black church in Charleston, South Carolina in a racially motivated act of terror. He was welcomed in, participated in a Bible study, and then opened fire. Many of the families and loved-ones of the victims, weary with heartache and violence, had no more room for hating, so they chose forgiveness.[636] The swell of grace offered to Roof is a tremendous act of "quest and daring and growth"[637] able to convert even the most powerful urge to hate. Such is the cathartic effect of transpersonal love. It does not have to approve of or even like a person to say, "You, too, deserve immeasurable grace."

There are those in the Black church who disagree with the mostly women-led offering of public forgiveness in the face of immeasurable pain. Some wanted distributive justice. We have so much to learn. Not only from a Brown-skinned Jewish Rabbi White Christians claim to follow, but from communities like Mother Emmanuel AME church in Charleston, whose radical act of love is one to memorialize as a national standard to emulate in all arenas. It is another point of tension that a culture of whiteness so often relies on absolution from historically

---

[635] Lighthart, "The Second Music," 3.

[636] Schiavenza, "Hatred and Forgiveness in Charleston."

[637] Baldwin, *Fire Next Time*, 44.

marginalized groups instead of doing the work of transformation and taking personal responsibility from within.

White churches have been so complicit with racism and white supremacy such that disaggregating the two will require a great force of will. Predominately White churches could consider forming information gathering committees dedicated to unearthing the history of specific buildings and denominations concerning racism and slavery. Such excavation should include examining hymns, readings, liturgy, and the church or denomination's role in working for, against, or remaining neutral to issues of injustice. A process of discovery initiates truth-telling and reparations to communities harmed. We simply cannot afford to deny church allegiances to a culture of whiteness.

"Father, forgive them; they know not what they do."[638]

While many would argue that institutionalized religion has done more harm than good, it serves the purpose of building community and engaging in rituals, both necessary to the praxis of liberation. The colonization of White Christianity can be reversed if churches deepen their relationship to mysticism, liberation, and reconciliation with their histories. By going through the dark, we access the light, we come to know our true nature, and we open ourselves to the oneness of being, to communion. Having turned from unconscious darkness to the day, we will be dazzled by the light.[639] Besides the internal work, we would be served by listening to those so often marginalized and following their examples of empowered community

---

[638] Peterson, *The Message*, Luke 23:34.

[639] Plato, *Allegory of the Cave*, 12.

and radical grace. The White church can reorient itself to the cross as a message of hope and liberation rather than a symbol of supremacy. The credibility of a radically inclusive Christian gospel is at stake if we do not take ownership of healing the wounds of racial violence.[640] Imagine, if you will, how a "Mature We" consciousness, philosophically, psychologically, and spiritually, can lead us toward greater love.

---

[640] Cone, *The Cross and the Lynching Tree*, 15.

PART III:

TRANSFORMATION

In depth psychology, transformation helps us to reimagine our relationship with a presenting problem. This section offers simple-yet-powerful practices and methods for becoming and being antiracist. It is a dialectic between the two. On the one hand, as long as we are alive, being human involves continuous becoming. On the other hand, "to be" draws us into greater consciousness and resulting action.[641] To be transformed requires that we take certain collective action in untangling the knots of whiteness. Inspired primarily by bell hooks and Martin Luther King, Jr., I outline actions inspired by love that must be undertaken in the public and political sphere to transform society. This section is, in many ways, a work of radical imagination that calls a future world into the present.

> They must be made to descend again among the prisoners in the den, and partake of their labours and honours, whether they are worth having or not. . . . Wherefore each of you, when his turn comes, must go down to the general underground abode, and get the habit of seeing in the dark. When you have acquired the habit, you will see ten thousand times better than the inhabitants of the den, and you will know what the several images are, and what they represent, because you have seen the beautiful and just and good in their truth.[642]

---

[641] Benner, *Human Being and Becoming*, 11.

[642] Plato, *Allegory of the Cave*, 18–19.

To love someone is a human experience bonding one in a human way to another being. It is seeing that person truly, and appreciating [them] for the ordinariness, failures, and magnificence of human personality. If we can ever cut through the fog of projections in which we live so much of our life . . . we can perceive an ordinary creature as magnificent.[643]

---

[643] Johnson, *She*, 38.

CHAPTER 6 | HUMAN BECOMING AND HUMAN BEING

Our struggle to become more human is unfolding within an evolutionary cosmos whose creativity pulls everything toward greater complexity and consciousness. Our physical beings already exist in this evolutionary stream, but our psycho-spiritual becoming demands intention that is far from automatic or inevitable.[644] The ways in which we participate in or resist our own development has consequences for the planet as a whole and our relationships with one another. Our job is not to become more than human, but to become the best possible version of ourselves. In this chapter, I offer practices that facilitate unbelonging to systems of domination and oppression.

My inquiry began with a child's question: What does it mean to be human? I aim to operationalize love as the creative core of human being and becoming. If human becoming means consciously participating in our evolution and reimagining our reality, then the being of love resides within. As awareness increases, so does the potential for reactivity. If we choose to participate in becoming more aware, we need tools to lessen reactivity. Recall that I have borrowed James Baldwin's definition of love as "quest and daring and growth"[645]; in this chapter, I outline practices to grow into a transpersonal, mutually liberating love that aids both the psycho-spiritual and social process of unbelonging from whiteness. It is a cyclical, ongoing process. In Benner's terms, "being human involves continuous becoming."[646] The hiddenness of

---

[644] Benner, *Human Being and Becoming*, 11.

[645] Baldwin, *Fire Next Time*, 44.

[646] Benner, *Human Being and Becoming*, 11.

our innermost being manifests through action, and love begins to take concrete form when acted upon.

Love in Action

Paradoxically, love is both indiscriminate and discerning. It is indiscriminate because when we embody love, we cease to see people as good or bad, racist or anti-racist. Instead, we see them as unaware or ignorant but no less deserving of love. The sun does not withhold its light; those who walk in love do not withhold the actions of love from the unaware.[647] Love is discerning because it encourages us to continually scan circumstances and determine what behaviors of love are required. Discernment is not an effort to control, but to submit to how love moves through us so that freedom arises. Love and freedom are synonymous and increase in relation to one another.[648]

It matters how we think about and develop language around structures, institutions, and each other. Language shapes experiences and spaces. It is one way of operationalizing and giving form to love. If we can imagine public love as a particular kind of kinship that intertwines the social, spiritual, and practical, then a love revolution depends, in part, on a language revolution.[649] Love needs to be part of our social and political rhetoric, nurturing a language devoid of dominance.[650] In

---

[647] de Mello, *The Way to Love*, 106–7.

[648] de Mello, 109.

[649] Van Horn, "Kinning."

[650] C. Keller, *Face of the Deep*, 203.

describing love earlier as both maternal and transpersonal, the language of love depends less on how we feel about one another interpersonally and more on how we respectfully recognize one another as co-participants in this magnificent, mysterious web of life. We need a more supple vocabulary about love that extends beyond the intimacy of interpersonal relationships to imagine a culture that values it in both theory and practice.

Love is known by our actions. Ultimately, I want our thoughts about love to inform what we begin to create a transformed society. If we can start to think about love as an action rather than a feeling, then using the word as a verb automatically assumes investment, accountability, and responsibility.[651] It brings mind and body into union. Further, if we are to understand how to love the self, we must also confront how we have experienced lovelessness in own lives. Examination is the first act of "being" love.

Love cannot coexist with abuse or neglect, but it heals both. Once we individually recognize how we understand and experience love and not love, we can better extend the self to nurture another's growth and eek our way toward love of the transcendent other.[652] Learning to love self and others exemplifies our inseparability as both intensify in tandem. Words, definitions, explanations, and symbols create maps; however, we cannot mistake the map for the terrain. It is a tool

---

[651] hooks, *All About Love*, 36.

[652] hooks, *All About Love*, 10.

that readies the mind for "quest and daring and growth."[653] The real work, the vulnerability of this entire exercise, is our willingness to walk the path.

Love requires sacrifice and struggle, a kind of death, lament, care, honesty, justice, mutuality, and a commitment to repair. The behaviors of love are transpersonal and interpersonal. Adopting the language and practicing behaviors of love opens us in two directions. Gazing inward, we may humbly recognize when we are "not love." Strengthening an intrapersonal hermeneutic, or inner observation, helps us better discern when we are out of alignment. Turning outward, we engage in communion with the world around us.[654] Love is considered a "soft skill," and it is rarely taken seriously in the sociopolitical sphere. Thus, to love in a radical, public way is subversive and nonconformist. Nonconformity by itself has no redemptive power. It often manifests as little more than performance and exhibitionism.[655] Consider the vast numbers of businesses that issued statements after George Floyd's murder or joined marches during the height of the subsequent Black Lives Matter protests. Though responsive to the moment, most efforts fell flat as sustained allyship, meaningful reflection, and continued financial support bolstered by steps toward change did not occur.[656]

---

[653] Baldwin, *Fire Next Time*, 44.

[654] hooks, *All About Love*, 13.

[655] King, *Strength to Love*, 26.

[656] See, for example, Williams, "A Year After George Floyd's Killing;" Horowitz, Hurst, and Braga, "Support for the Black Lives Matter Movement Has Dropped;" and Jan, McGregor, and Tiku, "As Big Corporations Say 'Black Lives Matter,' Their Track Records Raise Skepticism."

The consensus is that White people enter liberation movements with the idea of helping "them," the separate other, in hopes of being seen as a "good White person." This type of virtue-signaling maintains the primitive narcissism I speak of in Chapter 3. When we show up as helpers rather than co-participants with our own needs for liberation and transformation, the depth and breadth of our involvement remains shallow. Often White people "help" as an act of charity or allyship without understanding that we, too, need help. In the wake of the murders of George Floyd, Ahmaud Arbery, and Breonna Taylor, my mother wrote me a letter expressing that she had warned me that marrying a Black man would make my life harder. She wrote, "I am so sorry you have to deal with this." Her line of thinking—that White people should remain untouched by racism—is not uncommon, but what I have come to understand is that it is precisely ours "to deal with." Racism makes all our lives harder.

We need to adjust our minds (by seeing racism as a societal problem involving all of us, not a "them" problem), our bodies (by turning toward one another's suffering), and our souls (by allowing ourselves to be converted by love). We need to realize that the dysfunction caused by racism is everyone's problem. As I write through the behaviors of transformative love, I have my mother in mind, but she could be anyone's mother. She could be any one of us, seduced by the belief that racism has nothing to do with whiteness and that we are powerless to change it. On the contrary, a culture of whiteness depends on racism. Dismantling one undoes the other. Though not exhaustive, the behaviors outlined offer opportunities to attend to the social-emotional profundity of the "human element."

Sacrifice and Struggle

To this point, I have defined love with Baldwin's words as "quest and daring and growth."[657] The colonization of this continent and the subsequent dehumanization of the non-white other is full of a different quest and daring and growth defined by land- and asset-acquisition. The story of my first paternal ancestor who arrived in Jamestown, orphaned and alone, amplifies that narrative. I cannot argue that he was without an internal sense of quest or daring or growth. However, in terms of a grander, societal transpersonal love where liberation from oppression of any kind is central, his vision remained limited. He was formed, as most of us are, by the social and cultural milieu in which he came of age, but there is no evidence of a radical departure from the spreading tendrils of white supremacy. "White as normal" became so ubiquitous in our society that I inherited the unconscious learnings four centuries later. Throughout this dissertation I have attempted to define "quest and daring and growth" not in terms of the unjust acquisition of material and political power but as a psycho-spiritual process of growth, repair, and transformation.

I've described love as the practice of freedom—philosophically, psychologically, and spiritually. Each of these have personal and communal implications. I mentioned an asterisked ancestor, Elizabeth Margaret Chandler, a Quaker-abolitionist-poet, who worked on behalf of the Underground Railroad in Michigan and called for the immediate and total integration of Blacks and Native

---

[657] Baldwin, *Fire Next Time*, 44.

Americans into society.[658] The conscientious consumer choices she made entailed a great deal of sacrifice, as so many of the country's goods were entangled with enslaved labor. She never married, bore no children, and died tragically young. But she lived for ideals beyond the self, embodying the ethics of the Beloved Community. Documentation of her contributions and her lineage are relatively scant, but some of her poems remain. She practiced love as freedom, and her story was not heralded throughout my family line. Her relation to the Chandler family is a question mark because of her marital status and childlessness. And yet, hers is a lineage I am not only trying to reclaim but emulate.

In reply to the men and naysayers who contended that women lacked the power to abolish slavery; Elizabeth countered that, as maternal figures, women were in a unique position "to give the first bent to the minds of those, who at some future day are to be their country's counselors."[659] Elizabeth practiced radical imagination. She lived as if freedom were not only possible but imperative. She cast a ladder in the sky for me to live as I do today.

I arrive at another critical aspect of love as sacrifice. There will be loss of previously unquestioned positions of privilege and further erosion of certainties. We will experience discomfort, insecurity, and challenges to belonging. But there is also a tremendous opportunity, a cooperative journey into something unknown that

---

[658] Information about Elizabeth on the Chandler Family Association website is a single name that, when clicked, takes you to another website. All information about her retrieved from *History of American Women*, "Elizabeth Margaret Chandler."

[659] *History of American Women*, "Elizabeth Margaret Chandler," par. 6.

embraces "quest and daring and growth."[660] If White people want to participate in co-creating a radically different society, we must be willing to sacrifice some of the less-concrete aspects of white supremacy that keep us in a privileged position. Sacrifice is an aspect of unlearning and unbelonging, and it is critical to activating love as a political and social force.

Love is the decisive word that marks the distinction between humans in disunion and humans seeking union. What some point to as evidence of love, such as conviction, devotion, sacrifice, service, and action, also arise without love. There is often a residue of selfishness, a need for recognition in human behavior even though we reference God in our righteous doings and equate them with sacrificial love.[661] Such efforts to appease God are often driven by the ego. Belief in God is not necessary to understand love, but love is essential if we are interested in reorienting understandings of God. Love acts in accordance with cosmogenesis as it seeks wholeness. It is the counterbalance to chaotic violence and the very basis of connection and creativity. Reconciliation is the purpose and direction of liberatory spiritualities, the practice of which may coincidentally restore our relation to a God of love. After all, we are commanded to "Love one another. In the same way I loved you, you love one another. This is how everyone will recognize that you are my disciples—when they see the love you have for each other."[662] We will become like

---

[660] Baldwin, *Fire Next Time*, 44.

[661] Bonhoeffer, *Ethics*, 48.

[662] Peterson, *The Message*, John 13:34–35.

gods when we learn to love. Such a transformation extends beyond a particular religious domain and racial category.

Religious language is helpful to understand love as sacrifice and sacrifice as giving something up for the sake of a larger whole. Sacrifice is a kind of death. White people sacrifice social belonging when we challenge injustice. It may occur as an emotional loss if family or loved ones respond to difficult conversations with fear; financial loss if we seriously consider our obligation to participate in reparations; or positional loss if we share or give up power to include those previously excluded. Loss makes space for rebirth. We will inevitably have to sacrifice formerly held limiting beliefs and behaviors for enlarged belonging.

Sacrifice means extending love beyond the myopic, often-warped needs of the integrated self. It is the ultimate occasion for "unselfing," what Iris Murdoch refers to as piercing the veil of self-centered consciousness and joining the world as it is.[663] Here we are called to sacrifice romantic notions of a post-racial society and nostalgia about an imaginary past to consider that the most powerful kind of love enables us to exist in a state of immanent transcendence. Love contains us, moves between us, and flows from us. We cannot experience it without yielding to bodies.

Consider the image of Jacob wrestling the enigmatic angel from the Hebrew Scriptures. One of the radical elements of the story is his willingness to struggle, to wrestle with the shadows of fear, doubt, anger, loss, and denial. Jacob is like us, grappling with the most profound queries of being human. Am I good enough? Am I forgivable? Am I lovable? *Can I change?* Jacob struggles through the proverbial dark

---

[663] Murdoch, *Sovereignty of Good*, 131.

night and emerges transformed. We are privy, here, to the wisdom of a religious myth that paints a universal truth: to love is to struggle with the things that matter most. Struggle is the language of transformation, the path to metanoia. Baldwin placed this truth in a cultural context for us. He challenges us:

> To trust and to celebrate what is constant—birth, struggle, and death... and so is love... to apprehend the nature of change, to be able and willing to change... not on the surface, but in the depths—change in the sense of renewal. But renewal becomes impossible if one supposes things to be constant that are not—safety, for example, or money, or power. One clings to chimeras, by which one can only be betrayed, and the entire hope—the entire possibility—of freedom disappears."[664]

Consciousness is a human virtue, and the pursuit of freedom is a hallmark of it. We cannot talk about freedom without talking about love, lest we confuse freedom with domination. Here the entire project coalesces for me. If we are to get free from a culture of whiteness, ideas about a love beyond self-interest and a willingness to struggle for it will pave the way. Love is struggle, not against but with the very idea that anything at all is fixed and certain. Jacob never lets go of the angel. He struggles through the night. He sacrifices his certainty. At daybreak, he receives a new name—Israel: "He who wrestles God"—and discovers something quintessentially human about himself as he limps toward self-transcendence without ever leaving the earthly plane.[665] Sacrificing his selfhood makes him whole, which is

---

[664] Baldwin, *Fire Next Time*, 65.

[665] Peterson, *The Message*, Genesis 32.

not to say perfect. He is willing to confront and be confronted with hard truths. His struggle and subsequent transformation are the destiny of an entire people.

The most common critique of White people who enter the struggle for racial equity and justice is that we easily tire and walk away. We let go. We treat it with the luxury of choice and disengage when challenged. It should not be a choice, but like Jacob with the angel, the destiny of a people. We must learn to take some modicum of responsibility for our people, our ancestors, our choices, the society we've built and benefitted from, and work to give it a new name. Moving through darkness into light, integrating the two, as with Plato's *Allegory*, Jacob and the angel, and every great quest, is the story of love. It transcends space and time. It is also immanent, inherently indwelling. As such, the everlasting impact of humans directly relates to how well or poorly we love. In the words of the great mystic-poet Hafiz:

"Time will slay your body no matter what, but

with love the impetus of your final movements

will make eloquent your demise."[666]

If we are willing to sacrifice and struggle through the process of change rather than resist the idea of it, we will ready ourselves for the kind of death necessary to undergo transformation. If a culture of whiteness can lay down its needs for domination, then power becomes less forceful, reckless, and abusive. It begins to correct everything that stands against love.[667] When love enters the public sphere

---

[666] Hafiz, "A Day Too Great a Force," 80.

[667] King, *Where Do We Go from Here?*, 41.

and the halls of power, the possibilities for reimagining who we are, who or what God is, and what freedom can be, become limitless.

Death

Death is a metaphor for unbelonging from whiteness. Becoming antiracist, as opposed to doing or performing anti-racism, requires dying fully to an old self entangled with a culture of whiteness. It is a psycho-spiritual death in that it requires unbelonging. I assert that whiteness is incongruous with wholeness because of its tendency to exclude and compete rather than include and integrate. Whiteness is intent on making difference negative rather than embracing Mayra Rivera's concept of difference as transcendent.[668] In dying to whiteness, a new self emerges, a more human self that understands our entangled liberation.

A psycho-spiritual death is the beginning of individuation, a step forward in the evolution of consciousness toward embodied transcendence.[669] Depth psychology and spirituality intertwine with love by calling us forth into a higher self. By acquainting ourselves with our own nature and wrestling with the defenses of the ego, we transform the self and the world. In the process of "dying" we grow up, an essential tenant of love.[670] Jung envisioned the process of dying or individuation as

---

[668] Rivera, *Touch of Transcendence*.

[669] Carl Jung expressed this idea in a previously unpublished letter toward the end of his life. Parts of it retrieved from Beach, "God as Trauma."

[670] Reference to James Baldwin, *Nobody Knows My Name*, 72; see fn. 167 in Chapter 2.

the human recognition of the divine within.[671] While I am not concerned with how we relate to or what we name the divine, I am asserting that death to the small self (in this case, the self-created by a culture of whiteness) requires some recognition of a reality much deeper and broader than our singular experience. In dying we accept personal responsibility for our ethical decisions and ways of being in the world that either turn toward or away from love.

The social death that may accompany divesting from whiteness is the crux of unbelonging. There are people, some with a lot of power and influence in our lives, who are not ready for or actively resist anti-racism. It hurts to be rejected, questioned, or minimized by people with whom we have shared histories. The tension to bear is accountability to maintaining inclusive values while not succumbing to attacking or judging those we perceive as racially unaware. "We unbind from limitation through seeing, through direct realization at the level of our own hearts."[672] Once recognized, the new insights gained by learning to *see* at the level of the hearts, are virtually impossible to turn away from. Silencing new understandings is a form of complicity and harm done to the higher self. I don't have a way to soften the blow of unbelonging to familiarity and comfort except by going through it. It is extraordinarily hard to leave the field of the known and venture into the unknown. However, greater belonging is not only possible, but it also already

---

[671] The Jungian concept of individuation as a kind of death is echoed in Edward Edinger's works, *Ego and Archetype* and *The Christian Archetype: A Jungian Commentary on the Life of Christ*. Of course, Jung himself wrote and taught about it throughout his career. See Jung, *Psychology and Alchemy*.

[672] Singh and Rodney Smith, *Unbinding*, 13.

exists. These are the margins that bell hooks points to, the place where death is transformed into new life and shared liberation.

Lament

> "Before you know kindness as the deepest thing inside,
>
> you must know sorrow as the other deepest thing.
>
> You must wake up with sorrow.
>
> You must speak to it till your voice
>
> catches the thread of all sorrows."[673]

Unbelonging from whiteness will stir up grief, an emotion that Francis Weller considers a "threshold emotion." Further, if we compress grief, we compress joy. In Western civilization, denial of grief triggers amnesia (forgetting or denial) and anesthesia (numbness).[674] Talking about racism unravels us because it strikes the heart of human vulnerability, evoking a fear that we are flawed and "other" than who we thought we were. Shame is among the lowest emotions. Though it is necessary to acknowledge the presence of shame, wallowing in it is useless to liberation from a culture of whiteness and White racism. The moment we accept that a racist system is not as much about personal wrongdoing as it is about the legacy we inherit, is the moment we begin to become free. Then we might experience anger. Deeper than anger, however, is sorrow. Grief. Lament. These are "shadow" emotions, but unlike

---

[673] Nye, "Kindness," 42.

[674] Weller, *Wild Edge of Sorrow*, 22.

the stuck-ness of shame, they break us open to our depths and transmute into fertile ground.[675]

Dussel remarks that the "feast of the dominators" is anguish masked by fictitious triumph that distracts itself by fetishizing the other.[676] Distraction causes shame because we feign happiness while denying anguish about the unrecovered aspects of the self. Shame disrupts and destroys while grief restores a connection to life. The depth of our laments correlates with the strength of our love and the essence of our vitality. Grief often arouses unbearable pain. It is a type of self-emptying, or *kenosis*, that is a necessary threshold for entering into transformative, loving action. Paradoxically, emptiness is a key to unlocking freedom and creativity.[677] Grief potentially fills us with tender empathy for ourselves, others, and the world. Emptiness allows for a genuine encounter with the Self.

Grief work is soul work, a gateway for experiencing extraordinary lightness and ease on the path of love. Grief might require the most daring because if faced, we see the world as it is without turning away.[678] The root of disunion with others is a disconnection from the ground of our being resulting from modern industrial consciousness. Our complete "othering" of the planet, seeing her as our right rather than our responsibility, limits an ability to encounter the beautiful, transcendent

---

[675] Weller, 8.

[676] Dussel, *Philosophy of Liberation*, 105.

[677] Weller, *Wild Edge of Sorrow*, 62.

[678] Weller, 7.

other. We limit access to strange and beautiful otherness by cutting off our instinctual needs for connectedness, mistaking our isolation for a failure of personality.[679]

In Weller's work with the five gates of grief, the one most relevant to a culture of whiteness is ancestral grief. We carry their sorrows and transgressions in our bodies; it lingers in silence, often unacknowledged and untransformed.[680] To be enslaved is an atrocious ancestral wound that needs its own tending, but to be the enslaver or complicit with it is to cut off one's humanity. That humanity is what we must recover in grief work, otherwise it is retained as heaviness and shame. Left untouched, it becomes our destiny, a hum of sorrow in the background of our lives.[681]

I discern that disconnection from the source, one another, and the dramas and traumas of our ancestors disables authentic lamentation. I wonder if we manufacture happiness in part because of a deep longing created by sorrow. I perceive that something essential in us is starving, and soul starvation drives behaviors like mass shootings and acts of violence against the self and others. We become strangers to each other when our shared otherness is precisely what ought to connect. Like Weller, I propose that if we touch the grief of separation, we immediately realize that we are not alone. Weller writes that "a grief-laden

---

[679] Weller, 75.

[680] Weller, 88.

[681] Weller, 94.

emptiness" emerges in our soul when we banish others from our imaginations.[682] On the contrary the experience of shared grief creates community and reconnects the discarded, fragmented, and "othered" parts of the self. In the companionship of shared ritual, an essential activity of lamentation occurs: remembering. Grief prompts memory, and collective efforts to remember help "keep the past from slipping away in a present that continues to deny it."[683]

How communities respond to memory should be unique, whether a mural, garden, ritual, shrine, or something else entirely.[684] I point again to the spontaneous, months-long ritual in Richmond, Virginia, around a Confederate monument. Like so many murals, vigils, and performances, it began as an act of collective grief honoring Black Lives in the wake of George Floyd's murder. When the portal is open, grief, ritual, and creativity weave together the personal and communal so that we may connect with the larger, often unseen world..[685]

I am inviting White people to lament the things unknown, the histories untold, including our own moral wounds around inherited beliefs. We need to recognize and lament how our intentional and unintentional ignorance causes harm that furthers disunion. We must mourn that many of our ancestors, however much they provided for us, also robbed others of provision and opportunity. Periods of

---

[682] Weller, 75.

[683] Watkins and Shulman, *Toward Psychologies of Liberation*, 122–23.

[684] Watkins and Shulman, Part IV, especially chapter 12, offers many examples of creative responses to grief within communities.

[685] Weller, 102.

lament are opportunities to show grace and gentleness to ourselves and others, to hold space for transformation. Poetry can be extremely useful for dropping into strong emotions quickly. The lines that began this section invite the questions, What are the sorrows I have known or shown? What are the kindnesses? What are the sorrows and kindnesses I have inherited? One awareness is to observe the slippery dance between grief and anger. The latter is an activating emotion, but if we cannot examine and be with the driving emotions beneath the anger, we tend to react destructively rather than with care and creativity.

Tremendous grief arises for me in reconciling my longing to belong with my commitment to racial justice. In many ways, whiteness has protected me. Consciously trying to individuate from it can lead to the type of social death previously described. Sometimes I feel intense shame and rejection when I teach how racism distorts our souls or speak to the prevalence of unconscious microaggressions in White spaces. People are so quick to anger when challenged or uncomfortable, and I am conditioned to placate. In the South, a culture of whiteness operates with unspoken rules. One of them, particularly for women, is to "be sweet." In other words, don't rock the boat or trigger controversy. Don't talk politics or current events.

I regularly uncover histories I did not learn in school, and the effect is like ripping off Band-Aids: hurt followed by relief, mixed with anger and grief. Learning truths ultimately feels like a balm and, in some cases, confirmation of something long intuited. My naïve assumption is that most people long for honesty, but our cultural learning leads us to prioritize comfort over truth. My sorrow, then, is about how difficult it can be to form a community of other White folks—especially those who are educators or leaders—willing to grieve our legacies and deep disappointments that the world is not as many of us were taught. These sorrows may be particular to my social location. They trigger profound grief for the impact on generations of non-white people of White people looking the other way. Neglecting grief furthers disunion from ourselves, others, and the world, whereas attending to it "dares us to love once more."[686] When we speak to grief, we open gateways to love. Once through this threshold, we can speak with more honesty and care.

Care

Care for self and others is foundational to love as a basic stance of kinship that presupposes every person's right to freedom and dignity. Similarly, if we care about the world, we know that our lives and fate intimately connect to everything on the planet.[687] Care is a mindset and a practice that is neither enabling nor permissive, but acts with intention to set clear boundaries. We are already part of a boundless vitality that makes for a universal kinship among all beings. In his meditations, Thurman offers that dwelling in our relatedness contributes to joyous overtones among human relations.[688] When we act from a liberated mindset that honors relatedness, the quality of our care reflects choice and freedom rather than obligation and duty. Responsibility for and with others is a value rather than a chore.

The diminutive feminine form of care is often represented as selfless, and the caregiver can become invisible and resentful. Care from an angry person who is not

---

[686] Weller, *Wild Edge of Sorrow*, xiv.

[687] hooks, *All About Love*, 87.

[688] Thurman, *Meditations of the Heart*, 100.

grounded in love—as in the case of a borderline mother—feels suffocating or harmful. Strangely, I felt cared for by the same mother whose emotional unpredictability I feared, but who made my sack lunch every school day of my life. Love is inclusive of care, but care alone does not create or sustain love.

On the contrary, powerful feminine care rooted in love is bidirectional, extending toward the self and others. It is to hold the oneness of life, to understand that "they, as part of us, have done this to us."[689] When we really get this, it is no longer possible to view harm or care of the self as separate from harm or care of another, nor is it possible to view another as immutable. Human relations are inherently dynamic and capable of deepening.[690] As a quality of love, feminine care is both tender and fierce. Especially in circumstances where the "nice girl" is expected but does not oblige, holding these two qualities in balance can feel like a challenge to the status quo. Transformative love is a paradox that requires the shrewdness of a serpent and the inoffensiveness of a dove.[691]

A practice of self-care tends to the inner world so that thoughts and behaviors better align with values. When regular time is scheduled for encounters with the self, through meditation, learning, creating, yoga, or the like, inevitable tensions arise, and previously unacknowledged aspects of the self emerge. A robust daily practice strengthens the tools and tough-mindedness needed to respond to the resulting tensions. Self-awareness grows in tandem with an ability to soften the heart

---

[689] Thurman, *Meditations of the Heart*, 117.

[690] Thurman, *Meditations of the Heart*, 118.

[691] Peterson, *The Message*, Matthew 10:16.

toward others.[692] In an integrated state, blending tough-mindedness with a tender heart, we are better equipped to show up for justice and freedom, both public forms of love. We can also better recognize our limitations and extend grace to ourselves in uncertainty.

The care of others extends from self-care. In what follows, I call attention to several practices that address racial injustices and microaggressions with care and integrity. They are metacommunication, "emotional judo," and clarity. Each strategy minimizes defensiveness and maximizes integrity. They are for those who ask, "But what can I do?" and recognize there is seldom a single grand gesture that will "cure" racism. Instead, like a daily practice, it is a persistent willingness to attend to present injustices in small ways.

Metacommunication in these instances does not cast blame but expects accountability. As a tactic, it is the communication beneath the communication. In this case, it is intentional rather than unconscious or nonverbal. It makes the invisible visible and educates and disarms the speaker(s). The following are examples from actual conversations.

Speaker: Sometimes [he] just sounds so Black.

Me: I'm not sure I understand what you mean. Can you explain?

[Subtext: I'm pretty sure I know what's implied, but I'm disarming by asking the speaker to explain.]

Speaker: Oh, you know what I mean. He just sounds Black.

[Offers no explanation but wants me to comply. Here it is important to remain resolute, not to laugh or offer agreement.]

---

[692] King, *Strength to Love*, chap. 1.

Me [option 1]: I'm still unsure I know what you mean. I don't think you meant it this way, but what you said offends/confuses/bothers me. There isn't one way to "sound Black," just as there isn't one way to "sound White." In some sense, all Black people sound Black, and all White people sound White.
[Provides the benefit of the doubt, offers a clear statement, disarms, and educates the speaker.]

Me [option 2]: I just read an article about microaggressions, which helped me understand how to identify and respond to them. Do you want me to share it with you?
[The goal here is to let something neutral do the educating, especially if the speaker is already agitated or defended.]

I have had some version of this conversation more than once. The response to my final statement is usually silence, befuddlement, or some attempt to walk it back. Sometimes I get a question and more dialogue. Without overtly saying to someone, "That's racist or problematic," the speaker comes to an understanding on their own. At the very least, there is the potential for reflection. In metacommunication, I care for my values, the speaker, and the one who is absent but being othered.

Emotional judo is a playful way to handle difficult conversations with the minimum use of force. Judo means "the gentle way" in Japanese. It is an especially useful tool within relationships, professional or personal, that diffuses attack energy.[693] Judo uses the energy of the attacking opponent to knock them off balance. In conversation, it looks like non-reactivity and avoiding a battle of wills. Both emotional judo and metacommunication find healthy and respectful ways to navigate complex topics in which we feel emotionally invested. Because race is connected to identity, talking about it is almost always charged. When self-care is a daily practice,

---

[693] I learned of emotional judo from my mentor, but literature and training exist for it as well. See Higgs, *7 Sneaky Tricks of Difficult Conversations*.

awareness of patterned responses to conflict increases. Whether it arouses antipathy or empathy, these tactics help us engage with challenging emotional energies. They are useful in the range of normal behaviors. In contrast, more rigid boundaries or disengagement might become necessary when dealing with a sociopath, an abuser, a committed racist, or a narcissist attempting to seize power.

People try to gain the upper hand in conversation by trivializing, shifting the context, reacting emotionally, manipulating, and silencing.[694] Based on how I define care, none of these behaviors uphold another person's dignity. They are neither curious nor loving. When dealing with racialized comments or microaggressions, I don't always feel curious or loving. It is challenging to remain playful in emotionally charged situations. Before offering an example of judo, I will say that an entirely appropriate response, if conversations become attacking, could be, "I am unable to have this conversation with you right now." A clear boundary demonstrates care of the self and others. Boundaries can also make the recipient angry, but consistency breeds respect overtime.

> *Setting:* A birthday dinner at a restaurant with my parents. Dialogue is not exact but very close to what was said. Parts of the exchange are seared in my memory.
>
> *Characters:* My mother, my mostly silent father, my husband Josh, and me.
>
> *Mother:* Tell me why Black people can't seem to move on from slavery?
> *[This question, right off the bat, trivializes a significant injustice.]*
>
> *Me:* Enslavement impacted generations of Black Americans. Their enslavement lasted longer than their freedom. As I understand it, unresolved trauma impacts individuals, families, and communities for up to seven generations.
> *[Attempt at education rather than emotional reaction.]*

---

[694] Higgs, 20.

Mother: Well, slavery wasn't all bad. Some slaves were happy.
[Again, trivialization.]

Me: I'm shocked to hear you say that. I wonder if you would have felt happy being enslaved.
[States feeling and poses a reflection.]

Mother: Oh, Holly. Why do you always have to make things so personal? I want to hear what Josh has to say.
[Shift of context from the original question to my tendency to dramatize situations then redirects to another person.]

Josh: Linda, it's a good question. Do you think you would have felt happy being enslaved?

Mother: Well, I think I would have moved on already.
[Trivialization.]

Josh: I wonder if part of the issue is that we haven't moved on. We have never truly repaired as a society, but it's my experience that many Black families still suffer from generational poverty and endemic racism.

Mother: I just don't understand why everything must be about race. I mean, you all seem to think that everyone is racist.
[This comment teeters somewhere between trivialization, manipulation, and emotional reactivity. I am also not sure if "you all" meant Black people generally or Josh and me specifically.]

Josh: Racism is hard to talk about and has definitely impacted my life.

Mother: Well, I can't pretend to understand . . .
[Silence.]

Father: Check, please!

Emotional judo does not necessarily change someone's mind or win arguments. It honors the dignity of all persons involved without succumbing to personal attacks. If even just one person in the conversation employs it, tension nearly always diffuses. I want to point again to the importance of a daily self-care practice and how it protects in challenging situations. My husband Josh possesses tremendous equanimity; truth be told, my shoulders were up to my ears during this conversation. I had to take many deep breaths and squeeze his hand. I listen to many people proclaim how much harder conversations about race and racism are with family. Emotional judo is a strategy that essentially says, over and over, "I hear you, and I think/feel . . ." so that neither person is stripped of their integrity and basic humanity. It uses empathy, acknowledgment, and validation as acts of care.

There may also be times when you are the person who unintentionally commits a microaggression and find yourself on the receiving end of attack energy. Emotional judo applies in these situations, as do the spiritual practices of curiosity and personal responsibility. Without moving through an entire dialogue, the intent in such a situation is to reply with humility. A response to being "called out" could be, "Wow. I did not realize what I said came across this way. I am so sorry." Sometimes it may be appropriate to add, "I'm not sure I understand what a microaggression is. Can you explain it to me?" If the response is "No" or further hostility, then it is incumbent on you to learn. So much of this is paying attention to cues, prioritizing connection, and honoring integrity.

When neither emotional judo nor metacommunication work, either because you are dealing with an emotionally volatile person or because group or individual safety is at risk, it is important to show care to all persons involved by setting clear boundaries. I am not interested in conversing with a White person about why they can't casually call my child the N-word or tell a racist joke in my presence, for example. There are times when clarity about values supersedes dialogue and drives behavior. In this sense, boundaries are healthy for everyone involved. They demonstrate love's ferocity.

I once chaperoned a field trip with ten students, ages twelve to eighteen, only two of whom were not White: my twelve-year-old son and a seventeen-year-old

Latinx woman. The kids were aware of my presence and pushed the edges of "appropriate language" in a discussion about who had permission to use which words. The gist was that the queer kids (about half of the group) could refer to themselves as typically derogatory names, but straight kids could not. Language conveys power, and ownership of historically weaponized language is a way of reclaiming power. They ventured toward the N-word and who has permission to use it. I felt my son's body shrink beside mine. Before it went too far, I said, "It is not okay for a White person to use the N-word. Ever." One kid responded that White kids use it all the time, and I firmly but evenly repeated, "It is not okay for a White person to use the N-word." The conversation ended. In this case, I was not interested in an intellectual discussion about literature, poetry, or rap songs. I was interested in protecting my child, who later said, "I'm really glad you were there, mommy."

While I do not want to come across as the self-appointed racial justice and language police, I stress the point that White people need to get more comfortable challenging other White people regarding racism and microaggression. I hope my son develops the tenacity to address racism directly, but it is not the sole responsibility of non-white people. We change a culture of whiteness by challenging the ways it exploits power or stays silent. Individuation begins when we wake up to the power it has over us. When we choose silence, we harm ourselves and others and further disrupt the great chain of being. Choosing language infused with care upholds a basic "we-ness." It prioritizes connection over righteousness, curiosity over defensiveness, and personal responsibility over minimization.

Thus far, I have offered ways to use language to care for the self and others. There are also direct ways to demonstrate care for the world. Clearly, amid the climate crisis, we need clear regulations to mitigate continued harm to Earth. There is a strong relationship between racism, classism, and climate change, as the world's poorest are primarily non-white, have contributed least, and yet are the most impacted by it. A society that prioritizes love and exercises care for people and planet ensures meeting basic physiological needs, as defined by Abraham Maslow.[695] A shift from zero-sum thinking creates space to imagine how the care of the world involves feeding, educating, and housing everyone. We do not lack the resources to care for everyone's basic needs, only the will. Wise spiritual teachings rooted in transpersonal, transformational love are not evacuation plans from this world. They are equations, myths, and rituals for falling deeply in love with the world and caring for it in such a way that we experience it and everything in it as sacred.

Honesty

If love is in part a revelation, an unmasking, it must include a fundamental commitment to honesty. Speaking truths instantly reveals our vulnerabilities and struggles. As a public practice, hooks writes that "the heart of justice is truth telling, seeing ourselves and the world the way it is rather than the way we want it to be. More than ever before we, as a society, need to renew a commitment to truth telling."[696] Truth telling is a public act of love. We live in a nation where truth is negotiable, and facts are filtered through ideology. No wonder we find ourselves in a

---

[695] See McCleod, "Maslow's Hierarchy of Needs."

[696] hooks, *All About Love*, 39.

contentious relationship with truth. Historian Edward E. Baptist asserts that the dominant narrative of the rise of capitalism in the United States and its relationship to slavery is riddled with holes and withholding. The story of this country is of untold sacrifice in which non-white bodies became currency and collateral, contributing to economic expansion more than any other innovation. Yet, our financial success is chalked up to American (read: White) excellence, exceptionalism, and superiority.[697] Robert Bellah reminds us that if we are to repair our covenant with one another, "if we are to free ourselves for the future we must remember what we would rather forget."[698]

The rise of capitalism in the United States is synonymous with brutality. Until recently, as more perspectives rise to the forefront, our history has been told through invisibility and negation. The Texas State Board of Education recently proposed calling enslavement "involuntary relocation," which completely misses the atrocities of the "peculiar institution."[699] We need to give ourselves and our children more credit for holding complexity. Realizing we have been lied to by our schools and institutions is deeply unsettling. It casts a veneer of inauthenticity and leaves students without critical thinking tools.

Recalling atrocities of the past does not negate positive contributions. Our possibilities for wholeness rest on holding these two in tension. When he wrote about integrating the "double self" that Black folks experience in a White-dominant

---

[697] Baptist, *The Half Has Never Been Told*, 19–34.

[698] Bellah, "Birth of New American Myths," 144.

[699] B. Lopez, "State Education Board Members Push Back."

culture, Du Bois proclaimed, "In this merging [we] wish neither of the older selves to be lost. . . . The Nation has not yet found peace from its sins; the freedman has not yet found in freedom his promised land."[700] As stated earlier, White people committed to anti-racism benefit from adopting a type of twoness in which we integrate the pains of our past with commitment to a different future. Developing an honest inward and backward gaze informs social change through practicing psycho-spiritual liberation, as discussed in Part II. Increased self-awareness reduces harm to others. As Baldwin points out:

> The truth about us is always at variance with what we wish it to be. The [human element] is to bring these [inner and outer] realities into a relationship resembling reconciliation . . . we know, in the case of the person, that whoever cannot tell himself the truth about his past is trapped in it, is immobilized in the prison of his undiscovered self. The same is also true of nations.[701]

Developing capacity to search for and reflect upon the contradictions in the world and ourselves challenges dominant narratives, exposes self-delusion and amnesia, and breaks open old paradigms so that we may begin to reconcile and re-member the multitude of selves within a larger whole. Truth telling reconstructs history be recovering alarmingly different perspectives out of the ashes of a violent

---

[700] Du Bois, *Souls of Black Folk*, 11, 13.

[701] Baldwin, "Creative Process," 318.

past.[702] Embracing difference is a dialectic that brings a radically reimagined future into being.

If we remain invested in collective amnesia, dedicated to White impunity, we become assassins of memory, conspirators with silence. We choose distortion over clarity and allow ourselves to be emotionally manipulated. In such a state, we live without the benefit of potentially deeper understandings.[703] Transformative justice cannot happen without honesty. Engaging in prophetic truth-telling that is not self-pitying or sentimental names systems of harm and diffuses their power over the population. Public truth-telling is not a confessional or tell-all that burdens historically marginalized people with tears or needs for forgiveness. It is strategic about revealing histories ignored and harm done to hold people and systems accountable for wrongdoing while remaining in touch with our shared humanity. Each of us is a witness to our social communities, able to awaken to issues of oppression and injustice in such a way that reflection, ritual, and repair are normalized and supported. Integrating experience with academic research, the spiritual with the political, is a path toward healing mind, body, and soul.[704] Truth-telling is a pathway to wholeness, personally and collectively. It is a strategy for being with what is, rather than colluding with denial.

Truth telling in the public domain emancipates those who actively participate in it from unjust structures. Truth telling subverts the status quo. My family and I

---

[702] Watkins and Shulman, *Toward Psychologies of Liberation*, 94.

[703] Watkins and Shulman, 73.

[704] Arora, "Women's Spirituality at CIIS."

recently made a pilgrimage to Montgomery, Alabama, to visit the Equal Justice Initiative (EJI) and The National Memorial for Peace and Justice. They utilize personal narratives, historical accounts, and stark visuals to invoke memory and create a sacred space for truth telling about a legacy of racial terror. Disembodied voices that wail, sing, and groan float among the din of tourists, student groups, and other pilgrims. Standing between the cool, brick walls with traces of moss and runnels of rust that once held the sweat, blood, excrement, and tears of human bodies as they awaited purchase is a living, sensuous experience. The rooms beckon viewers to listen to the unvarnished accounts of the ongoing impacts of a culture of whiteness that created race-based enslavement. In this space, remembering is a shared experience, and viewers encounter honest history. It is painful, jarring, and even grotesque. It is also restorative, moving, and beautiful. Truth is always multilayered, a study in holding the tension of opposites.

EJI is holy ground. Jars of dirt, excavated by hand from known lynching sites, line shelves and provide evidence of Earth's witness to pain and suffering. An exchange occurs between the collector and the earth, a knowing or retelling. It is an accounting with history that requires care and lament, too. Those who collected and consecrated the dirt, White, Black, and Brown alike, share in that memory as they unearth buried truths. When history belongs to the privileged, when we avoid seeing the suffering imposed, amnesia becomes part of the pathology of a nation and its people.[705]

The dead have truths to tell.

---

[705] Watkins and Shulman, *Toward Psychologies of Liberation*, 127.

We are their witnesses and their mouthpieces.

A commitment to honesty in the public arena counters complicity and denial. Just as it is with individuals and family systems, lies, secrecy, and withholding impact the health of the whole group. When we participate in it, we contribute to dysfunction.[706] Contrary to popular belief, the truth does not have to hurt or alienate. Carefully handled, it is an expression of love. "People who imagine that history flatters them," Baldwin wrote, "are impaled on their history like a butterfly on a pin and become incapable of seeing or changing themselves, or the world."[707] If we are content to be like the preserved butterfly, we are deceived by idealization rather than in active relation with our becoming. A willingness to hold history's ugly, brutal aspects with its incredible, creative ones with wide-open eyes creates more space for beauty and healing. Choosing to believe that people *deserve* their histories invites destruction if we continue to shut our eyes to reality by manipulating and misinterpreting information. A commitment to White innocence turns us into monsters; we remain trapped in our history and our history remains trapped in us.[708]

I do not think we want to be monsters.

There are several ways to imagine a truth and reconciliation process in the United States, and it behooves us to think about it in terms of past, present, and future. It is not a one-time event but an ongoing, cyclical commitment to addressing racialized trauma and abuse. While there are obstacles to a national movement—

---

[706] hooks, *All About Love*, 45.

[707] Baldwin, "White Man's Guilt," 410.

[708] Baldwin, "Stranger in the Village," 81.

extreme partisanship, lack of buy-in, a long history of injustice versus a singular event, denial, and the persistence of White racism in daily life—local, small-scale versions are already happening. Projects like EJI's Peace and Justice Memorial seek to bring forth truths about the past that connect people to the present. EJI's founder, Bryan Stevenson, maintains that truth-telling must always precede reconciliation, reparation, and restoration.[709] It is essential, here, to reiterate my insistence on using "we." All of us—our entire nation—inherits White racism, and all of us must address. The second we distance ourselves from it, we trip back into the denial that allows racist systems to endure.

After enslavement, there was neither a truth and reconciliation process nor a transfer of power in the United States that indicated a commitment to end white supremacist rule. Instead, it was allowed to exist and remain powerful alongside a nominal freedom from enslavement. Truth telling about our past and how it impacts the present is not a punishment. It is liberatory. I earnestly believe something more awaits us: a culture that embodies genuine freedom, justice, and equality. These are qualities that will guide us toward a future Beloved Community.

Patience and Persistence

Change is slow. It took billions of years for the cosmos to know itself in human form. However, humans have the capacity to make an idea tangible within minutes. Our ability to take immediate, effective action impacts institutional change in immediate and long-term ways. We water the seeds of yesterday as we plant them for tomorrow. In Dr. King's words, "We are not faced with the fact that tomorrow

---

[709] EJI, "Report: Reconstruction in American."

is today. We are confronted with the fierce urgency of now.... Now let us begin. Now let us rededicate ourselves to the long and bitter—but beautiful—struggle for a new world."[710]

Dismantling racism is urgent because it affects peoples' lives every day. It is not something we can necessarily take a break from even if we believe we have the privilege to do so.[711] When one awakens to racial privilege, it can lead to shame and denial, as previously discussed, and it can also lead to acting with increased haste. At times it may cause us to become judgmental, critical, or impatient with those we perceive to be at different points in developing race consciousness. We might also castigate ourselves for not doing enough or feel compelled to separate from White peers because of our own internal conflicts. In so doing, we perpetuate disunion. I am not suggesting that we take a "both sides" approach or soften a sense of integrity in responding to racial injustice. However, cultivating patience and compassion for the process is necessary. As such, it is imperative that White people do this work together, unpack the difficulties and insecurities in spaces where non-white people will not be burdened.

When Dr. King confronted us with "the fierce urgency of now," he proclaimed that "in this unfolding conundrum of life and history there is such a thing as being too late. Procrastination is still the thief of time.... Over the bleached bones and jumbled residue of numerous civilizations are written the pathetic words:

---

[710] King, *Essential Martin Luther King, Jr.*, 165–66.

[711] Tochluk, *Living in the Tension*, 68.

'Too Late.'"[712] Further, he expressed disappointment in the White moderate "who paternalistically believes he can set the timetable for another man's freedom; who lives by a mythical concept of time and who constantly advises the Negro to wait for a 'more convenient season.'"[713] Now is that time. The issues that divide us need our pressing attention. While we can exercise patience and empathy for our continued learning as well as for those who have yet to grasp the pervasive harm of racial injustice, we can also persist in taking imperfect action to continue building worlds characterized by deeper belonging. We must be patient for a quantum leap in enlarged consciousness to occur but remain persistent in in our efforts to push it past a tipping point.

Justice

While I recognize that some will always believe justice is retributive, earned, or deserved, I also think that each of us is more than the worst thing we've done.[714] I can already hear the "What about . . ." questions surfacing. Yes, those people too. Available resources and traumatic events impact our trajectories in life, among them the type of care received in the early years. In the family unit, care without love feels confusing to a child. Love without boundaries or reciprocity teaches entitlement. Beyond the early years, if we do not learn to take personal responsibility for our behaviors, we ultimately lead violent, defensive, or generally egocentric lives that cause harm to self and others to varying degrees. The path of individuation is vital to

---

[712] King, *Essential Martin Luther King, Jr.*, 165.

[713] King, "Letter from a Birmingham Jail," 73.

[714] Stevenson, *Just Mercy*, 18.

creating more just and loving societies. Otherwise, we continue to perpetuate "eye for an eye" principles of justice, which are the antithesis of love.

Implementing distributive and restorative justice requires a radical departure from how most of us learned to think about consequences. Distributive justice is concerned with members of society having equitable access to resources. A loving society attends to every person's basic needs such that poverty and its challenges are not determining factors in one's success or failure. I appreciate that the Blackfoot people measure wealth by generosity rather than asset acquisition. A shift in our mindset about wealth alone would be an enormous undertaking in this country, but suffice to say that we have more than enough to meet every person's basic needs. Eradicating poverty is not an act of charity but justice, underscored by a fundamental respect for interconnectedness and human dignity.

While distributive justice is concerned with fair allocation of resources, restorative justice is concerned with relationships and belonging. It focuses on healing victims and perpetrators so both can be restored to the community. Truth and reconciliation commissions, for example, are restorative efforts. The five basic tenets of the restorative process are as follows:

1. *Relationship:* This goes beyond the specific relationship between victim and perpetrator, and outward toward the relationship to society at large, taking into consideration the conditions that perpetuated the harm done.
2. *Respect:* Implement measures to ensure safety, such as deep listening, mirroring, shared goals, and a commitment to process.
3. *Responsibility:* Everyone involved must grapple with responsibility in each situation, so self-reflection and honesty are imperative.

4. *Repair:* This step is partly guided by facilitators and seeks to mitigate tendencies toward revenge and punishment. Repair cannot happen without establishing respect and taking responsibility. Repair may entail serving a consequence, but it is related to the misdeed.
5. *Reintegration:* Once the person who caused harm accepts responsibility, they can begin reintegration. Here community involvement is necessary, whether provided by family, school, workplace, or legal system. Reintegration counters coercion and isolation. It requires a community willing to take both forgiveness and accountability seriously.[715]

My experience with restorative justice emerges from my work as a middle and high school teacher. I was trained as a facilitator for peer mediation and taught groups of students to execute restorative processes in their school. I have many examples of when it worked well and only a few when it did not. The latter were largely a function of not following through with accountability measures. I wholeheartedly believe in restorative discipline and counter any assumptions that it equates with a lack of consequences for wrongdoing. Facing the person to whom harm was done is often much more difficult than separation via suspension, expulsion, or jail time. Separation does not allow for closure and leaves far too much room for shame and denial to fester. Even though specific interventions change, the concept of the "5 Rs" remains consistent whether restoration happens interpersonally, in families, in schools, or in the courtroom.

---

[715] For a basic overview, see: Maynard and Weinstein, *Hacking School Discipline.*

Principles and practices of philosophical, psychological, and spiritual liberation are vital to imagining a more loving society that prioritizes care, honesty, and justice. These seem straightforward, like mere switches to flip. An earnest commitment to love and dying to a culture of whiteness are complete shifts away from our conditioning. As I work through imagining a culture committed to anti-racism, I am aware of how little our society values process and forgiveness. We often want quick fixes that feel easy, but like anything thoughtful and meaningful—love, democracy, liberation—justice is a process.

Every one of us is broken in some way. The most vulnerable aspects of our imperfect nature are the most universal. We all hurt; we have all hurt someone. This tension in us creates and sustains our capacity for compassion and mercy. Blindness to our own brokenness and potential for wrongdoing minimizes our humanity. Compassion is not complicit with wrongdoing. It simply acknowledges the fallibility of humans while still prioritizing accountability. Even though justice is associated with deference to the law, one meaning of the root *jus* is "to join" or "bind together."[716] When justice is rooted in restoration, it is relational. It binds us to one another. The guiding question in restorative systems is, "How do we hold people accountable for wrongdoing and yet at the same time remain in touch with their humanity enough to believe in their capacity to be transformed?"[717] Accountability promotes change and growth.

---

[716] Boatright, "History, Meaning, and Use of the Words Justice and Judge."

[717] hooks and Angelou, "Angelou," par. 60.

Implementing restorative justice in schools is crucial because every person intersects with the education system at some point. Schools use more punitive measures against Black male students than any other demographic, resulting in higher suspension and expulsion rates across the board. Evidence shows that students who experience punishment involving removal from school or displacement to corrective environments have higher disengagement, lower confidence, and a greater possibility of dropping out altogether.[718] I don't think school is a panacea for avoiding jail. Still, students affected by disenfranchisement, retributive punishment, and zero-tolerance policies have an increased likelihood of entering juvenile justice or prison systems. Black students are suspended or expelled at three times the rate of their White peers.

It is not their failure.

It is a failure of the system to create belonging, safety, and justice.

I mean the kind of justice that binds.

I mean the kind of justice that transforms.

…

I tell you these stories, two chapters in two different schoolboys' lives, to illustrate the impact of a justice system that retaliates rather than ameliorates. When my middle son was in kindergarten, only five years old at the time, he was trying to get the attention of a little White girl at his lunch table. Finally, out of frustration, he said, "If you don't play with me, I will kill you!"

The little girl and her friend reported him, and ten minutes later, the school called me.

---

[718] Maynard and Weinstein, *Hacking School Discipline*.

The school pulled my son into the front office, thrust paperwork into my lap upon arrival, and the administrator immediately issued him a suspension because he was considered a "Red-Level Three Threat," according to the handbook. My mouth hung open. My son cried big, fat tears and crawled into my lap. This kid was not going to kill anyone, and with what? A sandwich? They told me to take him home. On the floor of the principal's office with my heart in my belly, I modeled restoration with him. It was perhaps more for the administrator, who at the end of our dialogue also had tears in her eyes. I asked what had happened. He told me. I asked him what he was feeling. He told me. I wondered what he meant to say to the little girl, and he said, "I just wanted her to play with me." And I asked if he could think of any other words, he could have used to meet his request. He came up with several.

That conversation was enough for me. He got it. I am aware that so much of motherhood is repetition, and over the years, I have had many versions of this conversation with him, how to say what you mean directly and intentionally without doing harm. The administrator was undeterred. She stood up, wiped her eyes, handed us the proverbial pink slip, and sent us home. My husband and I must continuously parent with a combination of hypervigilance and tenderness.

Mine is a kid who longs for belonging and approval from his peers. He has big emotions, a huge heart, and like many young kids, poor impulse control. He is also big for his age, Black-White biracial, and, as stated, male. No matter what we say consciously, implicit biases are stacked against him. White educators who work with Black children need to be aware of biases that inform responses and perceptions. Just naming the possibility makes it conscious and offers our minds a different pathway and perhaps a different outcome.

Let me emphasize: my son was five years old.

A second schoolboy in my life, also Black, was impacted by a conflation of circumstances: an absent father, poverty, a wonderful, hardworking mother who worked multiple jobs, and the influence of peers seduced by the very American values of instant gratification and materialism. He engaged in petty theft and eventual aggravated robbery that landed him in the Orleans Parish Prison System at age sixteen. He came of age in a prison system with a documented history of cruelty and neglect of its inmates and has been subject to numerous federal court-ordered consent decrees for years.[719]

While some jail time may have been a normal consequence according to our legal system, there is nothing ordinary about a child having to fight grown-man battles or protect himself from them. He left prison at age twenty-four with no applicable life skills, no money, no GED, and nowhere to go. To leave old friends and old ways behind, he arrived at the previously absent father's house and has since attained a high school equivalency degree and training in truck driving. I don't know if he has ever talked openly about his experience in prison.

Today this man is developmentally and emotionally arrested. He never received any therapy or opportunity for restoration and reintegration into the community outside of the grace offered by his family. It is incredibly problematic that our society thinks this is acceptable. In this case, justice did not bind him to anyone, restore him to his original condition, or transform his sense of belonging. Distributive justice caused further separation from healthy social networks. If we are better than the worst thing we've done, then we need to rethink prison as a pathway for self-discovery, repair, and forgiveness. They'd do better to be guided by the families of Mother Emmanuel AME. Those who participate in upholding abusive prison practices are not issuing justice but furthering harm.

It is a well-documented fact that Black people consist of over thirty percent of US prisoners while comprising only thirteen percent of the total population. A one-in-three statistic is troubling to a mother with three Black-biracial boys. I know many Black people, and I am confident that thirty

---

[719] See American Civil Liberties Union, "Orleans Parish Prison."

percent of them are not criminals, but Black men are five times more likely to be accused of a crime. The targeting of Black men dates to the "slave patrol" as early as the 1700s that pursued, apprehended, and returned runaway enslaved people to their enslavers and allowed the use of excessive force to control and produce subservient behavior.[720] *A long history of bias in the legal system needs to be deconstructed and corrected. We need to reorient our thinking about justice and how our practices to illustrate this country's commitment to behaviors of love and liberation.*

In his work with violent offenders in prisons, Marshall Rosenberg found that once these (mostly) men could connect with their feelings and unmet needs, once they learned different strategies for communication, massive shifts in compassion toward themselves and others occurred. Given the opportunity, they could conceive alternative methods to address conflict rather than violence. Of course, these seismic shifts did not happen overnight, but with support and group accountability over time. Rosenberg writes of witnessing the most hardened men experience catharsis through tears, often by connecting with the little boy inside who simply wanted the attention of a schoolmate but was not taught the words to express it.[721] *Compassionate communication is a strategy that decreases violence and paves the way for peacemaking, even in the most heightened conflicts. Words can heal; words can harm. Being love is, at least in part, a language revolution.*

…

The most egregious misconception of restorative justice is that it lacks consequences and accountability. On the contrary, it upholds concepts of natural and

---

[720] There are many reputable resources regarding implicit bias, racism, and abuses in the legal system. The NAACP, ACLU, EJI all keep up-to-date information in their websites. Perhaps one of the best concise documentaries regarding the issue of justice and race is *13th*, directed by Ava Duverney.

[721] Rosenberg, *Nonviolent Communication*.

appropriate consequences with the added effort to reintegrate the wrongdoer. It is committed to personal responsibility, which is also a premise of psychological individuation and spiritual liberation. From my work with middle- and high-school students, I can attest to the difficulty of standing in front of their peers, acknowledging guilt, asking for forgiveness, and repairing relationships. It is easier to disappear into a secluded room for suspension or a whole new environment because of expulsion. On the other side of repair, however, is the opportunity for disrupted relationships to strengthen and grow. Without repair, shame and resentment bloom. Suspension and expulsion are consequences, but neither stress personal responsibility nor repair. Even if suspension is sometimes appropriate, there are restorative ways to reintegrate students upon return.

A restorative system requires more process on the front end. It requires compassionate, skilled individuals to mediate, facilitate, and mentor at every level of intervention, from schools to law enforcement. Changing the paradigm requires sacrificing previously held notions about justice, but ultimately—I believe and have seen—restorative systems create safer, healthier, and more loving communities. Societally, by addressing the failings and discriminations inherent in our justice system, we begin to correct issues of systemic racism. The more we mistranslate justice as punishment that isolates and increases suffering rather than consequences that educate and restore, the further from love we stray.

Mutuality

"Being love" requires individuals to adopt new ways of seeing and being so that more expansive, inclusive behaviors become endemic at the level of community and society. Transpersonal love depends on mutuality. Contrary to popular notions of sacrificial love in which we sing along with some version of "I would die for you," love is (a) never violent and (b) never one-sided. Mutual love has clear boundaries and values, beginning with those I just outlined. It is also the ability to see oneself in another and the other in oneself, to recognize the paper-thinness that separates one from the other despite the chasm we often mistake it to be.

> "Before you learn the tender gravity of kindness
>
> you must travel where the Indian in a white poncho
>
> lies dead by the side of the road.
>
> You must see how this could be you,
>
> how he too was someone
>
> who journeyed through the night with plans
>
> and the simple breath that kept him alive."[722]

We are all, in one way or another, just travelers trying to get through the night.

On the one hand, radical love is self-emptying, and egoic desires do not guide it. It is not focused solely on the needs of "Me." On the other hand, radical love is not self-less. A strong sense of I grounded in we-ness, in the interconnectedness of all things, drives it. Radical love does not cause pain to the self or another. The path of love is the path of growing up, learning to take personal responsibility, and being guided by care, honesty, and justice to strengthen mutuality in everyday life. Mutuality as a behavior of love will not prevail when one party wants to maintain control or codependence.[723]

---

[722] Nye, "Kindness," 42.

[723] hooks, *All About Love*, 152.

Immature love wounds so many. The idea of love might feel utterly unsafe or even life-threatening. I precede the section on love with philosophies, psychologies, and spiritualities of liberation to propose frameworks to help us stretch beyond our personal wounds and into the world's wounds. We can heal them. White people need to unearth ancestral pasts rooted in colonialism that continue to breed shame, fear, resentment, and division. Where truths emerge, love thrives. Truth-telling fosters mutuality between the present and the past. The past is a wise teacher that can guide us toward a more courageous, inclusive, and liberated future.

Central to "being love" is listening to the still, small voice that whispers and protects from what is *not* love. Lamenting the impact of lovelessness and pain is one way of beginning again on love's journey. Acknowledging, listening, being with, and responding to hurt from a place of tenderness allows for reciprocal dialogue with our understanding of love. One of the responsibilities of mutuality is deep listening, especially to voices long silenced. Listening in a devotional way allows healing to occur, and in the process, we become better communicators.[724] Listening strengthens our ability to rise above sectarian political and ideological positions so that we may attempt to see the person inside.[725] Attentive silence is sacred and may arouse grief about disconnection, again ushering in the opportunity to practice lament. The hope is that the interconnected, interlocking, and cyclical nature of active, transformative love becomes more apparent.

---

[724] hooks, *All About Love*, 157.

[725] Freire, *Pedagogy of Hope*, 36.

Mutuality should not be confused with quid pro quo. It is a broad sense of interdependence where participants commit to dynamic interactions that do not rely on perceived or actual hierarchies nor upon convincing another to accept a particular opinion. It begins with the premise that interpersonal and transpersonal relationships involve commitment to the growth and well-being of every other being. When we practice mutuality, we are more likely to be generous and forgiving. Mutuality honors the interwoven nature of our suffering and liberation.

In a multicultural society, tolerance is a precondition for mutuality. Tolerance acknowledges differences, and mutuality engages with them. Where mere tolerance is not necessarily sustainable in conflict, robust mutuality recognizes and embraces multiple perspectives and wrestles with them. It extends beyond refraining from harming others and asks citizens to consider the viewpoints of those with the least power and influence so that some form of social solidarity becomes possible.[726] Asking for acknowledgment of multiple views and agreeing to engage despite them is unlike the expectation to celebrate and champion difference. While celebrating and enthusiastically valuing the "different other" is ideal, the commitment of a mutual democracy first accepts the fact of differences; second, recognizes the right to have varying perspectives; and third, compromises with others to meet the most needs.[727] In any case, tolerance is the minimum expectation in a pluralistic democracy. It feels like a tall order to the most orthodox conservatives and hardly enough for the most

---

[726] Rosenblith and Bindewald, "Between Mere Tolerance and Robust Respect."

[727] Rosenblith and Bindewald, 593.

radical activists. As tolerance evolves toward mutuality, communities must learn to work together to address common values with social and political solutions.

Mutuality abides by the tenets of pluralism and creates an aura of gratitude and grace. It does not ask others to do away with their convictions but to refrain from imposing them upon others in harmful ways. The hope is that proximity and genuine engagement increases empathy and builds new containers of possibility. Mutuality is also a willingness to bear witness to the visible and invisible forces that create our realities. When we surrender to mutuality, we surrender to reality. When we fight against it, we cause suffering that may emerge as denial, scapegoating, silencing, or overt harm. These are behaviors stemming from lovelessness and racism that allow oppression and dominance to thrive.

We live in a time that represents an evolutionary shift in consciousness about the pervasiveness of racism in our society. Moment to moment, we choose whether to move toward or away from the issue and, therefore, toward or away from one another. I believe the onus is upon White people to lean into convergence, into how we are all knotted together by the problem of racism. We need to move away from seeing it as "us versus them" and toward "us with them," again highlighting the need for a language revolution that emphasizes mutual belonging.

Entire states and public school systems are tightening the reins on what is acceptable to discuss or even say in shared spaces, from classrooms to board rooms. Progress toward tolerance and inclusion has more recently acquiesced to those who feel threatened by exposure to different sets of beliefs or lifestyles, and many schools choose to avoid challenging topics altogether so as not to create controversy. Such a decision favors exclusion and primarily benefits a culture of whiteness. Anyone who exists at the margins of whiteness knows the sting of omission. Exposure does not amount to indoctrination. Mutuality is not about forcing views but advancing the capacity to make space for those different from our own. A civic sensibility creates experiences that broaden horizons. Among the democratic state's responsibilities is to ensure the rights and freedoms of all citizens and prepare them to lead and thrive in an increasingly pluralistic society.[728] I do not imply citizen as a legal status, but as people in a society who come together in shared spaces to form traditions, values, laws, and customs.

Mutuality values equal citizenship and the fact of diverse perspectives and experiences. It is ultimately a "will to relationship" with the different other in the face of disagreement. The focus is not necessarily on establishing agreement but collective decision-making that does not sacrifice individual religious or cultural values.[729] In a society that values mutuality, citizens retain their identities while simultaneously committing to civil discourse and retiring superiority of one identity over another. It is imperative to create values and processes that increase mutuality and empathy in public schools. They are the single greatest intersection of shared learning in our society.

Mutuality folds into care, honesty, and justice because it upholds the dignity and sanctity of all persons. Relationality and the fact of plurality are starting points. The state should establish and enforce parameters that protect individuals or groups from harm, discrimination, or prejudice. Our nation and perhaps our world are

---

[728] Rosenblith and Bindewald, 594.

[729] Rosenblith and Bindewald, 596.

presented with an enormous opportunity to seek ways to live with ourselves, one another, and the planet with greater love and peace. As we acknowledge and heal national and personal wounds, we strengthen the ties that bind us. We strengthen the path of communion, which is neither painless, linear, nor easy. Rarely does one heal in isolation; healing is an act of communion.[730] As we practice love in the ways outlined in this dissertation, we can cultivate an awakened heart better able to see and hear our mutual pain and joy. In such a state, we can engage in authentic acts of repair.

Repair

In 2010, the United Nations issued a paper that outlined guiding principles and frameworks for societies to "come to terms with a legacy of large-scale past abuses, to ensure accountability, serve justice, and achieve reconciliation."[731] The guidelines included judicial and nonjudicial processes and mechanisms to inspire institutional and national reparations and reform. Again and again, the paper notes the importance of truth-telling and accountability. There can be no repair without honesty. There can be no accountability without repair. I read the UN paper and think immediately of South Africa, Syria, and Rwanda, of what a godsend transitional justice is to war-torn, obviously corrupt, autocratic nations.

What about the United States? Does not a foundation of Native American genocide and African enslavement that resulted in generations of disproportionately

---

[730] hooks, *All About Love*, 147.

[731] United Nations, *United Nations Approach to Transitional Justice*, 2.

high rates of poverty, discrimination, health inequities, mass incarceration, and unequal treatment before the law warrant acknowledgment and repair?

The UN paper states that efforts toward repair "should further seek to take account of the root causes of conflicts and the related violations of all rights, including civil, political, economic, social, and cultural rights."[732] Such a mandate applies to countries with longstanding issues of racial injustice. It is difficult to implement here because the injustice is neither singular nor particular to a specific time, nor did we undergo a dramatic shift in governance from military to democratic rule. However, we have not shifted away from or fully acknowledged the force of white supremacy woven into the fabric of the United States. Over the course of 400 years, racial injustice became endemic and normalized. Congress issued an apology in 2008 for slavery and Jim Crow, ironically mere months before the first Black man became president of the United States. Barack Obama would then become the first president (rather meekly and without fanfare) to sign an official apology to Native Americans.

> Whereas the arrival of Europeans in North America opened a new chapter in the history of Native Peoples;
>
> Whereas while establishment of permanent European settlements in North America did stir conflict with nearby Indian tribes, peaceful and mutually beneficial interactions also took place;[733]

---

[732] United Nations, 3.

[733] S.J. Res. 14, 111th Cong. (2009).

Whereas the story of the enslavement and de jure segregation of African-Americans and the dehumanizing atrocities committed against them should not be purged from or minimized in the telling of American history;[734]

Whereas many Native Peoples suffered and perished—[735]

Whereas on July 8, 2003, during a trip to Goree Island, Senegal, a former slave port, President George W. Bush acknowledged slavery's continuing legacy in American life and the need to confront that legacy when he stated that slavery "was . . . one of the greatest crimes of history. . . . The racial bigotry fed by slavery did not end with slavery or with segregation. And many of the issues that still trouble America have roots in the bitter experience of other times;

The United States, acting through Congress— . . .

(3) recognizes that there have been years of official depredations, ill-conceived policies, and the breaking of covenants by the Federal Government regarding Indian tribes;

Whereas President Bill Clinton also acknowledged the deep-seated problems caused by the continuing legacy of racism against African-Americans that began with slavery when he initiated a national dialogue about race;

---

[734] H.R. 194, 110th Cong. (2008).

[735] Each successive line alternates between an excerpt from S.J. Res. 14 and H. Res. 194.

The United States, acting through Congress—...

    (4) apologizes on behalf of the people of the United States to all Native Peoples for the many instances of violence, maltreatment, and neglect inflicted on Native Peoples by citizens of the United States;

Whereas a genuine apology is an important and necessary first step in the
    process of racial reconciliation;

Whereas an apology for centuries of brutal dehumanization and injustices
    cannot erase the past, but confession of the wrongs committed can
    speed racial healing and reconciliation and help Americans confront
    the ghosts of their past;

(b) DISCLAIMER.—Nothing in this Joint Resolution—

    (1) authorizes or supports any claim against the United States; or

    (2) serves as a settlement of any claim against the United States.

Native American poet, Layli Long Soldier responded to hollow apologies when it became clear that conditions for Native Americans would remain unchanged.

> Whereas a string-bean blue-eyed man leans back into a swig of beer work-weary lips at the dark bottle keeping cool in short sleeves and khakis he enters the discussion;

> Whereas his wrist loose at the bottleneck to come across as candid "Well *at least* there was an Apology that's all I can say" he offers to the circle each of them scholarly; . . .

> Whereas like a bird darting from an oncoming semi my mind races to the Apology's assertion "While the establishment of permanent European settlements in North America did stir conflict with nearby Indian tribes, peaceful and mutually beneficial interactions also took place"; . . .

> Whereas I could've but didn't broach the subject of "genocide" the absence of this term from the Apology and its rephrasing as "conflict" for example;
>
> . . .
>
> WHEREAS the word *whereas* means it being the case that, or considering that, or while on the contrary; is a qualifying or introductory statement, a conjunction, a connector. Whereas sets the table. The cloth. The saltshakers and plates. Whereas calls me to the table. Whereas precedes and invites. I have come now. I'm seated across from a Whereas smile. Under pressure of formalities, I fidget I shake my legs.[736]

Apologies are absolutely part of repair. It signals that one is at least awakened to the reality of harm done. As with any relationship, acknowledgment addresses the broken spaces and must be revisited repeatedly. Whereas an apology is an opening for further dialogue, empathy, and action, we mustn't stop there. Repair is a continuous cycle of becoming that includes education, elucidation, and transformative action. It is an ongoing cycle of lament, care, honesty, justice, and practicing mutuality that asks us to consider the needs of our specific communities. Genuine repair enables psycho-spiritual liberation, especially the ability to take personal responsibility for our histories and abide in interrelatedness. Dussel suggests that it is no longer enough to simply become informed that "the oppressed are hungry; it is necessary to give good bread to the hungry."[737] Good bread implies work on behalf of the other's growth, development, and happiness. It extends beyond enthusiasm for a single project and toward continuous, sustained activity in service of liberating the other, which in turn liberates the self.[738]

---

[736] Soldier, "Whereas," 72, 79.

[737] Dussel, *Philosophy of Liberation*, 152.

[738] Dussel, 152.

The full acceptance of the atrocities committed in the name of the United States is paramount to changing a culture of whiteness and the basis of any monetary, legal, psychological, and spiritual repair. While there are definitive reparative actions, such as land repatriation, renaming or removal of tributes to confederates, financial investment, and historical accounting, these remain limited if the interior commitment to repair is hollow. Over time, efforts toward reparations have occurred, but liberty remains exclusionary, justice is not yet blind, and White narratives dominate history books. Results are temporary and fickle.

On the one hand, reparations require the tandem efforts of citizens, consistently demanding that local and federal governments act while supporting and participating in grassroots movements. On the other hand, a deeper spiritual and moral commitment to a more equitable society begets reparations. Journalist and cultural critic Ta-Nehisi Coates warns that "until we reckon with our compounding moral debts, America will never be whole."[739] She will never be free.

While I support local and federal government initiatives dedicated to financial, psychological, judicial, and educational reparations, my primary purpose is to address the moral and spiritual reparation necessary to ensure their perseverance. Our wrestling publicly and personally with these issues matters as much as the outcome. *Through wrestling, we will receive a new name.* As we evolve, we become conscious agents of change, bending toward communion, toward a unified diversity. Coates challenges us:

---

[739] Coates, "Case for Reparations," par. 1.

Imagine a new country. Reparations—by which I mean the full acceptance of our collective biography and its consequences—are the price we must pay to *see* ourselves squarely. The recovering alcoholic may well have to live with his illness for the rest of his life. But at least he is not living a drunken lie. *Reparations beckon us to reject the intoxication of hubris and see America as it is*—the work of infallible humans.[740]

I am obliged to acknowledge several limitations of repair. First, we cannot force it. The prerequisite for voluntary participation is a desire for change. A relatively small percentage of White people may enter the path initially. That number need only grow to twenty five percent of a group to reach a tipping point that impacts large-scale social change.[741] It does not require critical mass, only critical consciousness. Second, I focus primarily on repair as it concerns the Black–White binary in this country. There are many to whom we owe much. Third, we are a culture impatient with process. If we do not experience immediate, visible change, we grow bored or weary, eager for the next cause. It is a marathon, not a sprint, and we must pace ourselves accordingly. Fourth, we live in a time of broken covenants with one another and remain unconvinced that changes are possible or that we are powerful enough to make them. We possess tremendous power to do good.

We cannot confuse repair with charity or philanthropy, which often centers donors. It is less kindness than restitution, correction, and making things right. A

---

[740] Coates, par. 143, emphasis mine.

[741] There is a range of percentage points assigned to a tipping point from ten-forty percent. For reference, see Berger and Sloane, "Tipping Point for Large-Scale Social Change? Just 25 Percent."

substantial piece of repair is the interrogation of self, family, and community that involves deconstructing a culture of whiteness and the harm it has caused. There is a risk to our belonging, comfort, and acceptance in challenging whiteness. "If one cannot risk oneself, then one is simply incapable of giving"[742] and loving. Repair is not the happy ending in which we skip off into the twilight holding hands, but the long-overdue next step. The work is iterative, communal, and personal. We need to be honest about our motivation for participation, decenter the need for recognition as "a good White person," and trust it as the just course of action. If feelings of hopelessness, grief, or shame arise, we are called to sit in the soft, dark middle of it all. Hope and renewal emerge from wrestling the fertile dark. We will transform only by our willingness to push through discomfort.

> "There is a sorrow
>
> beyond all grief which leads to joy
>
> and a fragility
>
> out of whose depths emerges strength."[743]

Humans have a remarkable ability to harm. Parallel to this is a remarkable ability to heal and adapt, but even more specifically to choose and imagine. Yes, our bodies are patterned, perhaps long before we were woven into being. We inherit templates and believe them to be true. Our responses to the "different other" are often based on subtle or overt blueprints of old. Nevertheless, our saving grace is an ability to grow in awareness, become more conscious, observe ourselves, and rewrite

---

[742] Baldwin, *Fire Next Time*, 46.

[743] Rea, "The Unbroken."

the script. If we can learn a pattern, we can also unlearn it. We can shift and reorient ourselves in ways that honor both our differences and similarities, our autonomy and embeddedness.

We arrive here, burdened by a present rife with hate and division that some speculate is as intense as before the last Civil War. We arrive here, burdened because we never faced the shadows in our cave with courage and honesty. One wonders what is left to build on. Decades ago, in a time of other broken covenants, Robert Bellah cautions:

> The recognition of the broken covenant does not mean to me the rejection of the American past. We are not innocent, we are not the saviors of mankind, and it is well for us to grow up enough to know that. But there have been Americans at every point in our history who have tried to pick up the broken pieces, tried to start again, tried once more to build an ethical society in the light of a transcendent ethical vision. That too is part of our tradition, and if we can find no sustenance there, our prospect is even darker than it now seems.[744]

There have always been broken pieces. We are in desperate need of those willing to reassemble them. Repair restores an object, a person, to its original condition. Transformation moves it beyond. We are the ones called to do the repair furthered by transformation. There is no superhero waiting in the wings, and we do not wake up one day and become transformed. It is a process, a practice. The quest for transformative, restorative love is always daring, and there is always growth. Love

---

[744] Bellah, "Birth of New American Myths," 141–42.

is a stance, a philosophy of life in which we honor the fundamental dignity and worth of every being while understanding that not everyone can honor either their own or others' dignity and worth. They remain trapped in the cave in an unintegrated state. We hold space for their pain and possibility, knowing the cave's "mouth [is] open towards the light."[745] Love is a practice that attends to cycles of grief, honesty, care, justice, mutuality, and repair. It integrates the dark of the cave and the light of the world and makes something like wholeness out of our experiences. The entire time we are in wild pursuit of love, we realize it was in and between us all along.

Unbelonging to Belong

In our society, "White" is a claim of belonging, a special but elusive membership, and the racialized "other" bears the stigma of non-belonging.[746] Challenging White racism requires that we challenge an exclusive definition of belonging. Unbelonging from whiteness to create greater belonging is the purpose and destination of transformative action centered in love. Authentic transformation changes how we see and show up in the world more than what we see. It furthers itself at the boundary of self and not-self, ultimately enlarging self and shrinking who we perceive to be "other" and how we ostracize "them."[747] When I talk about unbelonging from whiteness I do not mean we ought to deny the aspects of it that shaped us. If we retreat to denial, we run the risk of lapsing into "we are all just

---

[745] Plato, *Allegory of the Cave*, 10.

[746] powell, *Racing to Justice*, 195.

[747] Benner, *Human Being and Becoming*, 13.

human" tropes without acknowledging how our racialized experiences inform us. My argument thus far has illustrated how belonging to a culture of whiteness is incongruous with wholeness and liberation because of its tendency to exclude others and define standards for normalcy. Unbelonging is a type of resistance, a willingness to stand in the margins with historically marginalized populations as well as a willingness to see how whiteness subjugates White people with narrow definitions of humanity.

There are several pathways that inspire my understanding of unbelonging. One is the mystical path of unknowing the known, egoic reality to discover what is real. In the New Testament of the Christian Scriptures, it is most succinctly described as, "Whoever wants to save their life will lose it."[748] It is an invitation to sacrifice what we think we know in favor of deeper knowing. It is to die before we die, to die to the false self so that we might live as the True Self. It is the type of death James Baldwin suggests whiteness fears and masks itself against.[749] "Dying to live" is a mystical concept not specified to a particular religious tradition.

I am rooted in the Christian tradition, but I draw from a lineage of interfaith mystics. A common misperception of mysticism is that it is rooted in transcendence or "out of body" peak spiritual experiences, when it is actually rooted in our embodied humanness. As Benner writes, "Mystics start with human longings and follow them to their transcendent source."[750] I propose that the "transcendent

---

[748] Peterson, *The Message*, Matthew 16:25.

[749] Baldwin, *Fire Next Time*, 65.

[750] Benner, *Human Being and Becoming*, 16.

source" is both our beginning and end that evolves from a singularity to differentiated unity. My experience of reading the mystics is that they are interested in how we might become more human and more embodied and increase our capacity for dignifying the transcendent other.

A second inspiration is poetry. It is a genre able to succinctly hold concrete images with abstract ideas. Poetry recognizes our potential for wholeness and ability to sit with the gravity of deep questions while relieving us of the need to have all the answers. It leaves room for mystery, growth, and wonder in the space of its natural pauses. Especially the mystic poets I read write beautifully about the underlying oneness of all things. Eighth-century mystic poet Rabia wrote, "I died a thousand times before I died. . . . Have wings that feared ever touched the Sun? I was born when all I once feared—I could love."[751] Our human becoming and the creation of greater belonging requires that we learn to love what we once feared. And from Hafiz, "I wish I could show you, / When you are lonely or in darkness, / The Astonishing Light / Of your own Being!"[752] We are both the darkness and the astonishing light in the darkness. That is, I think, the final meaning of Plato's allegory.[753] The prisoner who discovers the light within must dare to come back to the den and share it with the others.

Poetry is part of my daily practice. It expresses the ineffable and touches the breadth of human emotions. Reading it opens me to simultaneously intimate and

---

[751] Rabia, "Die Before You Die," 7.

[752] Hafiz, *I Heard God Laughing*, 1.

[753] Plato, *Allegory of the Cave*.

universal experiences. It can succinctly hold paradox and the tension of opposites. Lucille Clifton believed in "the poem as a way to wonder, wonder as a way to live."[754] Wonder and curiosity are elemental to reimagining a world of greater belonging. Poetry carries large stories of lament, loss, joy, remembrance, and so much more that taps into the wholeness of human experience.

A third inspiration is depth psychology, specifically the process of individuation, which, counter to its root, is not a devotion to the individual, separate self, but to the fully integrated self who becomes conscious of what has previously been concealed and furthers this work indefinitely.[755] For my purposes, the cultural concealment is addressing how fears of our psychic shadows were projected onto the non-white other. Left unaddressed, racism became our nation's pathology, and it is the internalization and repression of this pathology that a process of unbelonging seeks to remedy. Howard Thurman wrote of social integration, and it applies psycho-spiritually, too:

> To integrate is to unify, to combine, to become whole, to become one. It cannot be achieved, therefore, by any kind of mechanical rearrangement of persons or rules or regulations.... [It] can never be achieved as an end in itself but must emerge as an experience after the fact of coming together.... [It] has to do with the quality of human relations ... the private, personal experience of individuals and groups of varied backgrounds as they discover

---

[754] Clifton, *How to Carry Water*, xvi.

[755] Jung, "Problems of Modern Psychotherapy," par. 125.

that there is a unity among peoples that can contain and support diversity as an expression of itself.[756]

Legal and social integration are much more robust when we submit to psycho-spiritual individuation and integration. The process of individuating or unbelonging from whiteness may create the conditions for achieving the Beloved Community, and if submitted to, enables us to restructure the entire fabric of the social context and therefore create greater belonging.[757] Ultimately, the responsibility for creating this greater belonging is both individual and communal. Individuation, therefore, does not only help the self, but extends to the betterment of society.

Unbelonging is a move away from the false self, captured by essentialist identities, toward the true self who can hold complexities. It is, ultimately, about loving the lost aspects of the self and others. James Baldwin describes it as the difference between acceptance and integration. On learning to love those trapped by a culture of whiteness, he wrote to his nephew in 1961, "But these men are your brothers—your lost, younger brothers. And if the word integration means anything, this is what it means: that we, with love, shall force our brothers to see themselves as they are, to cease fleeing from reality and begin to change it."[758] Unbelonging is a commitment to truth telling and presupposes that we see one another as brothers and sisters, as interconnected beings. Even though he writes of social integration relevant to the 1950s and '60s, his words pertain to psycho-spiritual integration as

---

[756] Thurman, "Desegregation, Integration, and the Beloved Community," 14–15.

[757] Thurman, "Desegregation, Integration, and the Beloved Community," 16.

[758] Baldwin, *Fire Next Time*, 12–13.

well. It is not necessary to accept bigotry and superiority as true, but to integrate them as shadow aspects of our social fabric so that they can be transformed by love.

Because individuation has a clear form, I apply it here to amplify the process of unbelonging. Carl Jung pioneered the psycho-spiritual process of individuation as the optimal direction of human development. While he foresaw it as a method of connecting the individual to a universal, archetypal, and ancestral collective unconscious, psychoanalysis was largely reduced to the individual work between the analyst and client. Mental constructs were separated from the cultural, social, and economic worlds in which clients were embedded.[759] We need to apply elements of depth psychology to resolving collective issues so that they can be understood beyond an individual life.

History has not properly honored the impacts of enslavement and Native American genocide on this nation's psyche. These are collective traumas, even though the resulting oppression and systemic racism got reduced to problems of specific, marginalized communities. The affected groups are often responsible for their own healing, whereas I am proposing that White people take on the responsibility for healing the internal dehumanization caused by perpetuating the dehumanization of others. Psychologically informed public practices can repair our social bonds as well as elucidate the narrative threads of an individual life.[760]

---

[759] Watkins and Shulman, *Toward Psychologies of Liberation*, 13.

[760] Watkins and Shulman, 14.

Individuation involves four stages: catharsis, elucidation, education, and transformation.[761] The initiation into unbelonging from whiteness is usually an apocalyptic moment that induces a personal or communal response, including an outpouring of intense emotions. Examples include any one of the recent, high-profile, state-sanctioned murders of an unarmed Black man and the ensuing public outcry. There is some debate as to whether Jung saw individuation as the destination of the human or an ongoing process, but as it relates to unbelonging, I assert it is ongoing and multilayered.

Transformation, or the reimagining of one's relationship to a presenting problem, is achieved (and I use "achieved" lightly because it is a commitment to process) by submitting to the following:[762]

1. *Catharsis*, or becoming conscious of what the ego has concealed. As it relates to unlearning racism, I equate this stage with truth telling, or a willingness to examine and bring forth the truths about the racist foundations of our society and, for many of us, our ancestors. In unbelonging from whiteness, this is the final stage in which we become aware of and want relief from the known and unknown ways we are shaped by a culture of whiteness. Many White people enter a period of confession after gaining an education and elucidation about how whiteness operates. We tend to look for absolution from non-white friends and colleagues, desperately wanting to be seen as "good" and

---

[761] Jung, "Problems of Modern Psychotherapy," par. 122.

[762] List items summarized from Jung, "Problems of Modern Psychotherapy."

separate from the culture that shaped us. The catharsis leans toward transformation once it is understood that the work requires more than individual exoneration but continued commitment to liberation and the behaviors of love mentioned in this chapter.

2. *Elucidation,* the process of illumination or discernment that allows one to begin to both personalize and depersonalize the shadow aspects of the self in the context of culture. Here we are learning to straddle the light and the dark. In the work of anti-racism, it entails noticing how pervasive racism is in systems and institutions and seeking deeper awareness of how they privilege whiteness on an individual and collective level. This stage alternates with education as one furthers the other. Each phase of elucidation reveals the long shadows of our country's evolution, how whiteness subverts race consciousness.

3. *Education.* One consciously interprets and understands the issue by exploring and learning through creative and intellectual endeavors. Regarding unlearning racism, it is engaging with literature, dialogues, editorials, and community participation. Following an apocalyptic event, it is the first stage of unbelonging from whiteness, as many are often propelled to learn more. If we commit to the educational stage even as it challenges us, we are more likely to sustain elucidation, which I understand to be a deeper, perhaps more experiential form of knowing in

which we engage the shadows.[763] Education is coming out of the cave, whereas elucidation is the return to it to illuminate the shadows in a new way. Each layer of unbelonging deepens a personal and collective transformation and makes way for new belonging.

Jung states that there is something curiously final about each stage, but that life itself is a living history that continuously illuminates manifold layers of awareness.[764] Unbelonging from a culture of whiteness is like individuation in that we must learn to hold both the manifold layers of new awareness and learn to live with the tension of opposites. In this case, the opposites might be critiquing and accepting how whiteness shapes us while choosing to remain in constant dialogue with it to imagine a society with deeper inclusion and equity. In addition, both depth psychology and unbelonging emphasize the vital role of imagination in disrupting internalized norms and suggesting alternative ways of being.[765]

Unbelonging is different from individuation in that it is consciously chosen and follows a different sequence. The stages are apocalypse, education and elucidation taken in turns, catharsis, and transformation. It happens simultaneously at the individual and communal level, thus deepening the understanding of the self within a social context. Very often the need to address historical wounds is precipitated by an apocalyptic public tragedy that reveals the shadow nature of a

---

[763] Jung, "Problems of Modern Psychotherapy"; applying these steps to anti-racism is my contribution.

[764] Jung, "Problems of Modern Psychotherapy," par. 159–63.

[765] Watkins and Shulman, *Toward Psychologies of Liberation*, 6.

culture of whiteness. It forces an education that is further elucidated by individual and communal attempts to learn, change attitudes, and make reparations. The major catharsis, or revelation to the self of deeply held learnings about whiteness, reaches a crescendo as we either return to the comfort of the status quo or submit to the process of personal and collective transformation.

Typically, the initial apocalypse reveals deep imbalances in the social and political milieu. Following the event, we immediately face a crossroads. We can choose, like the prisoner who unleashed his chains in Plato's allegory, to ascend toward the light of understanding[766]; we can choose to remain in the dark, seduced by the shadows on the wall, insisting the moment is grossly exaggerated; or we can choose denial. Regardless, such events and the resulting outcry disrupt the innocence of "normalcy," even if the seismic shifts are beneath the surface.

I recognize the callousness in equating a public tragedy to an educational moment, but it inevitably offers new ways of seeing and can intensify layers of learning that are intellectual, spiritual, and experiential. If we are willing to pay attention to the voices in the margins, to the incredible artworks, think pieces, and personal stories available—if we are willing to practice curiosity, wonder, and uncertainty—a rich and humbling education begins. Thus enters elucidation, or a conscious pursuit of new understandings at the heart level and a willingness to examine personal and collective shadows. The resulting major catharsis is the desire to purge unwanted, often unconsciously absorbed ideas about whiteness, race, and racism. The realization that they cannot be purged can trigger anger, helplessness,

---

[766] Plato, *Allegory of the Cave*.

shame, and grief—all emotions that if harnessed and integrated productively can fuel transformation. If ignored, we return to our shackles in the cave of denial. If attended to, we submit to the pain and liberation of change.

While depth psychology links the individual unconscious with historical conditions and suffering, the work of unbelonging moves beyond an exclusive focus on individual interiority to embed the self in a community context.[767] In Austria and other parts of Europe, psychoanalysts were initially engaged in holistic initiatives that included early childhood education, supports for women to mitigate forms of domination, psychology classes for laborers, and suicide prevention centers. They were involved in elucidating the importance of mental health and belonging in communities. They helped create solutions rooted in specific social and political contexts.[768] However, when European, mostly Jewish psychoanalysts migrated to the United States because of increasing antisemitism in Europe in the early twentieth century, two things happened.

First, they joined a White profession in the United States, even though Jews were not initially accepted as White. To assimilate, many adopted a White, upper-middle-class value system that resulted in suppressing their histories and previous socialist engagement in Europe to ease their transition to a country intensely skeptical of socialism. They retreated from interests in social justice and took refuge in disease and pathology models that focused on individuals.[769] In short, they

---

[767] Watkins and Shulman, *Toward Psychologies of Liberation*, 49.

[768] Watkins and Shulman, 56.

[769] Watkins and Shulman, 57.

sacrificed a sense of "cosmic belonging" that located the individual within a much larger context.

Second, they traded their "night vision," what Watkins and Shulman describe as "an ability to critique society and to examine its intrapsychic implications from the position of an outsider and critic [that] allows us to begin to see what of our psychological suffering is linked with the culture(s) in which we reside."[770] Instead of subverting the status quo and broadening the space of the margins, psychology became myopic, a phenomenon discussed in Chapter 3. Even though depth psychology provides some tools for unbelonging, it too needs to be subverted in its current form. Like White Protestant Christianity, it may have lost contact with its liberatory and communal origins and needs reinvigorating.

The very difficult aspect of choosing unbelonging is the potential for loneliness that results in an urgent need to educate and elucidate other White people about racial injustice. This is important and necessary work but is quite often ill-received by the uninitiated. Unbelonging, a feeling of being adrift in spaces once familiar and comfortable, is unsettling and requires deep trust that "something more" is available. William James defines this *moreness* as the surrender of the lower self to the higher self, a necessary surrender if we are to initiate social change.[771] I would add, however, that the higher self is inaccessible if we remain separate from community, unable to see how our individual growth and well-being is interconnected with the collective. The "something more" is the fertile ground of the

---

[770] Watkins and Shulman, 57.

[771] James, *Varieties of Religious Experience*, 385.

margin, a location of radical openness, possibility, and community.[772] Here live the world changers and ladder makers. Unbelonging is an active and ongoing process that requires repeatedly attending to the spiritually liberative practices listed in Chapter 5 and the behaviors of love in this chapter.

The psycho-spiritual process of unbelonging is transformative for the self and the world. It is a liminal space where all transformation occurs. Modern mystic Richard Rohr says that part of changing is learning "to stay with the pain of life, without answers, without conclusions, and some days without meaning."[773] That is the perilous path of psycho-spiritual liberation and transformation. Liminality is counter to the Western mind, and unbelonging is counter to whiteness. Yet I am asking us to consider undertaking voluntary displacement for the sake of transforming our racial consciousness in the hopes that we can create another world, "much bigger and more inclusive, that relativizes and reenchants this world [of whiteness] that we take as normative."[774] The dark uncertainty of liminality is creative and disruptive of "business as usual." Further, the liminal space pulls us out of our private, individualized center, toward a broader sense of belonging that thrives on differentiated unity. It pulls us toward the margins because it softens defenses and resistance and allows for shifts in perception to occur. It also pulls us toward the feminine aspects of converting the old into new, of the shadows into wisdom. When

---

[772] hooks, "Choosing the Margin," 23.

[773] Rohr, *Everything Belongs*, 45.

[774] Rohr, 47.

we experience our bodies and minds in different ways, in this space of in-between, we are carried into deeper awareness, which is an experience of the soul.[775]

As noted earlier, the margins are not sites of sameness. Belonging there is not homogeneous. Watkins and Shulman compare the borderlands to the restorative environmental work of assisted regeneration. Transformative solutions are specific to place. Just like renewing a population of native plants, they differ according to location, culture, social fabric, and histories.[776] Such an approach is based on deep trust, the regenerative capacities of communities, and the patience to allow incremental changes to seed larger ones. There is no waiting for an outside expert or dynamic leader, but attempts toward local, creative, participatory solutions to problems that begin with transforming relationships to the self and "transcendent other."[777] The margins are not just spaces for historically marginalized populations to regenerate and rest but also for those who have, to varying degrees, unknowingly participated in systems of oppression. Here we can commence unlearning whiteness, hold multiple realities at once, and co-create new paradigms.

Willingly choosing unbelonging is a leap of faith toward an unfulfilled longing that taps into the depths of our feminine origins and destiny. We began in a state of oneness; we are moving toward a diversified unity. Actively participating in unbelonging facilitates repairing our cultural and personal mother wounds that has kept feminine knowing and trusting our fundamental interconnectedness in

---

[775] Watkins and Shulman, *Toward Psychologies of Liberation*, 136.

[776] Watkins and Shulman, 15.

[777] Watkins and Shulman, 16.

darkness.[778] In a newly discovered place of belonging, our relationships with one another are governed by curiosity rather than suspicion, creativity rather than sterility, complexity rather than simplicity. Living in the margin, whether entered by choice or imposition, is a critical response to dominator patterns. It is a mental and physical space as well as a radically creative space, which gives us a location from which to articulate a new sense of the self, community, and the world. To echo hooks, "Let us meet there. Enter that space. We greet you as liberators."[779]

---

[778] Jung, *Archetypes and the Collective Unconscious*, 94.

[779] hooks, "Choosing the Margin," 23.

www.ingramcontent.com/pod-product-compliance
Lightning Source LLC
LaVergne TN
LVHW011927070526
838202LV00054B/4518